Ecclesiological Investigations

Series Editor

Gerard Mannion

Volume 9

Being Faithful: Christian Commitment in
Modern Society

Other titles in the series

Being Faithful:
Christian Commitment in
Modern Society

Judith A. Merkle

t&t clark

Published by T&T Clark International
A Continuum imprint

The Tower Building, 11 York Road, London SE1 7NX
80 Maiden Lane, Suite 704, New York NY 10038

www.continuumbooks.com

First published 2010
Paperback edition first published 2012

Judith A. Merkle has asserted her right under the Copyright, Designs and Patents Act 1988, to be identified as the Author of this work.

British Library Cataloguing-in-Publication Data
A catalogue record for this book is available from the British Library.

ISBN: 978-0-5673-8900-8 (HB)
        978-0-5670-9504-6 (PB)

Typeset by Pindar NZ, Auckland, New Zealand
Printed and bound in Great Britain

CONTENTS

PREFACE

This book is for all those seeking to be faithful in our age. Students, married people and singles, members of religious orders, pastors, professionals, and those active in advocacy organizations face the daily challenge to live their Christian commitment in a time when yardsticks of faithfulness are difficult to come by. We live in a time of transition. The challenge of our particular life situation, our context, calls us daily to faithfulness, yet the forces which pull us in many directions often remain unconscious and unaddressed when we consider the moral life. At times one's very acts of faithfulness are judged as betrayals by those who see the Christian life with a different lens or emphasis. We know that the basics remain the same in every age. The commandments, the Golden Rule, the challenge of membership in the Church, the following of Christ, the call of personal integrity form a consistent moral compass for the discerning individual. However, the pressures of work and family or community added to the call to engage in social transformation can cause many to feel not up to the task of being faithful. The trap of postmodern living can leave one isolated but free to invest in what appears to be worth the effort; yet without a sense of what really counts. The pressures of modern culture often shackle our moral imagination, without our permission. They enter into contemporary moral experience unannounced to cloud a sense of moral fidelity, making faithfulness appear as an illusion too difficult to even attempt. A type of cultural desolation can set in as drifting, a modern form of unbelief, through which one can evade the challenge of moral commitment all together, or deaden the desire with distractions. The endeavor can appear as too high to hope for, to difficult to begin. This book does not explore every context of modern living. However, it does speak to the desire to be morally committed as a Christian and the difference being situated at this time in history makes in our assessment of moral experience. It is offered as a contribution to ongoing reflection on this important topic.

I wish to thank Gerard Mannion and those involved in Ecclesiastical Investigations for their encouragement with this text. I also wish to acknowledge the support of my colleagues at Niagara University and the assistance received through faculty research grants. My sabbatical time spent at the Catholic

University of Louvain allowed the completion of this text, and I am grateful to members of the theology department, Catholic Social Thought Center and other colleagues for their hospitality. The American College welcomed me into their sabbatical program. Finally, I am indebted to my family, friends and sisters in community, the Sisters of Notre Dame de Namur, whose daily commitment to the Christian life inspires my own journey.

DOCUMENTS CITED AND ABBREVIATIONS USED[1]

Rerum Novarum: The Condition of Labor (Leo XIII, 1891)	RN
Quadragesimo Anno: After Forty Years (Pius XI, 1931)	QA
Mater et Magistra: Christianity and Social Progress (John XXIII, 1961)	MM
Pacem et Terris: Peace on Earth (John XXIII, 1963)	PT
Dei Verbum: Dogmatic Constitution on Divine Revelation (Vatican II, 1963)[2]	DV
Lumen Gentium: Dogmatic Constitution on the Church (Vatican II, 1964)	LG
Gaudium et Spes: Pastoral Constitution on the Church in the Modern World (Vatican II, 1965)	GS
Dignatatis Humanae: Declaration on Religious Freedom (Vatican II, 1965)	DH
Presbyterorum Ordinis: Decree on the Ministry and Life of Priests (Vatican II, 1965)	PO
Populorum Progressio: On the Development of Peoples (Paul VI, 1967)	PP
Octogesima Adveniens: A Call to Action on the Eightieth Anniversary of *Rerum Novarum* (Paul VI, 1971)	OA
Justice in the World (Synod of Bishops, 1971)	JW
Evangelii Nuntiandi: Evangelization in the Modern World (Paul VI, 1975)	EN
Documents of Ecclesial Conferences of Medellin (1968), Puebla (1979) (Bishops of Latin America)[3]	
Redemptor Hominis: Christ the Redeemer (John Paul II, 1979)[4]	RH
Dives in Misericordia: On the Mercy of God (John Paul II, 1980)	DM
Laborem Exercens: On Human Work (John Paul II, 1981)	LE
Sollicitudo Rei Socialis: On Social Concern (John Paul II, 1987)	SRS
Redemptoris Missio: On the Permanent Validity of the Church's Missionary Mandate (John Paul II, 1990)	RM
Centesimus Annus: On the Hundredth Anniversary of *Rerum Novarum* (John Paul II, 1991)	CA

Veritatis Splendor: Regarding Certain Fundamental Questions of the
    Church's Moral Teaching (John Paul II, 1993)   VS
Evangelium Vitae: On the Value of Inviolability of Human Life
    (John Paul II, 1995)   EV
Deus Caritas Est: God is Love (Benedict XVI, 2006)[5]   DC
Caritas in Veritate: Charity in Truth (Benedict XVI, 2009)[6]   CV

Notes

1 All social encyclicals are cited from *Catholic Social Thought: The Documentary Heritage*, ed. David J. O'Brien and Thomas A. Shannon (Maryknoll, NY: Orbis, 2002).
2 *The Documents of Vatican II*, ed. Walter M. Abbott, S.J. (New York: Herder and Herder, 1966).
3 As referenced in the text.
4 *The Encyclicals of John Paul II*, ed. and intro. J. Michael Miller, C.S.B. (Huntington, IN: Our Sunday Visitor, 1996). All quotes from the encyclicals of John Paul II are from this source.
5 Benedict XVI, *Deus Caritas Est* (Vatican City, *Liberia Editrice Vaticana*, 2006).
6 Benedict XVI, *Caritas in Veritate* (Vatican City, *Liberia Editrice Vaticana*, 2009).

PART I

FOUNDATIONS OF THE CHRISTIAN
LIFE IN THE WORLD

Chapter 1

LIVING INTO A NEW PARADIGM

The struggle to be faithful is at the core of the Christian life. Like the young person in the gospel, the modern Christian asks, what must I do to inherit eternal life? (Lk. 10.17). However, today Christians ask this question in a very different set of circumstances. Changes in the world and new ways of thinking impact our approach to morality. Today we operate with an expanded understanding of Christian ethics because of these changes. Traditionally Christian ethics focused primarily on an analysis of human acts, what specific behaviors were right and wrong. While this is a perennial need in guiding human life, today Christians, as all people of good will, are also morally responsible to shape the forces which impact the modern world.

Lewis Mudge states the shift succinctly. Formerly, moral issues were seen as having to do mainly with personal conduct within stable orders of value. Today Christian ethics include a new sense of responsibility. Now they also have to do with the life, or the death, of the human race as such: and the fate of the created order in which we live.[1] The planetary scale of our human struggle presents challenges beyond any the Church has faced before. In order to influence the twenty-first-century global civilization, Benedict XVI reminds us that we need to contribute to shared visions and institutional expressions for which we have few relevant precedents, as we are in a new moment (CV 24, 25, 26). The goal of this book is to explore this new challenge placed on us by our times and the forces of globalization and to ask how it impacts our understanding of Christian faithfulness. We will begin by looking more deeply into this shifting paradigm of moral understanding.

Secularity as Modern Human Experience

In *A Secular Age* Charles Taylor reminds us that the "background" for modern life has changed. Background refers to the context of our lives, the beliefs and outlooks which we take for granted and seldom even formulate into clear terms.[2] As a cluster of ideas or worldview, background is unconscious. Yet it forms the framework by which we interpret our experience, frame the conditions of experience, and answer the spiritual and moral questions of our lives. Taylor argues that today this background is marked by the experience of the secular. In contrast to people who lived five hundred years ago, we come to belief and assess whether we are faithful or not using a new set of conditions marked by secularity.

Taylor offers three indicators of secularity in modern experience. One, we live in societies where public space is emptied of the mention of God. Two, we notice around us the falling off of religious belief. But most importantly, three, the conditions of coming to belief have drastically changed. In contrast to a former age when it was difficult not to believe in God, we come to belief in a climate where belief in God is one option among others to explain integrity of life. We realize there have always been rival theories to the existence of God and the meaning of life.[3] Today we recognize that people live side by side with very different experiences of the same life. Taylor explains the diverse kinds of lived experience involved in understanding life in one way or the other, which impact what it is like to live as a believer or an unbeliever.[4]

Some human experiences all people hold in common. Every person seeks a type of fullness in their lives, not just those with a clear religious identity. They seek a condition which is fuller, richer, meaningful, more as it "ought to be." They also experience the opposite, a sense of exile or alienation from the condition which they seek and a powerlessness to reach it. Everyday language betrays these states. We hear, "I'm in a good space," or a "bad space." However, most of the time we live our day to day lives in a middle condition where we have managed to escape the pain of "exile" through routine, or contentment or meaningful aspects of our lifestyle, yet we know we have not reached fullness. Knowing there is more, gives our middle position meaning and purpose.

Theologian Edward Schillebeeckx mirrors Taylor's observations as he claims that people become aware of the search for fullness in their lives indirectly, or in a "contrast experience." Both believers and non-believers can experience something amiss in the world, and say, "this ought not be." Yet implicit in their "no" to the situation is "yes" to something better. People choose to work to make things better, believing love is worth their effort, and act from a vision of a better life which fuels their energies.[5] However, a believer also will sense in this event an experience of God. They will be reassured through their belief and the symbols of their faith community that their efforts equal progress on a path in this life which ultimately has meaning not only now, but in the next life.

Taylor argues that a non-believer might work very hard at the same struggle, yet hold that this life is all there is. The sense of fullness toward which he strives or she aspires is understood in terms of the potentials which human beings can accomplish in the here and now. Unlike the believer, they do not experience help from above, rather the potential to reach fullness is within.[6] The chaos of exile is warded off through the potential they have as human beings to make laws and to use their rational powers to order the world. Human beings can through reason act well and appropriately to promote human flourishing. Even those who have less faith in reason, as the postmodern critique of reason suggests, might find the power to achieve fullness in Nature, in their own depths or in harmony with Nature as deep ecology argues. The fuller element to which the rational mind must open, they claim, is perhaps just another side of human life, its deepest feeling or instincts.

Taylor's insights into the changed climate of our lives point to the paradoxical situation in which we live today. Even for the believer, the conditions of unbelief form the background of his or her self-understanding, as a religious outlook on life's meaning is generally absent from the public realm as well as from many of our daily associations with people who find religion unnecessary to a sense of a full life. Secularity, Taylor argues, is not only the background of the modern age, but the background of belief and morality today. This shift is a challenge to moral theology and to the churches.

Context as a New Condition of Moral Understanding

We are challenged as Christians to integrate the relevance of the world in which we live, or our context, into an understanding of the moral life, while also embracing the faith which grounds us. How does the situation in which we live "weigh in" with other standards of moral wisdom such as norms, and virtues to give us a moral compass? Awareness of the impact of our situation causes us to think differently about this question than in the past. In the history of Roman Catholic ethical reflection, context has often been limited to the situation which surrounds a particular moral action. In the tradition, these "circumstances" surrounding a moral action were seen as mitigating or aggravating factors which affected the nature of the moral situation.[7] I should not steal. However, if I am starving and stealing food is my only means of survival, this circumstance is morally significant. "Situationists" however, went beyond this common sense approach. Some argued that the situation, in all its concrete aspects, is so unique and unrepeatable, that it cannot be susceptible to generalization. These moralists claimed that general norms cannot have normative value in any essential way, but simply serve at best as guidelines for action.[8] Situations are so different from one another that no one could imagine a general set of circumstances which would define "stealing" from a moral perspective, allowing that common law might define it legally. This position, called situation ethics, has generally been rejected by the Church.[9] Yet the debates continue regarding the role of circumstances in determining the morality of an action.[10]

We sense that the moral significance of context today is beyond these debates of situation ethics. When we attempt to define moral action "in this world" we do more than balance the lights that norms or circumstances shed on the determination of right action. Today we must also assess how encounters with re-occurring elements in a moral situation in modern life impact moral freedom and responsibility. These circumstances "weigh in" more significantly than was accessed in traditional ways, when they were elements along with intention and moral object in the determination of moral behavior. Today we are aware that realms of activity in modern society form spheres of thinking and responding which shape moral understanding and moral behavior. Our moral experience, especially in a media-saturated culture, is often more complex than traditional frameworks of ethics might suggest.[11] The complexity of moral experience today drives us to ask anew, just what does it mean to be a faithful Christian?

What is Christian Faithfulness?

A signature of Christian fidelity is acceptance of the salvation God offers in and through Jesus Christ.[12] This acceptance has an ethical component. The gift of salvation is a summons or call that is to bring about a change in one's perception of reality and values. It is a call to ongoing conversion. Our efforts to live a moral life are a response to this gift. However, the summons of one's baptism is to live the Christian life not "in general," but in a particular context. Christians in a particular place and time understand their moral responsibilities and celebrate their Christian faith in a way peculiar to their situation and context.[13] The call to be faithful is more than one of personal moral rectitude understood as keeping universal moral codes, however relevant these are to the moral life. Christians in this world are to allow their Christian faith to animate and direct the situation in which they are inserted. They are to do all they can to transform their culture and to direct it to serve the common good. This call to Christian faithfulness involves one in a paradoxical situation. This worldly transformation is an essential part of the gospel, yet the gospel proclaims a salvation that is irreducible to our actions alone. In the words of John Paul II, "The Kingdom of God being in the world without being of the world, throws light on the order to human society, while the power of grace penetrates that order and gives it life" (CA 25). Christian faithfulness is more than following an ethical blueprint of the gospel. It is not only a call to avoid sin, but also to live constructively with and for others.

When people seek to be faithful as Christians, they do so in a way which is informed by the very light and power of God's redeeming grace operating in the conditions of their life. However, this light does not replace their call to this world to be active for the good, to use their reason, skills and best information to make decisions for human betterment. The divine realities give the light of the Kingdom and the power of grace which gives life to the temporal sphere (LG 39). To live in this light, the Christian is called to a life with the person of Christ as its center.[14]

God's gift in Jesus gives us a Christo-centric basis or context for understanding the world. We are assured by the gospels of the absoluteness and intimacy of the God-human relationship. Yet the insights this worldview renders are not specific to Christians. They can be shared by others.

Therefore, living in Christ is not done in spite of the world, but in this world. Christians also receive from the world. John Paul II saw living the gospel in this world as a two-way action. It involves not only creative action in this world, but also, ". . . the intimate transformation of authentic human values through their integration in Christianity in the various human cultures" (RM 52.2). Christian faithfulness, in imitation of Jesus Christ, will always assume an incarnational bias. It is at core faithfulness in this world. Since men and women today are not only passive observers of the world, as they may have been considered in the Middle Ages, but are responsible for the shape of the world, understanding the role of context in the moral life has increasing importance.

The Dimensions of Context

One way to understand context is the background or specific circumstances of a person or subject. An expanded understanding involves consideration of context in three main ways; that is, through its personal, social and cultural dimensions. Any of the three dimensions can enlarge or limit moral responsibility and the moral possibilities in a situation.[15] All situate one's moral experience and affect a sense of being faithful.

Personal dimensions include personal history, character or aptitude. Here context refers to elements in one's personality or life story which set the stage for their engagement with a moral decision. Someone raised in a Mennonite community is likely to have a disposition toward a non-violent rather than hawkish approach to war. A parent is more likely to perceive a situation of sexual abuse in the Church as a question of the safety of children, than a moral lapse of a member of the clergy or other adult.[16] A life event which precipitates a moral decision can be experienced as an existential call, the experience that "this needs to be done by me."[17] During the Second World War, a German farmer was asked why he risked the safety of his family to hide a Jewish family. He replied, "Because I was there." The actual shape of the trajectory of conversion in the Christian life is enhanced by the personal dimension of context. It shifts from the more general requirements of keeping the commandments and loving God and neighbor, to include the more personal challenges of integration of a particular life, in a particular place and with a particular set of gifts and limitations in one's following of Jesus Christ.

This awareness of the personal dimension of one's moral journey is not new in the Church. In the fifth century, Gregory the Great advised those who counseled members of the Church who wanted to grow in the Christian life to attend to specific areas of personality which were unique to the individual. In *Pastoral Care*, Gregory advised those responsible for the care of souls to encourage the timid to have more fortitude and the boastful to be more humble.[18] Over the centuries, this aspect of the Christian moral life has often been relegated to ascetical theology or spirituality, while moral theology focused on concerns of the confessional and the need to discern the specific nature of sinful actions.

Today some link the personal context to virtue ethics. James Keenan defines virtue ethics as placing the moral agent and not the moral act or its consequences at the center of moral reflection.[19] Questions such as "Who am I?" "Who ought I become?" and "How ought I get there?" are the heart of moral reflection in virtue ethics. The project of the moral life is to become a certain kind of person. Attention to the personal dimension of context assumes people can only become morally excellent persons (or faithful) by being themselves.[20]

The *social dimension* of context refers to transpersonal realities which enter into moral experience. One's place or power in a social situation; issues of race, class, gender; the impact of institutional arrangements on one's range of choice, all refer to morally significant elements of social context. Liberation theologians have reflected on the ethical significance of being called to engage in a project of national development, the sacrifices involved and their impact on understanding the Christian life.[21] Some First World theologians incorporate "option for the poor" into an understanding of moral fidelity.[22] The impact of social context can also be confusing, as some feel they must live a "split life" in modern society. The goals and standards of one's private life are constantly in conflict with the expediency and necessary compromise at work. The question "Am I faithful?" can arise from the attempt to assess the gap between who we ought to be and who we are amid the conflicting expectations of modern living.

While a sense of estrangement from self can come from not being the kind of individual we want to be, it can also stem from a lack of focus or meaning in life. When we contribute to and maintain organizational structures which do not promote conditions we experience as fully human, we feel alienated. We feel trapped by the need to survive and the pressure to conform. A life of "success" can also render a collapse of primary relationships, a decline of good health and a loss of spiritual roots, all "goods" humans seek.

For others, structures of race, class and gender play a major role in their life experience, and focus their moral struggle. Modern life contains unequal access in the institutions which support daily living, a situation which demands constant transformation. For this reason, assessment of the impact which institutions have and one's role in their creation, whether this is in the family, work or wider civic and political arena, is a significant area of moral life. Because these life contexts have major impact on our sense of meaning and faithfulness, the social dimension of moral experience is a key contextual consideration.

Cultural dimensions of life contexts are the assumptions that are the unnoticed and pre-reflective lenses through which people view life and their relationships. Dorothee Soelle articulates one such perspective on modern living in her book, *The Silent Cry: Mysticism and Resistance.*

> We live in a fragmented world which has a center and a periphery. In the center, where we live, life is productive and worth living. In the periphery, a place far from us, life is economically useless. We have rights, they are losers. Living in the center of the fragmented world means most things can be produced and bought, accessed and possessed.[23]

This view as to "how the world is" is reinforced in First World culture, often in ways that are not easily perceived. Attention to cultural context assesses how these and other assumptions shape an unconscious understanding of our moral responsibilities.

We understand moral problems such as the free market economy, security, war on terror, militarism, immigration, etc. in light of our understanding of the meaning of the world and essential relationships in it. Our cultural context impacts this ethical framework, telling us in subtle ways what the problem means. It provides an interpretation of what meanings underlie the problem and constitute it. Is this acceptable or unacceptable behavior? Is this an abuse? Are we responsible for this situation?

Cultural assumptions are often the focal point of gospel reflection and cultural criticism. Every culture has a sinful or shadow side to its construction of human life. This makes culture alone an insufficient moral foundation. Feminists challenge the culture of patriarchy which places women in a subordinate role. Black, white and Hispanic theologians point to the incompatibility of racism and the Christian life.[24] Sociologists have remarked on the individualized character of modern life, which ignores the dimension of human community.[25] Theologians have criticized consumer culture and its deadening effect on faith life, and call for critical reflection on the economy.[26] To leave culture and its impact out of our understanding of a faithful life is to fail to be serious about the project of following Jesus Christ in the real world in which we live.

Context and Languages of Catholic Morality

Since Vatican II, the essential vision in Catholic ethics is the moral life arises out of a total worldview which responds to God, self, others and the world. Yet the freedom which is at the heart of ethics is both personal and social. From the personal level, moral response always arises out of personal freedom, yet this personal freedom is situated in the real world. The challenge today in the faith community is how to integrate a new awareness of history and culture and their impact on the moral person, and the wisdom of traditional approaches to moral experience.

The major paradigm for understanding moral responsibility in the Church prior to Vatican II was the Scholastic view of the human person. It focused moral responsibility on the act of the individual and was very compatible with the need of a confessor in the Sacrament of Penance to assess moral culpability. The person is a substance, a being that exists in itself who has a rational nature. The person is one who thinks and makes choices. Sin is a deliberate act against the law of reason, which is inherent to one's own rational nature. Moral evil is created through free will, the ability to act or not to act and to act in one way or another. This focus on the individual and assessment of personal freedom remains the first language of moral theology in the Church.

This approach to the person emphasizes an act-centered rather than a relational and more biblical concept of sin. Sin is primarily personal, and secondarily has effects "in the world." There is less stress on the factors which influence personal choice, create a climate of sin, or foster a sense of responsibility. This basic structure underlies our moral imagination since it formed the main moral catechesis in the Church. However, it was not a system for believers only. The Church's strong natural law foundation held all accountable for their moral lives.

Core Convictions of the Church regarding the Natural Law

The Church at Vatican II affirmed that within the foundations of conscience of all human beings there are non-conventional, non-arbitrary moral standards which make possible genuine moral self-criticism and so true moral knowledge even for those who have not received the moral instruction of divine revelation. It is possible to know right and wrong. It is possible to freely choose right from wrong. Finally, there are moral standards which are not simply the results of personal preference or choice or of social conventions.[27]

This core conception of natural law supposes that human beings can discover within themselves an objective moral standard. They experience this standard, not necessarily as a list of rules, but as an obligation which is "given," not originating with them. In this sense, the natural law includes all the moral truths which exist prior to human decision or independent of revelation. No one has a complete knowledge of these truths. No one has knowledge of a list of commandments which correspond to the unlimited variety of problems regarding the realization of human reality.[28] For these reasons, it is a mistake to confuse the natural law with the positive law formed in society, or with laws which are created in the sciences.

Scientists note regularities in phenomena following the rules of scientific inquiry, naming some realities "natural." The relative objectivity of this process is confirmed through the scientific method. The natural moral law is different. The natural law is found within the conscience, it is written on the human heart. Knowledge of it is part of a person's self-knowledge and capacity for self-reflection and criticism. It provides a norm for action, and a standard for the reform of existing norms. Knowledge of the natural law requires that the human person makes an honest effort to seek moral truth.[29]

Vatican II saw the natural law in light of a more transcendent law, the divine law, through which God providentially directs all creation (DH 3). The natural law is God's plan for all creation. Human beings can participate in this plan, not as puppets, but through reason they can understand in some ways the plan of providence and provide for themselves and others a humanly well-established life. The plan of God in the natural law is not a detailed one, as in positive law. A better way to consider it is as broad principles which constitute the welfare of humanity, its dignity, and the good of all creation.

Human beings participate in the divine law, yet many do so without knowledge of God. Rather they experience the call of the natural law as one to seek the truth in their lives in order to make good judgments. Moral knowledge is not something one acquires once and for all, rather it changes and deepens. When the Church asserts that God is the transcendent ground of this search, it does not make explicit knowledge of God a necessary door to this human search. Rather it grounds the human quest for moral truth universally and locates its source immanently in the human conscience.

God's providential plan for human beings is carried out through people who seek to form their conscience in truth and act on it. God's light does not come to us revealing something transcendent to human nature, rather through reason we participate in the eternal law, and discover the goods of human nature, those basic aspects of human life toward which persons have natural inclinations. Through responsible reasoning, we participate in the processes where we discover what is morally true, what is good for human beings. Natural law is concerned with the reasoned direction of human life toward ends human beings understand as worthwhile. Aquinas taught that God is offended by human beings only when they act against their own welfare.[30] Aquinas assumed also that the designs of that welfare were written on the human heart through the natural law.[31]

It is a special kind of knowledge about human beings, their possibilities and perfection, not about God, which grounds natural moral obligation. In this sense, natural law is based on human nature.[32] Moral truth is not about God, it is about our lives in the created order, and our moral obligations. Obviously, people can be oblivious of these truths, either through ignorance or indifference. People in different times and places might differ in their level of moral awareness, and there will be disagreements as to what is the more human course of action. Growth in moral knowledge is gradual and involves a process of conversion, since what is true may not always be preferred. All need communities of conscience to help them to think about moral issues. But core convictions regarding the natural law hold that everyone is able to form the concepts necessary for moral judgment and to know the most basic principles of the moral life. This is "natural" to humans. It is natural for people to make laws to govern themselves, to regulate scientific discovery, to protect their families, to ensure financial stability. Everything which is accessible to us without revelation through right reason belongs to the natural moral law, as well as right moral judgment or human evaluative intelligence.[33] To act against this law is to act against right reason itself.

Beyond the Core Vision

Since Vatican II the Church has held to this essential paradigm of moral responsibility, but has also sought to integrate factors beyond the personal which influence good and evil in this world.[34] In this sense, the Church struggles to create a fuller language of moral theology to account for its experience in modern society and to integrate these experiences into its account of moral life.

For example, we experience evil today as reaching massive proportions, far beyond the consequences of the intentions of the individual to create it. In its early social teaching, the Church stressed that social evil was created primarily through a failure of charity by individuals, a reference to the classical paradigm of an act-centered morality. The wealthy class did not have concern for the worker, as they lacked a personal sense of justice (RN 20). However, later the Church shifted its attention from moral acts that create injustice to attention to the moral actors and the situation of sin in this world. The social dimension of sin was given new attention both by the Synod of Bishops in their document *Justice in the World* and the Latin American bishops at Medellin as they recognized the sinful influence of structures as situations of "institutionalized violence" against the poor in their country[35] (Medellin 2.16). They noted that structures in society not only induce individuals to sin but discourage and seek to defeat the human spirit from seeking its full humanity.

Voices which spoke out against racism and sexism drew attention to the unconscious nature of these societal prejudices. The Church noted that such "social sin," after being initiated by individual choice, appears to virtually take on an independent existence in the social world, unavoidably becoming part of the individual's experience of sin.[36] Sin was not just personal; it was by analogy also social. Just how the personal and social dimensions of sin interrelated has become a matter of ongoing theological reflection.[37]

Attention also shifted to the significance of the social aspects of human life in its power for good. Vatican II in *Gaudium et Spes* 53 reflected that human beings only come to their full humanity through culture, by cultivating natural gifts and values. "Whenever human life is involved, nature and culture are intimately connected." The call for freedom to become more fully human was intimately linked to the creation of culture and its institutions. Culture is not only an evidence of the power of human transcendence. It is also the carrier of the hidden energy of the gospel. In the 1970s Paul VI in his apostolic exhortation *Evangelii nuntandi* spoke of evangelization as the Christian transformation of culture. He did not mean the conversion of all to Christianity. Rather evangelization involves bringing the gospel's criteria of judgment to the cultural assumptions of people in order to affirm that which leads to integral human development and to oppose that which fosters dehumanization. Such a statement points to the need to take the cultural context of our lives seriously.

Pope John Paul II also reflected on the immense role of culture on people's openness or non-receptivity to faith. Dominant culture can promote flight from God, or foster the spiritual nature of men and women and the dignity of the human person. It can be a "culture of life" or a "culture of death." The Church also defined the moral life in a more nuanced fashion by acknowledging the social dimension of life. The human person only fulfills themselves through love within a concrete community and through social solidarity.[38] Recently, Pope Benedict XVI asks Christians to work for the common good through the complex of institutions which give structure to life in society. "This is the institutional path — we might also call it the political path — of charity, no less excellent and effective than the kind of charity which encounters the neighbor directly, outside the institutional mediation of the *polis*." (CV 7). In contrast to a vision of the moral life as focused on the individual acts of a sole moral actor, the Church grapples with the significance of how culture and other aspects of social existence determine the mode of one's existence and ultimately have bearing on one's moral life.

Research in social sciences has also alerted us to the realization that not all motivation arises from the human heart. Robert K. Merton described a functional analysis of human society as one which "conceives of the social structure as active, as producing fresh motivation which cannot be predicted on the basis of knowledge about man's native drives . . . It attempts . . . to determine how the social and cultural structure generates pressure for socially deviant behavior upon people variously located in that structure."[39] Research on theories of reference groups and their impact on the human personality, and social roles and their place in identity formation are simply two examples of how our understanding of the human person has moved beyond that of the "rational animal" of the Middle Ages.

Context and Vatican II's Call to Renew Moral Theology

Vatican II did shift from the act-centered morality of scholasticism to a more biblically based morality which stressed the following of Christ in the modern world. The council asked an important question about the Christian moral life. "What can and should Christ mean, if anything, in the moral lives of Christians?" This concern set the direction of the renewal of moral theology. In its *Decree on Priestly Formation* the council called for a renewal in the Catholic Church in the area of moral theology. It stated: "Special care should be given to the perfecting of moral theology. Its scientific presentations should draw more fully on the teaching of Holy Scripture and should throw light upon the exalted vocation of the faithful in Christ and their obligation to bring forth fruit in charity for the life of the world."[40] An overly legalistic style of moral theology was inadequate for the tasks before the Church in the modern world. Christians needed a vision of life which included the necessity to take responsibility for a changing society.

Bernard Haring was one of the first to respond to this challenge.[41] Norbert Rigali recalls that Haring did not perfect the Counter-Reformation science of moral theology; rather he initiated a new discipline centered on the Christian life. The moral life was "life in, with, and through Christ."[42] The effects of this shift, however, left the state of moral theology in a quandary. In Catholic circles, moral theology began to operate on two tracts. One the one hand, it continued to treat individual human acts in relation to God as humanity's ultimate end. Specific teachings were expressed in the important areas of sexuality, medical ethics and society. On the other hand, it treated human life in Christ. Catholic moral theology now involved diverse modes of moral reflection. There were more formal reflections on right actions and more thematic ones on the nature of the Christian life. As these shifts occurred, people began to question the changes in mentality which resulted. Some stopped asking, how far can I go? Others began questioning, whatever became of sin? The consensus as to what the science of moral theology was and how it was to be defined and pursued shifted. Christo-centrism entered into Catholic moral reflection as well as ambiguity. These changes affected how members of the Church measured their personal moral fidelity.[43]

Context and the Post Vatican Church

Revisionist Catholic moral theology sought to revise the moral norms used in the Church to distinguish unlawful acts from what was morally permissible; aspects of the Church's first language in moral theology. Discussions of autonomous ethics, the nature of conscience, fundamental option, natural law, principle of double effect, methods of decision making such as proportionalism and the theory of incommensurable goods occurred. These debates were possible because of shared assumptions and texts from an earlier moral system.[44] However, changes in the Church climate diminished interest in revising material norms.[45] Catholics in general did not ask for the kind of specific moral guidance from the Church that they did in pre-Vatican times. Confessional practice shifted. Instead of a more norm-centered moral guidance from the Church, members looked for a sense of meaning in a rapidly changing world.[46] In First World society as a whole, people experienced themselves in a new place as moral actors. On the one hand, they searched to take responsibility for the new powers they held in the modern world. On the other, they established their place in the world with each new decision.[47] People sought to face and transform the evil they encountered in the world. In the First World, this was experienced as a search for a vision of the Christian life and ways to unite to God and their neighbor in light of a changing society. What did it mean to live rightly in the modern world? In the Third World and in situations of oppression it was reflected in the quandary as how to respond to the poverty and violence which marked human life. How does the quest for emancipation, in all its forms, relate to the Christian life?[48]

Bernard Haring's later major work, *Free and Faithful in Christ*, named the acceptance of responsibility for creative freedom to love in fidelity to Christ as the starting point of the Christian life.[49] Moral theology's concern is not only with decision making or with discrete acts, according to Haring. "Its basic task and purpose is to gain right vision, to assess the main perspectives, and to present those truths and values which should bear upon decisions to be made before God."[50] Freedom in moral theology, however, is always freedom in a particular context, a freedom in this world. The Christian therefore would receive direction for moral decisions by attending to the word of God, and in light of his word, read the signs of the times. The normative values of the Bible were seen differently than the kind of norms fitting external controls, as they arose from a relationship with Christ. These norms are binding but at the same time liberating. They depend on faith and thus are distinctively Christian.[51] In other words, any norms used were understood in terms of a relationship with God. Haring did not exclude that generous people not professing Christian faith might be guided by the same dynamics, but his focus was on rethinking the following of Christ according to the new concerns emerging in modern society. We find in *Free and*

Faithful in Christ attention to such issues as responsibility for health care and policy, the urban ghetto, the consequences of colonialism and creating a better world order.

In post-Vatican II times, Catholic moral theology made steps to move from a sole consideration of acts and moral righteousness within the horizon of personal and church life, to an expansion of the call to do good and avoid evil to transform society. Attention to moral acts and their effect on the state of one's soul shifted toward a new consciousness of Christian responsibility for the state of the world, and the situation and circumstances in which "the other" lived.

Yet much of revisionist moral theology relied on the anthropology of transcendental Thomism, which focused on the structure of moral experience on the personal, intra-psychic becoming of the individual. New theology, through its reference to the individual, could function in a world where the consensus model of universal principles had been displaced. However, it could not deal with the multiple sense of self which society was constructing.[52] Social theologies began to restate a definition of the moral person by including the impact of the structures of society on self-understanding and human becoming.

Context and New Theological Expression

The liberation theologies in Latin America, Asia, and Africa, along with black, feminist and Hispanic theologies, began to affect Catholic life.[53] Primarily they articulated the experience of being human in modern society, which went beyond the classical and revisionist perspectives. Being human was influenced by social location, race, class, and gender. Human becoming depended on one's response not only to the traditional moral challenges of egotism; but also to the social conditions which marked one's own or another's possibility of human flourishing. The universal experiences of being human were made concrete in the particular struggles of a situated life journey. These theologies, which emerged from postwar emancipation movements across the globe, entered into the narratives of Catholic life, and further specified what it meant to be Christian in the face of the situation of one's neighbor. The following of Christ was not only an I–Thou relationship but involved response to the concrete quest for human emancipation arising in society and discernment of one's responsibility in regard to it. The concern of moral theology is the authentic life and the development of persons and societies toward the *humanum* within history and ultimately to a future with God.[54] The call to follow Christ remains. The question is how to follow Christ in an increasingly diverse society. What does it mean to be faithful?

Context and the Modern Moral Imagination

In addition to the above ecclesial and societal changes, culture itself changed. Cultures once provided men and women with a type of moral horizon. It offered a narrative of the shape and meaning of the cosmos and social and human life, moving beyond its former paradigm to integrate new experiences.

However, today our sense of embeddedness in a social world and a cosmos has shrunk. People are more unclear as to how they belong to the world. A result is that shared meanings in the world are more confused. Instead of finding ourselves in a world of set meanings and perimeters in which to interpret the world around us, we find ourselves having to create a world in which to belong. Increasingly, responsibility falls to individual choice, not just for action, but even for the construction of a world of meaning.[55] We live today in diverse contexts of meaning, which often vie with one another for our allegiance.

Religion, and Christianity itself, has provided some alternative to this state of affairs by offering narratives of meanings regarding the self, others and the world. Yet, the postmodern criticism of the patriarchal, colonizing, racially segregated, and militaristic tendencies of Christianity raises questions in the minds of believers as to the role of religious belief in forming human identity. Can Christianity challenge and counter the modern cultural practices of racism and militarism, or has it been too assimilated into this same culture?[56]

J. Mathew Ashley points to a radical pluralism that feeds the privatization of spirituality which de-links it from social and institutional contexts.[57] Ashley's observation is captured in the modern comment, "I am not religious, but I am a deeply spiritual person." Does this popular cultural stance and religious move away from the institution free a person from the pitfalls of association with the hypocritical, patriarchal, colonizing, racially segregated, and militaristic tendencies they might be trying to avoid? Likely, the answer is no. The move away from institution is not a move to a culture-free zone, but to a different climate of pseudo-embeddedness.

Vincent Miller argues that consumer society can become the real context of one's embeddedness. It actually shapes people to approach religious beliefs as if they were consumer commodities. The result is that when members of consumer cultures embrace religious traditions they encounter them in commodified, fragmented form. Beliefs, symbols and practices appear abstracted from their connections to one another. Religious ideas can be consumed in "spiritual" practice without any connection to the communal and integral religious practice they are meant to represent. They lose their capacity to convey the alternative logics and desires of the gospel which can provide a horizon of moral meaning and draw believers' lives away from conformity with the status quo. The gospel in turn fails to create a community of contrast to society. Miller charges that religious belief is always in danger of being reduced to a "decorative veneer of meaning" over the emptiness of everyday life, as it is already spelled out in advanced capitalist societies.[58]

Today traditional boundaries of identity, once set by family and community, are overshadowed by a culture of radical pluralism where most institutions of late modern capitalism are being rethought, including the family and the significance of the Church to one's life of faith. Facing the challenges of moral commitment in this new context reframes the question Pilate asked Jesus — what is the truth? It poses the question of how we can be faithful in speaking and living the truth today.

This book will explore how the Christian life today is lived in a pluralistic situation, where different contexts of belonging give rise to different moral challenges. While it is characteristic of modern life to exist in a postmodern situation where there is an erosion of comprehensive systems of meaning, we still live in contexts of belonging. We still seek to gather out of the fragments of modern life the sustenance of a network of belonging, belief and practice which comprise a faithful life. The construction of such a life, not only for us, but for others, serves as the framework for our moral commitments. The moral journey is only made in these real contexts of our lives. It is hoped that through a more sustained reflection on the interaction, conflict and contributions of various contexts of modern living we can contribute to a better understanding of how the two languages of moral theology in the Church today interact to better respond to the gospel search for faithfulness to Jesus Christ. The next chapters will explore theological topics which are foundational to our question: a theology of the world, sin and grace in this world, and fundamental beliefs regarding action in this world.

Notes

1 See: Lewis S. Mudge, *The Church as Moral Community: Ecclesiology and Ethics in Ecumenical Debate* (New York: Continuum, 1998).

2 Charles Taylor, *A Secular Age* (Cambridge, MA: The Belknap Press of Harvard University Press, 2007), 9.

3 St. Augustine remarks that there were 288 interpretations of right living in his time. See: Augustine of Hippo, *The City of God*, Marcus Dodds, trans. (New York: Random House, 1950), Book XIX, 1, 669. Here Augustine quotes Marcus Varro.

4 Ibid., 5.

5 Edward Schillebeeckx, *Church: The Human Story of God* (New York: Crossroads, 1990), 22.

6 Taylor, *A Secular Age*, 8.

7 Dominic M. Prummer, O.P., *Handbook of Moral Theology* (Cork: The Mercier Press, 1956), 21–22.

8 Situation ethics is not a monolithic system. It is a trend that gives primordial

importance to a situation and only a minor place to norms. Joseph Fletcher, *Situation Ethics* (Philadelphia, PA: Westminster Press, 1966) is a key representative of this school of thought.

9 *Acta Apostolicae Sedes*, 48 (1956), 144–45.

10 An early account of this conversation is recorded in *Norm and Context in Christian Ethics*, ed. Gene H. Outka and Paul Ramsey (New York: Charles Scribner's Sons, 1968).

11 John T. Noonan argues that societal changes can create a new context which makes a previous teaching intolerable, as in the case of the long approval of the Church of domestic slavery until recent times. Hence the significance of circumstances can be extended in some cases to changes which impact perception of moral requirements. See: *A Church That Can and Cannot Change: The Development of Catholic Moral Teaching* (Notre Dame, IN: University of Notre Dame Press, 2005), 158, 218.

12 John Paul II, *Sources of Renewal: the Implementation of the Second Vatican Council* (London: Collins, 1980), 87. The horizontal emphasis of Vatican II on the people of God is nuanced by John Paul II's assertion that the Church is the Mystical Body of Christ, and hence in need of redemption. Living in the consciousness of that essential creaturely relationship is logically prior. This would put him in tension with those who see the Christian life, or the role of the Church as mainly one of right action either personally or socially. John Paul II here provides an essential element of Christian faithfulness.

13 See: Peter Schnieller, *A Handbook on Inculturation* (New York: Paulist, 1990), 1.

14 Paulinus Ikechukwu Odozor, "An African Moral Theology of Inculturation: Methodological Considerations," *Theological Studies*, 69 (2008), 600.

15 In practice, some aspects of our discussion of context have been handled in what has been called the "pastoral dimensions" of a moral situation.

16 Norbert Rigali, S.J., "Moral Theology and Church Responses to Sexual Abuse," *Horizon*, 34, no. 2 (2007), 183–204.

17 Richard A. McCormick, "Does Religious Faith Add to Ethical Perception?" in *Readings in Moral Theology, No. 2, The Distinctiveness of Christian Ethics*, ed. Charles E. Curran and Richard A. McCormick, S.J. (New York: Paulist Press, 1980), 156–73.

18 Gregory the Great, *Pastoral Care*, trans. Henry Davis. *Ancient Christian Writers*, 11. (Westminster, MD: Newman, 1950).

19 James F. Keenan, "Proposing Cardinal Virtues," in *The Historical Development of Fundamental Moral Theology in the United States*, ed. Charles E. Curran and Richard A. McCormick, S.J. (New York: Paulist Press, 1999), 282.

20 Paul Waddel, *Friendship and the Moral Life* (Notre Dame, IN: University of Notre Dame Press, 1989), 136.

21 Thomas L. Schubeck, S.J., *Liberation Ethics: Sources, Models and Norms* (Minneapolis, MN: Fortress Press, 1993). An early statement of these aims is by Jon Sobrino, S.J., *Christology at the Crossroads: A Latin American Approach*, trans. John Drury (Maryknoll, NY: Orbis Books, 1978), especially chapter 4.

22 Bernard J. Verkamp, "On Doing the Truth: Orthopraxis and the Theologian," *Theological Studies*, 49 (1988), 3–24. For a critique of the notion "preferential option for the poor, see: Stephen Pope, "Proper and Improper Partiality and the Preferential Option for the Poor," *Theological Studies*, 54 (1993), 242–71.

23 Dorothee Soelle, *The Silent Cry: Mysticism and Resistance*, trans. Barbara and Martin Rumscheidt (Minneapolis, MN: Fortress Press, 2001), 179.

24 *Interrupting White Privilege: Catholic Theologians Break the Silence*, ed. Laurie M. Cassidy and Alex Mikulich (New York: Orbis Books, 2007).

25 Robert Bellah, *Habits of the Heart: Individualism and Commitment in American Life* (Berkeley, CA: University of California Press, 1985), 143.

26 Vincent J. Miller, *Consuming Religion: Christian Faith and Practice in a Consumer Culture* (New York: Continuum, 2004). Joerg Rieger, *No Rising Tide: Theology, Economics and the Future* (Minneapolis, MN: Fortress, 2009).

27 Joseph Boyle, "Natural Law," in *The New Dictionary of Theology*, ed. Joseph A. Komonchak, Mary Collins and Dermot A. Lane (Collegeville, MN: Liturgical Press, 1987), 704–5.

28 Josef Fuchs, S.J., *Christian Morality: The Word Becomes Flesh* (Dublin: Gill and Macmillan, 1981), 34.

29 The natural law tradition would claim that each human being has three core inclinations, to self-preservation, to procreation, and to seek the truth.

30 *Summa contra Gentiles*, 3.122.

31 S.Th. I–II, q. 94, a.2.

32 Boyle, "Natural Law," 706.

33 Josef Fuchs, S.J., *Personal Responsibility and Christian Morality* (Dublin: Gill and Macmillan, 1983), 71.

34 To some degree the social teaching of the Church belongs to this effort. As moral teaching, it seeks to incorporate life in society and the special issues which exist there, into the Christian life.

35 *Second General Conference of Latin American Bishops, the Church in the Present-Day Transformation of Latin American in Light of the Council: II Conclusions*, 2nd edition (Washington, D.C.: Division for Latin America, United States Catholic Conference, 1973).

36 John Paul II, apostolic exhortation *Reconciliation and Penance* (Washington, D.C.: United States Catholic Conference, 1984), 16.

37 Judith A. Merkle, "Sin," in *The New Dictionary of Catholic Social Thought*, ed. Judith A. Dwyer (Collegeville, MN: Liturgical Press, 1994), 883–88.

38 Michael Paul Gallagher, *Clashing Symbols: An Introduction to Faith and Culture* (New York: Paulist Press, 2003), 52.

39 Robert K. Merton, "Social Structure and Anomie," in *Social Theory and Social Structure*, revised edition (Glencoe, IL: The Free Press: 1957), 132, 155–56, 464ff.

40 "Decree on Priestly Formation," in *The Documents of Vatican II*, ed. Walter M. Abbott, S.J. (New York: Herder and Herder, 1966), no. 16, 452.

41 Bernard Haring, *The Law of Christ: Moral Theology for Priests and Laity*, trans. Edwin G. Kaiser (Cork: Mercier Press, 1963–67).

42 Norbert Rigali, "New Horizons in Moral Theology," in *New Horizons in Theology. College Theology Society Annual Volume 50* (New York: Orbis Books, 2004), 43. I am indebted to Rigali's reflection here.

43 For instance, some sensed they could keep the moral law, yet be lacking morally, as they passively stood by before injustice, family disintegration, government corruption and other markers of modern living.

44 Paulinus Ikechuskwu Odozor, C.S. Sp., *Moral Theology in an Age of Renewal: A Study of the Catholic Tradition since Vatican II* (Notre Dame, IN: University of Notre Dame Press, 2003), 230.

45 In the West personal autonomy and mutual consent became the only public standards in sexual morality. To take another path a person would need a vision of "the kind of person" he or she wishes to be, distinct from the culture. The relevance of virtue ethics and natural law theory was re-examined in light of this quandary.

46 Rigali, "New Horizons in Moral Theology," 48.

47 Judith A. Merkle, "Social Ethics in the New Millennium," in *Ethical Dilemmas in*

the New Millennium (I), ed. Francis A. Eigo, O.S.A. (Philadelphia, PA: Villanova University Press, 2000), 85.

48 "... it is a fundamental question for modern Christology to decide the relation between redemption understood in a Christian perspective and emancipation understood as the modern age understands it." Walter Kasper, *Jesus the Christ* (London/New York: Burns and Oates/Paulist Press, 1976), 42.

49 Bernard Haring, *Free and Faithful in Christ: Moral Theology for Priests and Laity.* 3 vols. (Slough: St. Paul Publications, 1978, 1979, 1981).

50 Ibid., 1978, 6.

51 Faith, hope and love in this sense are emotional components of moral discernment. Through emotions we become attached to those great goods that inspire our lives, and without them "we become incapable of understanding any moral argument at all." See: Thomas Ryan, S.M., "Revisiting Affective Knowledge and Connaturality in Aquinas," *Theological Studies*, 66 (2005), 52.

52 See: Jean Porter, *Nature as Reason: A Thomistic Theory of the Natural Law* (Grand Rapids, MI: Eerdmans, 2005), 219.

53 One would also need to include the political theology of Johann Baptist Metz, although that is beyond the scope of this work.

54 Fuchs, *Christian Morality: The World Becomes Flesh*, 116–17.

55 Ronald A. Mercier, S.J., "The Holy Spirit and Ethics," in *Moral Theology: New Directions and Fundamental Issues*, ed. James Keating (New York: Paulist Press, 2004), 52.

56 J. Denny Weaver, *The Nonviolent Atonement* (Grand Rapids, MI: William B. Eerdmans, 2001).

57 J. Matthew Ashley, "New Horizons for Mysticism and Politics," in *New Horizons in Theology*, ed. Terrence W. Tilley (New York: Orbis Press, 2005), 63.

58 Miller, *Consuming Religion*, 225.

Chapter 2

TOWARD A THEOLOGY OF THE WORLD

There is perhaps no category of thought more challenging in the field of Christian ethics than the subject of the world. Deep in the intuitions of the Christian life is a basic paradox. One is called to live authentically in this world, yet also called to follow Jesus whose "kingdom was not of this world." How can one be faithful, and live in the tension of being worldly and other-worldly in the right balance?

How we understand the world impacts the role the world plays in the Christian life. Is the world to be avoided? Can the world be transformed? Do we live as Christians waiting for the better world of heaven? Can we attend to the "essentials" of Christian living, the commandments and the rituals of the Church, and avoid the messy business of involvement in the world, yet still claim to be morally good? Can we become fulfilled without "putting something back" into the world which is our only context for knowing ourselves, others and God? We will explore here five "moments" in the history of Christian thought which revisit this tension in Christian morality, to ask how they illumine the search to be faithful as Christians in the world today.[1]

The Greek Moment

The world, or the totality around us, was for the Greeks something well ordered and beautiful. For them, the order of human life, individual or social, was patterned on the order of the world.[2] While Plato saw the sensible world as only the image of a true world accessible to the Spirit, Aristotle saw nature as the principle of all things. The world was unconscious of nature, but God guaranteed the order of all things in the cosmos through his full self-consciousness. For the Greeks, cosmology — not anthropology — was the more fundamental of the sciences.[3] The perpetual revolutions of the stars in the universe more closely imaged the immutability of God than men and women. The Stoics saw God as the all-pervading reason (logos), the soul of the world, making His providence the law of the universe. The world for the Greeks is the ultimate divine space.

Yet, the Gnostics did not share this great appreciation for objective sensible reality. They focused on "another world," one of the spirit, apart from the laws of nature, above the vicissitudes of early life. Such a world was above injustices. It was more reliant than the drives and decay of the body and its vulnerability to sickness and death. Since matter threatened the world, flight from the body and the sensible world became the road to salvation, or the life of the soul. Introspection rather than involvement in this world was emphasized as the key to new life. The core ambiguity in Greek thought regarding the world contributed to Christian ambivalence regarding embrace of the world and flight from the world in spirituality and morality.

The Christian Moment

The early Christians were grounded in the Jewish sense of a created world. Gen. 1.31 named the world as non-divine but good. God, who lives beyond the world, guarantees its consistency. Creation is God's first saving deed which is continued in the covenant, and the election of key figures of the Hebrew Scriptures. The world of human beings and the cosmos is good but it is also fallen creation. Christians recognized Jesus Christ as the light of this world. While the world is fully redeemed, it remains the realm of the evil one. Humankind's ambivalent experience of the world is mirrored in New Testament thought.

St. Paul presents a world where sin reigns as a power.[4] While created good, the world through sin has turned away from God. The individual person cannot escape this (Romans 5–8). Insofar as the world is the context of the human condition, it is marked by the sin of the world.[5] Jesus came from another realm to be the light of the world and to save it (Jn 3.17). The cross of Jesus discloses the evil of the world, as well as the boundless absolute love of God for the world. Since the world was accepted by God in Jesus Christ; this brought a new age to the world. Christians are not to flee the world. They are to live in a world which is both open to and distant from God's acceptance of it. They are to use things of this world and recognize the goodness of creation, yet also to bear in mind that the world is passing away.

St. Augustine tried to synthesize the positive and negative attitudes toward the world which remained in both Christian and Greek thought. Augustine thought better of the world than the Greeks, who admired the structure and order of the world, but who viewed its matter as deficient. Augustine knew the world was created by God and was in itself good. The human person was not just to fit into the world as a niche in the cosmic order. They were to be persons before the face of God. The world was important, but more important was to live in God, one's supreme good. This was done through faith, hope and love. Augustine recognized that God's creation of the material world gave it beauty and order, however, for him this order was perceived in contrasts.

Augustine's world was comprised of three dimensions: the world that was external, the human soul, and that above the soul and in its depths, God.[6] The three existed in dynamic tension. The cosmos itself was divided into two realities, the city of God and the city of the earth. The *saeculum* is the realm in which the carriers of the two cities are intertwined.[7] It is important to note that for Augustine the earthly city has two dimensions, and is not limited solely to sinful humanity. On the one hand, it is the world which is profane, and rejects God. It is the realm of the impious and reprobate. On the other hand, the earthly city is simply the material world. It is the actual space of life, the empirical city where good and bad mix. The earthly city and its institutions have a moral dimension; they can be better or worse in their service of human life. The care of the *saeculum*, or the realm in which the two cities intertwine, thus has importance for both the believer and the non-believer. It is the real world in which all have to live. Augustine's vision of the two cities both validates the institutions and activities of the earthly city and relativizes their importance and purpose. Both aspects of his synthesis impact their role in understanding Christian faithfulness.

The institutions of the earthly city are validated as remaining intact until the end of the world (Romans 13). They are not morally neutral. Augustine holds that societies, institutions and practices are incapable of salvation or damnation, the realm of the heavenly city.[8] Human intentionally marks all morality. Impersonal institutions have no eschatological destiny, no intentions which can be directed to ultimate ends. Yet, shared meanings and consensus on a value system remain essential features of a society and form part of what the heavenly city recognizes, sanctions and fosters for its own ultimate purpose, the true worship of the one God.[9] For Augustine, the only true *res publica* based on the only true justice is the heavenly city. The values to which human groups are committed in this way are relativized by this ultimate reality, but not invalidated. Practices, customs, institutions form a complex which shapes and conditions human action and behavior even though they do not determine it.[10] Thus they have bearing on human welfare and ultimately on the options available to them to work out their salvation. To this degree, they reflect a consensus which promotes response to salvation, or negates it.

It is impossible given Augustine's synthesis to relate every aspect of the world directly to the sacred, even though he holds that all creation is good. He states: "In truth, these two Cities are entangled together in this world, and intermixed until the last judgment effect their separation."[11] The *saeculum*, or the secular, the shared space in which Christian and pagan both have a stake, retains its own autonomy and validity in this ambiguity. It is not a third city between the earthly and the heavenly, but rather their mixed, intertwined state in real life.

This middle ground between the sacred and the profane can neither be included in the sacred, by Christians or pagans, nor repudiated as profane and demonic. Political institutions, social practices, and customs can be directed either to the enjoyment of eternal peace by members of the heavenly city or wrongly directed to lesser goods, the earthly city. Between the two exists a sliding scale of better and worse. Augustine claims if you want to discover the character of any people, you have only to observe what they love.[12] Political institutions, social practices and customs, even of non-Christian origin, can foster proper loves. In this they have value.[13] Augustine validates the world by noting the importance of these institutions in human life.

Augustine's world was one of great pluralism.[14] However, it turned into the sacral society of the Middle Ages, or Christendom. An ascetic impulse fostered other-worldly emphasis in Christian spirituality. The political transformation in Western Europe led to a society which was organized around religion in the form of the Church. The Church in this sense swallowed up the world. Instead of the tension in Augustine's world between those inside and outside the Church, the Middle Ages was a time when the conversion process of the Christian, who was to become perfect, was stressed.[15] Christianity was endangered by becoming too closely identified with the culture and social structure of its social matrix. The danger to the Christian was a spirituality which embraced "flight from the world" yet had to face the inevitability of life in this world.[16] Physical withdrawal from the world became a symbol of the division between the perfect and the imperfect spiritually. The world lost ground as a viable place of Christian faithfulness, while Christendom was viewed by some as the growing together of the heavenly and earthly cities. The eschatological "gap" between Christ's lordship and the world narrowed, in the paradoxical situation of the de-valuing of the world.

However, the Middle Ages also held the tensions of this impossible synthesis. Aquinas opened the door to the independence of secular reason to the degree that "the philosopher" Aristotle is treated in his work as an authority with his own underivable principles.[17] Reason entered that incomplete but real space of human well-being which both the believer and the unbeliever had interest in preserving. The state gradually emerged as independent from the Church. Nature itself became a field for human experimentation, made possible by its freedom from a quasi-mystical status of magic and taboos. Nature created by God was free to have its own laws which opened it up to human investigation and study.

As modern times dawned, people shifted in their perception as to how the human person gained access to God. One no longer had to sit passively seeking God by observing the movement from cause to effect, as the only faithful stance. Rather human action changed nature, the world and lives in it. Discernment of how the world and its transformation entered into Christian faithfulness did, however, remain a question. How should the human person hold in balance both the obligation to become through love and work, and to transform the conditions by which others do the same, while also acknowledging one's finitude before the world?[18] Recognizing the inevitability of death itself as a signature of human identity, the Christian community had to ask how their growing consciousness of freedom before this world called them to be both this-worldly and other-worldly. How were they to follow Christ in this world and through this world, and also to surrender to Christ in love and hope, whose promise of a Kingdom not of this world was only his to fulfill?

The Moment of Modernity

For the theologian Reinhold Niebuhr, the problem of faithfulness in the Christian life is inextricably tied to the process of human freedom before the world. The problem of sin, or of lack of faithfulness, resided for Niebuhr, not in the world as we find it, or society, but rather in the contradictions within the human person. Niebuhr, living in the disillusionment between the world wars, reflected on a new state of humankind before the world which had been developing since the Enlightenment. Human nature is unique in that it can envision new possibilities and achieve them in this world. But this very freedom is prone to entertain the illusion that the human person is not limited, but rather is self-sufficient.

Human freedom in this world has both creative and destructive elements which cannot be separated. He remarks:

> The two are inextricably bound together by reason of man being anxious both to realize his unlimited possibilities and to overcome and to hide the dependent and contingent character of his existence.[19]

When the person feels the power of the creative potential of being human in this world, they can also deny the contingent character of human existence in pride and self-love. Another response is to ignore the moral call of this creative power before the world. The person escapes from this freedom in sensuality.[20]

Pride or sensuality is involved in every human act. One falls into pride when one seeks to raise one's contingent life to unconditioned significance. One falls into sensuality to escape from the freedom and possibilities of the human spirit by becoming lost in the detailed processes, activities and lesser interests of life. The result is that human beings have unlimited devotion to limited values and apathy toward what is truly good, including the social good, the call to transform the world.[21] Human sinfulness is more than a sheer act of defiance of God. Sin involves blindness to limitation. Sin is the deception that covers up the insecurity and anxiety people feel as they stand before the potentials of their freedom vis-à-vis this world. This deception inevitability leads to actions that stretch human power beyond its limits.[22]

Since the person stands before God in the paradoxical situation of freedom and finiteness, the person never really knows the limits of his or her possibilities. Only a sense of God and God's will can provide a boundary where freedom can find a balance between its drive for self-transcendence and its inherent creature-liness.[23] Niebuhr's anthropological turn places the tension of Augustine's two Kingdoms in the internal spirit of the person vis-à-vis this world. However, it leaves unanswered the paradox of faithfulness in this world.

For Niebuhr, Christian faithfulness is an impossible ideal, one taken on in faith and love, but never accomplished. Since it is impossible to achieve, it is better to focus on strategies to live with its challenge. He debates with his brother H. Richard, who sees faithfulness in a more other-worldly manner. Faithfulness depends on the disinterestedness of love which trusts in God, and seeks pure intentions and methods, in the many situations which frame modern living, H. Richard Niebuhr argues.[24] Reinhold is more this-worldly in his approach, and urges concrete action. Faithfulness involves the humble acknowledgment that we are never pure, and conflict and coercion is inevitable in the face of the evil of this world. The Kingdom of pure love in society is always partially expressed, and imperfectly practiced. The cross of modern living is the willingness to invest in societal change even though imperfect results may follow. In Reinhold Niebuhr's words, "Love may qualify the social struggle of history but it will never abolish it, and those who make the attempt to bring society under the domination of perfect love will die on the Cross."[25]

Niebuhr's world emerged through the processes of modernity which challenged both the human capacity to know the world as it is, and to experience its "givenness" as a normative element in the quest for faithfulness. The world of nature of the Greeks was now the world of culture, the world as we find it plus the human element of re-making it. However, the man-made world of technology, forces of domination and lost enchantments were as threatening as the untamed nature appeared to primitive people. What did it mean to be faithful in a world where history recounted no longer the cyclic flow of the inevitable, but the consequences of the chosen?

The Moment of Vatican II

John XXIII's vision of the value of this world liberated the Church from a Catholic cultural ghetto created as a retreat from modernity. The search for an enclave of faithfulness apart from this world ended.[26] Acknowledgment of the secular as an autonomous realm entered into Catholic spirituality in a new way.

Encouragement to invest rather than withdraw from the world as a measure of discipleship caused members of the Church to re-examine priorities and strategies for expressing faithfulness. In contrast to the suspicion in the pre-Vatican II Church to developments in science, technology, and modes of social organization associated with the modern world, the documents of Vatican II reflect an appreciation for the changes which were sweeping the world. The Church recognized the expansion of human capacities to act. There was a deepening confidence that humankind could face the challenges of the time through new forms of social and political organization (PT 44–45). These insights also energized the Church to face the possibilities of this new context.

However, the *Church in the Modern World* document acknowledged in its introductory paragraphs the ambiguous character of life in the modern world:

> Never has the human race enjoyed such an abundance of wealth, resources and economic power, and yet a huge proportion of the world's citizens are still tormented by hunger and poverty, while countless numbers suffer from total illiteracy . . . political, social, economic, racial and ideological disputes still continue bitterly, and with them the peril of a war which would reduce everything to ashes . . . Finally, man painstakingly searches for a better world, without working with equal zeal for the betterment of his own spirit.
>
> (*Gaudium et Spes*, no. 4)

Appreciation for the expansion of human agency at the heart of great changes sweeping the world was tempered by insight into misery which could be avoided with other priorities and modes of organizing human life. The "peace," which for Augustine was the order and tranquility sought in human life, had to be found again in a new age of human agency and massive inequities marking global progress.[27] Concomitantly, how to take responsibility for this new context posed a new challenge to visions of Christian faithfulness.

Because of massive cultural changes, the council called for a renewal in the Catholic Church in the area of moral theology. It called for the Church to integrate not only its new understanding of the Scripture into moral theology but also to orient it to the task of Christians to love, to bring forth the fruits of charity "for the sake of the world."[28] Moral theology needed to stress responsibility for the new world that the modern person was creating. The Church's social tradition, both in its social encyclicals and in the theological voices of Christians at the margins of global progress, illuminated this reading of the signs of the times. A more just and fully human development was named "another name for peace" (PP 76, 83). The moral challenge of Augustine's *saeculum*, that world of the human well-being that both the believer and non-believer share, was given the normative vision of the *humanum*, the dignity of the human person.

God's Kingdom is ultimately God's final action at the end of time. However, in the in-between times, Christians are called to look at decisions in the social political order not just expediently but in terms of their ultimate meaning for the other. In this way, the Kingdom also enters into time to shape it. John Paul II offered a measuring stick of Christian faithfulness in an ambiguous world through the humanistic criterion. This is a standard for evaluating and choosing between social systems, institutional reforms or legal reforms in terms of how they enhance human dignity. In his words, the humanistic criterion is:

> the measure in which each system is really capable of reducing, restraining and eliminating as far as possible the various forms of exploitation of man and of ensuring for him, through work, not only the just distribution of the indispensable material goods, but also a participation, in keeping with his dignity, in the whole process of production and in the social life that grows up around the process.[29]

The coming of the Kingdom in the *saeculum* is always partial and incomplete. In this sense the other-worldly dimension of Christian spirituality remains intact in the Christian imagination. However, the lack of ultimacy of the *saeculum* did not reduce the urgency of the quality of its decisions. To be a faithful Christian in an increasingly interdependent world, the maxim to do good and avoid evil is not enough. One has to search out how to embrace responsibility for the "other" in a manner that respects the other and his or her good as carrying the face of one's own moral obligation.

The Postmodern Moment and the Challenge of Liberation

The challenge of Vatican II was to embrace the world without submitting to a false incarnational optimism. The world has not yet been "divinized," therefore a positive posture toward the world could not overlook its pitfalls. The eagerness to embrace the world and interpret salvation history itself as the growing divinization of the world by thinkers such as Teilhard de Chardin was tempered by voices from the margins. These lives were marked, not by the inevitable progress of the developmentalist mentality of the sixties, but by situations of "institutionalized violence" (Medellin 2.16).

Theologian Teilhard de Chardin saw the cosmos as a process which mirrors the inner life of God. Despite its pain, failure, and apparent absurdities, all life is developmental and moving in a process of cosmogenesis. Chardin saw the universe as a cosmos or whole developing in a precise direction. It goes from the Alpha point to the Omega point, under the ever present care of God the creator and preserver.[30] However, as positive and inviting as Chardin's view of the world was, many used his optimism as a theological foundation for prevailing cultural views which overstated just how well the world was progressing. They drew an analogy between continuous evolutionary process in nature and economic, social and political systems in the *saeculum*. What for Chardin was a process which had to be discerned, was for others a belief in a mechanical vision of progress in this world which was inevitable and divinely sanctioned. Such an overly optimistic view of the international community understated the conflict and interests protected by the status quo and the countervailing histories of women, the poor, minorities and whole continents left out of the post-Second World War prosperity experienced in First World countries. Such visions lost ground in the modern outlook as both postmodern and liberation thinkers held the inconsistencies of human progress and the intractability of human suffering before the Christian imagination.

Experience of massive cultural change in the *saeculum*, the world shared by believer and non-believer alike, raised questions of faith for the believer. Christians pondered the future of faith itself and the meaning of moral faithfulness. How was one to be faithful in this new world? How was one to pass on faith to new generations? Moral theology stressed the following of Christ in the modern world. What can and should Christ mean, if anything, in the moral lives of Christians? Systematic theology probed the penetrating consequences of these questions in its own field of inquiry. How does the quest for emancipation, in all its forms, relate to the Christian life? In the words of Walter Kasper, ". . . it is a fundamental question for modern Christology to decide the relation between redemption understood in a Christian perspective and emancipation understood as the modern age understands it."[31]

These questions were coupled by even more troubling ones surrounding the significance of human agency, its relevance to faith, and even to knowledge of God. Those from the Third World, for whom little movement seemed possible in the North-South divide, asked, "What possibilities remain for Christian faith if Christians have no possibilities of changing their history?"[32] What is the meaning of Christian freedom if people cannot be free; have no concrete options, before the conditions of their lives?[33] Practices of Christian asceticism were questioned regarding their significance for the order of this world. Asian theologian Aloysius Pieris comments regarding voluntary poverty, "the few who renounce their possessions are not 'founded and rooted in Christ Jesus' if the many who have no possessions to renounce are not the beneficiaries of that renunciation."[34] Debate ensued as to the nature of Christian spirituality. What part is the practical conclusion of theology and what part is the radical involvement with the poor and oppressed? Does one know and unite with Jesus Christ through faith, seeking understanding, or by following Jesus as the way, especially the way of the cross, in involvement in social and political change in this world?

Profound was the assessment of the impact of modern society on evangelization, or the link between Christian faithfulness and the handing on of the gospel. Since influences on people's receptivity for faith were so different to pre-modern times, a type of "shaping of culture" was imperative for believers. John Paul II alerted the Church to a world situation characterized by a "culture of life" and a "culture of death." "We find ourselves not only 'faced with' but necessarily 'in the midst of' this conflict" (EV 28). Here it is not enough to simply analyze the world or flee it in search of moral faithfulness. Rather the future of the believing community depends on discernment and action that can actually mould cultural reality. Christian faithfulness is marked in the *saeculum*, the world both believers and non-believers share, by a sense of transcendence and compenetration on the part of believers and the Church.[35]

The Church continually reiterated that growth of this world into God's Kingdom is not a progressive development, nor arrived at solely through the modern theories of human power over nature, evolutionary progress, science and technology, or even modern liberal rights.[36] Rather it is a process often marked by radical contradictions, violent transformations, and death-resurrection experiences. Latin American theologian Jon Sobrino terms this *rupture epistemological* — scripturally founded in the "transcendence of the crucified God."[37] Others, embedded in First World culture, stress that a non-conflictual encounter between faith and modernity is impossible in Christian faithfulness.[38] The encounter of God and humanity — the interplay of grace and liberty — is seen as the obligation to use all human potentialities to anticipate the Kingdom, which nevertheless remains God's gratuitous gift. What is involved is not a passive solidarity with the poor but also a dynamic participation in their struggle for full humanity. What is called for is not a self-righteous denunciation of modernity but a transformative influence on aspects of its culture which do not serve the *humanum*.[39]

For John Paul II the path to Christian faithfulness which takes the *saeculum* seriously is one of solidarity. Solidarity is "a firm and persevering determination" to commit oneself "to the common good; that is to say to the good of all and of each individual because we are all really responsible for all" (SRS 38). Solidarity checks those forces which ignore the fundamental equality of all and the purpose of creation and the goods of the earth. These are structures of sin that reside in cultural visions of what it means to be an adequate human being (SRS 36). He remarks that "hidden behind certain decisions, apparently inspired only by economics or politics are real forms of idolatry: of money, ideology, class, technology" (SRS 37). If those things which block development are not just inadequate theories or structures for human flourishing but human sin itself, genuine development requires a conversion. Development is more than economic;

it includes the trajectory of human growth toward otherness and depth. For Christians, this process is integral to the meaning of Christian faithfulness in the modern world. It is a call to conversion on a moral, affective, intellectual and religious level. "This conversion specifically entails a relationship to God, to the sin committed, to its consequences and hence to one's neighbor, either an individual or a community" (SRS 38). For our purposes, it is important to note that the spiritual conversion is not just an interior one. It has concrete manifestations in the individual and in society. A sign of conversion is a growing awareness of interdependence among individuals and nations and evidence that people "care" about injustices and violations across the world (SRS 38). Such conversion is also linked to a responsible use of human agency. The spiritual path of solidarity is reflected in a new imagination that creates systems that are more interdependent in economic, cultural, political and religious ways. These moral changes reflect a deeper growth in the spiritual path of solidarity. Finally, for the Christian, living the virtue of solidarity has a political-mystical dimension: it gives one access to God. As we find worth in our neighbor, respond to her or him as "other," we find God. The bonds formed in this way are deeper than the natural or human bonds we hope bind the world (SRS 40). These are the bonds of communion. Augustine might recognize this communion as that mix of the heavenly and earthly cities, one that requires the structures of a healthy *saeculum* but also is dependent on that gift of faith, hope and love which is only God's to give.

Openness to the World and the Cross

Johann Baptist Metz in his *Theology of the World* argues that the history of the person of Jesus Christ does illumine for us the question of our relationship to the world.[40] How does one follow Jesus Christ faithfully while living in the tension of being worldly and other-worldly in the right balance?

Jesus accepted the world in the "form of a servant" (Phil. 2.6-11). His death was accepted, an exposure to the fate which came to him from the outside. His life and mission involved both activity and the passivity of obedience before that which was contradictory. The wholeness of Christ did not protect him from human suffering and paradox. In his humanity Christ fully engages and accepts the world, but in its distance from God. His embrace of the world changed the world and its possibilities, but the world remained different from God, and not completely integrated and transparent. Christ in this sense revealed the transcendent God, not the God of the Greeks who was conceived more as a world principle or kind of cosmic reason and cosmic law. Rather God being God lets the world be the world. For the Christian, this means that pursuit of God in this world follows the path of the cross, as no matter how many transformations the world receives through human ingenuity, the world remains the world, and other than God. Its capacity to resist and subvert the embrace of God remains. Metz puts it this way:

> With the Father's acceptance of the world in Jesus Christ we have the radical and original setting-free of the world, its own authentic being, its own clear, non-divine reality. This process operates in history on the basis of the modern secularization of the world. The world is now universally given over to what the Incarnation bestows upon it in a supreme way: secularity.[41]

The historical course of this process of engagement with secularity or the *saeculum* is not free from ambiguity. The human propensity for evil grows alongside its real progress (GS 40). The prophetic call of Micah, "To act justly, to love tenderly and to walk humbly with God" (Mic. 6.8), reminds Christians that faithfulness is neither a self-initiated project nor a flight from this world. Rather Christians affirm that God gives a future to all the fragments of love and meaning they seek to bring into the world, even if it appears that their efforts are like footprints on a sandy shore, easily swept away by the currents of more powerful forces among them.

As they voice a "no" to the world as they find it, and seek to build a "yes" of a better *saeculum*, Christians take on the cross.[42] This is not the cross found only in one's own life, but the cross embraced for the sake of the others. Only love makes the cross possible, and sustains it in its meaning.[43] Trust is required to confront evil, sustain those who suffer and draw near to those who are vulnerable in this world.[44] Without it there is no entrance into the dynamism of hope and investment which marks Christian faithfulness in this world.

The cross is involved not only in the use of power for the good in this modern age of science and technology, arms and communications, but also when humans are impotent in the face of suffering. The choice which measures faithfulness is whether to turn to God in hope and trust and continued faithful investment, or to turn away. Characteristic of the ministry of Jesus was that he invited people beyond the externals of his various healings to its source, a relationship with God. Every miracle in the gospels required a change of heart. The problem in Nazareth was that people were asking for miracles which required no change of heart, no deeper fellowship with God. Today's technical solutions to the world's problems are not enough without the heart and will which reflect change in the human spirit (CV 23).

The meaning of the paschal journey in Christian life has too often been concentrated in the symbol of the cross taken out of context and raised up in an isolation that glorifies suffering and death for its own sake. This false asceticism plagues the Church at various times and leads to other-worldly spirituality which is non-productive for the world. The cross, on the other hand, must be seen in conjunction with Jesus' relationship with God as the defining experience of his life. Jesus' mission to proclaim the reign of justice and love was not a stoic goal of self-determination; it was a loving response to His Father. Jesus shows Christians that the cross always involves God as the positive ground and horizon of all negative experience of suffering.

The assurance of salvation which Jesus proclaims arises from the unbroken communion with God in which he lived.[45] There is no possible ground in the human history of disaster for the assurance of salvation that Jesus imparts. No plan, no form of government, no system or success which humans can create. There is no basis for the hope of a future opened up by God, except in the experience of contrast which Jesus himself knows in the depths of his own being in relationship with God. It is Jesus' love to the point of death, rather than death itself, which is salvific. The experience of the defeat of God's plan in him was the beginning of his experience of death. His sustained trust in God in the face of all resistance was the beginning of his experience of resurrection and the vindication of God's plan.

In the face of the cross, or personal experiences of negative contrast, the Christian is brought mysteriously to the heart of God's purposes for them and for the world. Faithfulness in the Christian life is woven with this inviolable thread of communion with God standing in resistance to evil in and of the world. This experience lies at the heart of Christian faith and is what resurrection faith proclaims. The communion which flows from such sharing is also a door to joy. Christian faithfulness calls for solidarity in both joy and suffering, a standing with one another in concrete communion in the face of all the dimensions of human life.[46]

Fidelity to God and God's cause, which is the cause of the flourishing of humanity, especially suffering humanity, has also been named as the path of the Church. John Paul II stresses that the human person is the primary and fundamental way for the Church. In the encyclical *Redemptor Hominis* (1979) he remarks that this "way" is "traced out by Christ himself," the mystery of the incarnation and the redemption is grounded in God's love for human beings (RH 14). Christ's own model of living through the paschal mystery is the model that the Church herself is to follow. The truth of Christian faithfulness is that we experience the resurrection only in light of our deaths. And these deaths are to be as Christ's, for the life of this world. Here Christians find the clues to true faithfulness.

Notes

1 This essay was published in another form in *Moral Theology for the Twenty-First Century: Essays in Celebration of Kevin Kelly*, ed. Julie Clague, Bernard Hoose, Gerard Mannion (London: T&T Clark, 2008), 20–33.

2 See: Gerd Haeffner, "World," in *Encyclopedia of Theology: The Concise Sacramentum Mundi*, ed. Karl Rahner (New York: Crossroad: 1975), 1,832–38.

3 *Nicomachean Ethics*, VI, 7.

4 Cf. Judith A. Merkle, "Sin," in *The New Dictionary of Catholic Social Thought*, ed. Judith A. Dwyer (Collegeville. MN: Liturgical Press, 1994), 883–88.

5 Cf. Piet Schoonenberg, *Man and Sin* (Notre Dame, IN: University of Notre Dame Press, 1965), 20.

6 *The Confessions of St. Augustine*, trans. F.J. Sheed (New York: Sheed and Ward, 1943), Book X, vi.

7 Robert A. Markus, *Christianity and the Secular* (Notre Dame, IN: University of Notre Dame Press, 2006), 48.

8 Ibid., 47.

9 Ibid., 62.

10 Ibid., 44.

11 Augustine, *The City of God*, trans. Marcus Dods (New York: The Modern Library: Random House, 1950), Book I, 35.

12 Ibid., XIX.14.

13 Markus, *Christianity and the Secular*, 38.

14 *City of God*, XIX.1.

15 Markus, *Christianity and the Secular*, 86.

16 Philip Sheldrake, S.J., *Spirituality and History* (New York: Orbis Books, 1998), 68ff.

17 Jean Porter, *Nature as Reason: A Thomistic Theory of the Natural Law* (Grand Rapids, MI: Eerdmans, 2005), 8.

18 See: Sheldrake, *Spirituality and History*, 213ff. for a typology of Christian spiritualities which address this tension.

19 Reinhold Niebuhr, *Nature and Destiny of Man Vol. II* (New York: Charles Scribner's Sons), 186.

20 See also: Erich Fromm, *Escape from Freedom* (New York: Avon Books), 1969.

21 Niebuhr, *Nature and Destiny of Man*, 185.

22 Ibid., 181.

23 Ibid., 57.

24 H. Richard Niebuhr, "The Grace of Doing Nothing," *The Christian Century* (March 23, 1932), 378–80.

25 Reinhold Niebuhr, "Must We Do Nothing?" *The Christian Century*, (March 30, 1932), 417. For an interpretation of Niebuhr's Christian realism in light of the new realities of the postmodern age see: Robin W. Lovin, *Christian Realism and the New Realities* (Cambridge: Cambridge University Press, 2008).

26 Judith A. Merkle, *From the Heart of the Church: The Catholic Social Tradition* (Collegeville, MN: The Liturgical Press, 2004), 110ff.

27 *City of God*, XIX.11–13.

28 "Decree on Priestly Formation," in *The Documents of Vatican II*, ed. Walter M. Abbott, S.J. (New York: Herder and Herder, 1966), no. 16, 452.

29 John Paul II, "Address to the United Nations on the Declaration of Human Rights,"

AAS 1156, para. 17, as quoted in Donal Dorr, *Option for the Poor, 100 Years of Catholic Social Teaching* (New York: Orbis Books, 1983), 275.

30 Teilhard de Chardin, *The Phenomenon of Man*, trans. Bernard Wall (London: Wm. Collins and Company, 1959). See also Denis Carroll, "Creation," in *The New Dictionary of Theology*, ed. Joseph A. Komonchak, Mary Collins and Dermot A. Lane (Wilmington, DE: Michael Glazier, 1987), 246–58.

31 Walter Kasper, *Jesus the Christ* (London/New York: Burns and Oates/Paulist Press, 1976), 42.

32 Hugo Assman, "Statement," in *Theology in the Americas*, ed. Sergio Torres and John Eagleson. Documentation and papers from the Theology in the Americas Conference, Detroit, Michigan, August, 1975 (New York: Orbis Books, 1976), 300.

33 Roger Haight, *An Alternative Vision: An Interpretation of Liberation Theology* (New York: Paulist Press, 1985), 34.

34 Aloysius Pieris, S.J., *An Asian Theology of Liberation* (Maryknoll, NY: Orbis Books, 1988), 21.

35 Merkle, *From the Heart of the Church*, 236.

36 Herve Carrier, S.J., *Evangelizing the Culture of Modernity* (Maryknoll, NY: Orbis Books, 1993), 119.

37 Alfred T. Hennelly, "Theological Method: the Southern Exposure," *Theological Studies*, 38 (1977), 721.

38 Michael Paul Gallagher, *Clashing Symbols: An Introduction to Faith and Culture* (New York: Paulist Press, 2003).

39 This concept would also include the totality of systems which foster the well-being of the human in its harmony with nature.

40 Johann Baptist Metz, *Theology of the World* (New York: Herder and Herder, 1971).

41 Metz, *Theology of the World*, 35.

42 Edward Schillebeeckx, *Church: The Human Story of God* (New York: Crossroad, 1990), 22.

43 Benedict XVI, *Deus Caritas Est* (Vatican City: Liberia Editrice Vaticana, 2006), 18.

44 Cynthia D. Moe-Lobeda, *Public Church for the Life of the World: Lutheran Voices Series* (Minneapolis, MN: Augsburg Fortress, 2004).

45 Kathleen Anne McManus, O.P., *Unbroken Communion: The Place and Meaning of Suffering in the Theology of Edward Schillebeeckx* (Lanham, MD: Rowman and Littlefield, 2003).

46 Christopher Lasch comments that the modern views of progress suggest life will get better and better with each succeeding generation. Success brings an upward mobility and individual autonomy which reward citizens with having to depend less and less on others or be influenced by their wills. Yet modern culture lacks a language of meaning when life's negative experiences occur. The rosy outlook of secular culture makes faith, salvation, and Church extra baggage on a non-conflicted secular life journey. *The True and Only Heaven: Progress and its Critics* (New York: Norton: 1991), 40–81, 529ff.

Chapter 3

UNDERSTANDING GRACE AND SIN IN THE WORLD

Our desire to engage the world leads us to experiences of its coherence and incoherence. In life, people or events concur with our deepest hopes, as well as thwart our dreams and plans. On the one hand we ask why we cause each other so much suffering, on the other we marvel at how often good people come to the aid of others, at a great cost to themselves. Theologically, this mixed quality of life engages us in the twin mysteries of sin and grace. The Church tradition testifies that the two are inseparable in life experience.

To be alive today is to recognize that things are not in order in the world. We observe continuing war and famine, shifting markets changing the lives of millions. Families fall apart and violence marks the streets of modern cities. Third World poverty, disease and political unrest make it impossible for people to find a home in this world. Yet good people are unwilling to give evil an equal footing with good. When they observe these disorders they seek to do something about it. This desire to reach out to the world to improve it is a reflection of the human experience of transcendence.[1] Every effort at moving beyond ourselves, improving our world, and shaping our lives opens the door to a new cycle of reaching again. We reach for more, but not just in consumer culture. It is the more of depth and mystery. Believer and non-believer differ as to their explanation of this experience. For the non-believer, the reach of transcendence is a call to explore the depth of human life. For the believer, this same reach of human depth can be an encounter with the divine.

Transcendence as a human capacity not only fuels our efforts to create a better world, it makes it possible for human beings in their creatureliness to know or experience the infinite God. The very structure of human knowing and the quest to understand the world contains in it the possibility of connecting to the divine. Karl Rahner claims that every time we know or choose anything in particular, we do so against a horizon of limitlessness. Through this reaching out, this horizon or mystery touches or connects with us. The presence of human transcendence does more than engage us in the continued cycle of growth and development. The term of our transcendence can be experienced as absolute mystery, as God.[2]

The experience of transcendence can bring with it the realization that we are finite and cannot bring about the fulfillment of our being. Constant striving alone cannot resolve the tension evoked by this core seeking. St. Augustine said, "Our hearts are restless, until they rest in Thee."[3] In our search for fulfillment we are engaged by Mystery, which is more than a motivational drive, it is a presence which confirms us. As faith assists us to reach out to life through love, more than the visible encounter occurs. Through this reach of faith a person "opens his heart to the nameless presence of a grace and favor still perhaps undefined."[4] We refuse this call to transcendence by turning in on self through egotism and sin. Bernard Haring frames faithfulness in light of this challenge. "In the bible, the main decision of salvation is the choice between a saving solidarity in Christ and a destructive solidarity in sin."[5] Solidarity in Christ is expressed in love.

The experience of transcendence sheds light on the nature of religious faith. Faith concerns not only a way to live in this world but the human search for meaning in it. We seek the meaning not only of our lives but of all of life. We search in the real world, with its ambiguities and its disorder, as well as its gifts and harmonies. Karl Rahner claims that faith in the Spirit of God is the positive and unconditioned acceptance of one's own existence as meaningful and open to a final fulfillment, "which we call God."[6] This is the experience of salvation. Ultimately, faithfulness is a response to this gift, meaning in life is offered as a gift of grace. Salvation is not generated by history alone, an easy life or things going our way. Rather faith responds to God as the ground of our lives in spite of all evidence to the contrary. We can see that salvation is not something we do, it is what God does. It is not achieved by the actions of human beings in history; salvation is always a pure gift of grace.[7] However, our response is necessary for this gift to be accepted. We respond to this gift of God and to the promise of our own life in this world, as we find ourselves in it. This is the core of a faithful life.

People use their reason to understand the world, to make sense of the world. Susan Neiman points out that they do so especially in the face of the fact "that things go intolerably wrong."[8] Belief that the world makes sense in the face of the experience of its complexity is the basis of every attempt to make it so and to assume responsibility for it. Believers reach out to this task with faith as well as reason. They journey to embrace the world with knowledge of the reality of God in their hearts. Yet they experience both hope and despair in engaging this challenge. Their journey engages them in the mysteries of grace as well as sin. However, today the conditions of our postmodern world lead us to approach these mysteries with new questions, yearnings, and challenges.

Does God Add Anything to our Understanding of the World?

Believers see God as relevant to understanding the world, in its wonders as well as tragedies. Faith leads us to see the world differently than the way the world is viewed in secular society. Today we have powerful disciplines which equip us to understand what goes wrong and right in this world, such as sociology, political science, philosophy, criminology, psychology, psychiatry. Talk of God can appear to be functionally redundant. A secular mentality alone assumes God's irrelevance to analysis and interpretation, and brackets God out of the picture. God is left to a private decision concerning personal values and motives. God's reality makes no difference to the frameworks through which we see the world.[9] Rather than a disbelief in God, this approach to the world is a practical exclusion of God from public rationality, reference and insight.

Yet, as believers, we can ask how a doctrine of sin and grace might explain something important about the world today. Therapeutic categories convey some aspects of human behavior we have traditionally discussed as sin. Yet, used alone, they do not make a doctrine of sin an explanatory factor of our world.[10] The therapeutic language is not wrong; it is not enough. A dialogue is needed between all the languages of our secularity and our language of faith to understand the world. The goal is to have God-talk enrich our lived understandings of the world with its light and shadow experiences, and not leave this task simply to secular disciplines and discourses.[11] Christians are challenged to show that reference to God holds explanatory and descriptive power in understanding the world and our role in it, that Christian doctrine sheds light on the human condition.[12] This can be done without reducing sin to an ideological tool to cast blame and pass judgment or calling on grace as a way to cloak the ambivalent nature of human realities.

Can We Do Anything about Good and Evil in this World?

Susan Neiman links the problem of evil with the problem about the intelligibility of the world as a whole.[13] She charges that if we abandon the effort to comprehend evil, we also abandon every basis for confronting it, in thought and in practice. Belief that the world should be rational is the basis of every attempt to make it so. "Without such a demand, we would never feel outrage — nor assume the responsibility for change to which outrage sometimes leads."[14]

The urge to unite what is to what ought to be stands behind every creative endeavor. She charges that those who never seek to unite them do nothing at all.[15] Christianity affirms Neiman's insights as it charges that following Jesus Christ requires that we discern right from wrong and act on it. The traditional moral commands found in the Scriptures and in the tradition aid us in this endeavor. At other times, we are called to confront the problems that plague our world through entering into dialogue between theology and the social sciences (CV 31).

The Catholic tradition holds that all, not just believers, are called to this challenge. Natural law thinking grounds the obligation to face evil in human experience. Natural law belongs to a broad tradition in the history of thought which refers to the human drive to understand *recta ratio*, what is humanly right. This sense of right is inscribed in human nature, and flows from what it means to be human. This does not mean that one can read off a moral regulation from natural reality.[16] The natural order, as raw nature, does not directly affirm or provide the basis for any moral laws.[17] Rather it is human nature as reasoning which grounds morality. Reason leads us first to understand ourselves and our reality in order to assess the significance of the alternatives for action available, and so to come to a sense of the right thing to do. Our Christian faith tells us that in this process, we also meet God. Christians attend to the values of revelation for this discernment. While we cannot find norms of conduct for complex modern problems stated in the Scriptures, faith informs our reason. With St. Paul in Rom. 2.15, we find the moral law "engraved on the heart," and call on our faith to illumine the search for what is right, a search that we share with all people of good will.

As we face evil in our world, as Christians we seek what is right with key assumptions in mind. We are called to be responsible, to live in harmony in our interpersonal and social relationships. We draw on our experience in various aspects of life, such as family, economics, sexuality and medicine. We assume we must respect life, that it cannot be destroyed at will, as all other rights are based on the right to exist. We recognize certain "givens" of human culture, birth, death, marriage, peace, commerce, art, and learning. All of these experiences lead us to search for the truly human in their ordering, while respecting the diversity which culture offers. We assume that values are not just personal, but hold interpersonal and social validity as well. Finally, we know we must weigh the priority and urgency of the different values implied in a judgment of right in order to determine which values must be addressed, so that the behaviors which most closely further human self-realization and development are realized in action.[18]

In this broad Christian vision of moral understanding we hold that along with our faith response to God, inherent in our action, the pertinent reality which forms the context of our decision making has to be understood as fully as possible. Both are necessary in order to come to an understanding of what we shall do. Often this requires the best information possible from the natural and social sciences. Understanding our nature and social context does not make our decision relative, it makes it truthful, as what is right must be in conformity with the whole concrete reality of the human person in this world.[19]

Understanding Evil and the Experience of Auschwitz

As we take responsibility for doing what is right and eliminating evil to the extent that we are capable, perception of what is at stake can shift.[20] Major events in history affect common understandings of good and evil. Think of how our view of the world has shifted since 9/11. We remember its horror as well as witness new forms of heroism in its events. For Enlightenment thinkers, the Lisbon Earthquake in 1755 had a similar effect of shifting their sense of the world. They asked how a Good God could allow such a senseless loss of life. They struggled to express what the terms good and evil meant. They made a distinction between moral evil, evil a human being intends, and natural evil, destructive natural experiences like earthquakes and sickness and death.[21] These expressions allowed them to integrate the negative event while also hold on to a belief in a Good God.

Yet Auschwitz, in its magnitude and horror, could not be held or explained even within these definitions. People recognized Auschwitz as moral evil, yet its magnitude far exceeded the evil the intentions of individuals are able to cause. All the improvements in a "civilized" society in social sciences, political science, international systems, and alliances were ineffectual in the recognition and containment of the carnage at Auschwitz. In fact, their resources were employed to fuel its efficacy. Auschwitz occurred right under the noses of the international community. The progressive tools of modernity, thought to be the highpoint of human civilization, "seemed as hopeless in coping with the event as they were in preventing it."[22] Auschwitz revealed, in Neiman's words, ". . . a possibility in human nature that we hoped not to see."[23]

This event forced the human community to continue their struggle to name evil. We observe today that a modern form of evil is characterized by its power to subject its victims to a process designed to destroy the very concept of humanity within them. Forms of contemporary evil destroy not only its victims but its perpetrators, who lose their own humanity in the process.[24] It denies its victims all the conditions of having a soul. In addition, evil can also appear as banal. Routines of thoughtlessness and inattention allow massive evil to be done in our day by ordinary people who do not let themselves acknowledge that what they do is evil.

When we alter our conception of evil, we also shift our understanding of our place in the world. People today can feel a sense of homelessness in this world. Their experience of life can be one of living not in a cohesive world but a fragmented one — facing at times a bleak, stark, and fragile existence. John Paul II names the situation in his encyclical *Redemptor Hominis*. Human beings as more creative, yet inherent to their creations is their capacity to destroy people and civilization as a whole (RH 15.2). The Pope here articulates a new challenge in the search to be faithful. Faithfulness must include the human drive to be whole in the face of the banality of evil and the feeling that evil is inevitable. This requires a conscious affirmation of the possibility of being faithful over the course of a lifetime.

Faithfulness calls us to resist evil in all its forms; yet our resistance is never complete. *Faithfulness is always partial on its way to wholeness.* The struggle to love and to understand the world challenges us to move ahead although we only have pieces of the whole. The desire to be faithful calls us not only to resist evil but to be creative in the face of it. Faithfulness is the search for the possible, knowing that God's incarnation into this fractured world is the paradigm also of all Christian faithfulness of investment and hope. Faithfulness demands a conversion which not only resists evil, but also evokes a new imagination that creates the world in a more human way. We seek to build systems that are more interdependent in economic, cultural, political, and religious ways in society, as well as build up family, community, profession, and Church.[25] John Paul II reminds us that because the world is both sinful and redeemed, the person seeking to be faithful must act within the horizon of the mystery of love:

> Without the help of grace, men would not know how to discern the often narrow path between the cowardice which gives in to evil, and the violence which under the illusion of fighting evil only makes it worse. This is the path of charity, that is, of the love of God and of neighbor.[26]

Benedict XVI claims that this charity must rest in the truth of human transcendence, that human beings are not self-sufficient nor the authors of themselves, their lives or of society. Rather we are accountable to a truth beyond ourselves, which requires our response but ultimately comes to us as a gift (CV 34). To be closed off from this truth is, in faith terms, an effect of original sin. Yet, we understand sin and evil most fully against the background of the mystery of grace.[27]

New Conversations about Grace

When the modern philosopher Frederic Nietzsche analyzed the world, he concluded that God is dead. Nietzsche expressed a concern about God which is different than in the past. In previous ages, people assumed the existence of God. Nietzsche asked, are we in this world without God? Today we envision our relationship with God differently than in the past. Since grace is God's relationship to us in this world, how we understand God's relationship with the world today impacts our understanding of grace.

In the Scholastic period of theology theological imagination conceived of two orders of life, the natural and the supernatural. Each appears as a separate and self-enclosed sphere of reality. Nature is devoid of anything supernatural and of any experience of it. Grace is conceived as being imposed on human existence by an external degree of God, completely from outside nature, outside history and outside human experience.[28] The connection of this religious sphere to a person's life is essentially achieved through authority and obedience.

Modern theology, as expressed by Karl Rahner, sees this relationship differently. For Rahner, orientation to God comes from within human experience in this world. Human beings have more than a mere passive ability to receive grace. Rather the potential to communicate with God is linked to one's active seeking and desiring in human life. As we try to be at home in this world, we question and search for meaning and fulfillment. Rahner suggests that our access to God is in this very process. As we pursue question after question of our lives, a previous solution shows itself to be only a finite horizon of the answers we seek. As we expand the horizons of possibility in modern life we become aware that the human person is someone with an infinite horizon. (This is not only true for individuals but for communities searching for solutions to their common problems.) Rahner states, "The infinite horizon of human questioning is experienced as an horizon which recedes further and further the more answers man can discover."[29] Engagement with modern life itself can lead the human person to experience themselves as called to more, as reaching out toward truth and reality itself, as transcendent. In seeking to know any and every reality, the structure of human knowing allows the human person to experience an essential openness to the created reality they try to understand and the uncreated reality, God's own Mystery, which grounds it. Key to understanding Rahner's thinking is the realization that in the single experience of knowing, we are simultaneously present to and in touch with the world of objective reality, with ourselves as knowers and with this larger, unlimited horizon in what Rahner calls the transcendental element in our experience. Because human beings are spirit in the world and in history, they are possible subjects of an encounter with God's word in history. Human beings have this potential because, in his words, "God can only reveal what man is able to perceive."[30]

Rahner claims that human beings operating in this world are capable of being open to a positive revelation of God in space and time. We do not have to leave the world and its concerns to find God, as if this were possible. Human beings experience their transcendence not just in knowing but in loving. When they go beyond themselves, they use their freedom to love, and in this love of neighbor, they express love of God.[31] A turn from this call to transcendence is the retreat into egotism, and a turning away from God. Rahner claims that every time we reach out to know or choose anything in particular, that is, make a categorical choice, we do so against a horizon of limitlessness. In this encounter, we actually make a transcendental choice, and meet God as mystery. Absolute mystery or

God is the term of our transcendence.[32] Faith is the surrender to this Mystery as the source of our own meaning and fulfillment. People surrender in faith, ". . . to the hope of an incalculable final reconciliation of their existence, marked by the presence of the One whom we call God."[33]

This active transcending of self takes place by the power of the absolute fullness of being, or grace. Rahner does not think of human nature as apart from God, yet he also wants us to understand that it is through the gratuity of God's grace that our relationship with the fullness of being, or God, is actually an enabling one in our lives. Through his use of the term "supernatural existential" he offers an explanation how this occurs. The term "existential" suggests a component of human existence which makes humans themselves, and distinct from others in creation. God created human beings in order to share God's life with them. God created them for a life of grace, grace as relationship with God. Creation itself is ordered to this goal of union with God. The offer of grace, a relationship with God, therefore is part of being human, it is an existential, an intrinsic component of the very definition of being human in this world.

Since God did not have to create human beings for this purpose and end, this existential is called a "supernatural existential." Grace is part of human nature only because God gifts us with this relationship. Created human existence is therefore in itself a gift from God; in being created God freely bestows upon human beings the gift of Godself in grace. Since human beings must freely accept this gift if there is to be a personal relationship of knowledge and love with God, it is the *offer and possibility* of grace which is the existential. God does not treat us as puppets and force us to respond. Grace is not a thing. Rather grace is a relationship which on the one hand is part of being human and an essential of human nature, but on the other is pure gift. This offer of grace is universal and comes with being human. It is an existential of human life also in that every aspect of human life is included in it. "The power of God's love and grace is stronger than the power of sin and cannot be conquered by it. The presence of grace is not eradicated by the presence of evil, but remains an ever-present existential of human existence."[34]

Rahner's thought stands in contrast to the worldview of those in the Middle Ages. Grace does not come to us from some order of the universe outside the world. Rather God communicates in grace within the structure of human knowing and loving, as limited, yet open to what is ultimate. It is in everyday existence where men and women listen for the possible Self-manifestation of God in a human word.[35] In this Self-communication, God reveals God's own Self as personal and loving and acting. God in this sense does not just give us power or help to know and love, but God's own Self dwells within us.

Revelation points to the reality that the horizon encompassing all human life is the saving God. Human life is the abiding presence of God in which God offers to humanity God's Self and the possibility of the free response of faith. Through the special revelation of Jesus Christ the believer knows that God is more than a Supreme Being who lives outside their world. Rather their field of knowing and loving can now be interpreted through faith as the presence of God and the ground of Christian hope and love. Religious faith in the Christian life is the identification of the ultimate possibilities and limits of human life and the world with the revelation of Jesus Christ. While all people seek meaning for their lives, religious faith interprets the process in relationship to God. We recognize that believers and non-believers question and seek fulfillment for themselves and the world as a whole. Believers, however, see the face of God in this experience and name the unfolding of a better history as God's gift.

Sin and Evil in a Fragmented Culture

The mystery of sin can be imagined as both personal and as situated in this world. A notion of sin, as personal sin alone, is inadequate to account for our experience of evil in this world. However, to view evil only as an ingredient of the world, in the situation, and not of our human spirit, is also lacking in depth. Through the centuries the Church has developed a language of sin which seeks to account for the human experience of sin and evil in this world.

The Council of Trent, in line with the early Council of Carthage, affirmed that each human being lives in solidarity with the sin of Adam, or original sin. Original sin is the primordial situation of guilt in which our freedom and its history are situated and embedded. Human nature exists in a state of sin and grace prior to human choice. Original sin refers to the human experience of resistance to grace expressed in the clouding of intellect, unruliness of desire and weakness of will. Original sin is present before any personal decision and self-chosen attitude of the person. The Church holds that original sin is a personal component of human existence and not simply a result of living in a sin-infected human environment. It is the grace of Jesus Christ that reconciles the divided condition of human freedom due to sin. It changes the condition of human freedom from a state where it is impossible not to sin, to one where there is the possibility of loving despite the power of sin.[36] Christians hold that the sacrament of baptism is key to entering into this transition from sin to grace.

However, the letters of Paul and the gospel of John refer to the entrance into the world of the rejection of God's initiative of grace through free choice, or sin of the world. "He came into what was his own, and his own people did not receive him" (Jn 1.11). Sin of the world is the objective condition of men and women insofar as they are beings conditioned by sin.[37] In other words, sin remains a power in this world, even when we individually avoid its influence on our behavior. Human freedom is limited by the sin of the world, in spite of the call and gift of grace. As a structure of human existence, the sin of the world affects all human actions in a manner that is prior to human decisions. One manifestation of sin of the world is blindness toward human actions as to their real import. Another is a system of personal or communal desires that is satisfied with less than human conditions in the world. A third is satisfaction with the lack of change in the human spirit.[38] Sin of the world is seen in the negative influence of one person on another. Theologian Patrick McCormick refers to it as the cyclic and dead-end approach to human problem solving, which is handed on to successive generations, groups, political parties, and governments.[39]

Awareness of the impact of sin of the world is not new; intuitions of its import can be seen in the Middle Ages. Theologians referred to different stages or situations in salvation history. In paradise humans experienced an original innocence, while in heaven their future is eschatological glory. However, in between humankind lives in a society burdened by sin and its effects, and norms and institutions reflect this state, not the state of perfection before the fall. Some argued that these institutions exist and are necessary only on account of the actual situation of humankind in that time and place. Bonnaventure, for instance, recognizes that certain "orders" of nature do not correspond to the ideal original condition of nature nor even to the more ideal situation of eschatological glory. Rather they are to be considered as "preternatural" modifications which reflect states and stages of existence on their way between the two above realities.[40]

Sin of the world affects moral decision making. Natural law does not refer to reason's search for the objectively right in an ideal situation, but a real one influenced by the sin of the world. The real will of God is not concerned with an ideal world that is different from the world we live in, instead it is concerned with the development of the human situation, including the influence of sin on it. Yet God's will is also connected to the dynamic thrust toward continual improvement, the restoration of all things in Christ. Such improvement means overcoming in grace the consequences of sin in the movement toward eschatological perfection. We pray for this grace in Our Father when we say, "your Kingdom come."

Structural Sin

The contemporary Church has reflected on the sin of the world in human experience through its depiction of structural sin. The Latin American Bishops conference at Medellin (1968) claimed that their reading of the "signs of the times" in their society required of them an "option for the poor," a redirection of pastoral energies to address the concern of poverty in their region.[41] They recognized the sinful influence of structures as situations of "institutionalized violence" against the poor in their country (Medellin 2.16) They noted that structures not only induce individuals to sin but discourage and seek to defeat the human spirit from seeking its full humanity. Those who are dependent on a structure for life sustenance or cultural support experience instead, through the very way the structure organizes and distributes goods and services, an affront to their basic human rights. Unjust structures are the place where the sins of lack of solidarity are crystallized (Medellin 1.2). The Church too was affected by these structures. Helder Camara described the situation: "The Spirit of God was with us pushing us to discover, in our continent, the most painful colonialisms: privileged internal groups who maintain personal wealth at the expense of the misery of their countrymen."[42] The Church was influenced by this situation to the degree it allowed existing political and social structures to leave it untouched by the situation of the people. Insight into these situations is insight into the mystery of sin.

A decade later at Puebla the Church consciously sought a new direction.[43] The bishops reflected that sin is a "rupturing force" which arises from the hearts of human beings and leaves its mark on the structures they create (Puebla 281). Structural sin reflects and incarnates the sinful condition of humanity and the sinful choices of individuals. Structures do not sin, people do. Later John Paul II clarified: no structure can force an individual to sin, but it can make it easier to sin than to be just.[44] A social structure is sinful insofar as, by the way it organizes the distribution of goods, services, or power it violates human dignity in a manner that could be avoided, or it facilitates and supports individual acts of selfishness.[45]

John Paul II commented that desire for profit and thirst for power ignore the fundamental equality of all and the purpose of creation and the goods of the human economy. These are more than destructive personal attitudes; they are structures of sin that reside in cultural visions of what it means to be an adequate human being. These structures are rooted in personal sin and are linked to the acts of individuals who socially reproduce them and make them difficult to remove (SRS 36). Structural sin goes beyond observations of human limitation made by social analysis. Rather these behaviors are linked to the mystery of evil and the heritage of sin. The thirst for power and the desire for profit "at any price" make human attitudes absolute in a manner that is really religious in nature. They are a form of idolatry. To see them as human short-sightedness does not grasp their depth (SRS 36–37). John Paul II remarks, "hidden behind certain decisions, apparently inspired only by economics or politics are real forms of idolatry: of money, ideology, class, technology" (SRS 37).

Structural Sin, Solidarity and Conversion

If those things which block human development are not just inadequate theories or structures for human flourishing but human sin itself, genuine development requires conversion. For John Paul II the virtue of solidarity is connected to the spiritual nature of all humans and to Christian spirituality. Men and women "without explicit faith" can see that the obstacles to full human development are not only economic, "but rest on more profound attitudes which human beings can make into absolute values" (SRS 38). As people work to change these attitudes to ensure a more human life on this planet, they should assume the depth of the human heart in which these attitudes reside, and the vigilance they require to eradicate.

For those who are Christian, this confrontation with structural sin requires a conversion on a moral, affective, intellectual and religious level. "This conversion specifically entails a relationship to God, to the sin committed, to its consequences and hence to one's neighbor, either an individual or a community" (SRS 38). The spiritual conversion is not just an interior one; it has concrete manifestations in the individual and in society. A sign of conversion is a growing awareness of interdependence among individuals and nations and evidence that people "care" about injustices and violations across the world (SRS 38). The spiritual change which leads to solidarity is reflected in a new imagination that creates systems that are more interdependent in economic, cultural, political and religious ways. Moral growth is externalized into facilitating a better life for others.

Finally, solidarity for the Christian has a mystical-political path, it gives one access to God. As we find worth in our neighbor as "other," especially one whom society rejects as worthless, we find God. As we see the image of God in the enemy, friend, and the unknown person who is allowed to impact our lives, we discover bonds with others deeper than the natural or human bonds we hope bind the world (SRS 40). The fragmented world needs a model of communion to heal it: "The 'evil mechanisms' and 'structures of sin' of which we have spoken can be overcome only through the exercise of human and Christian solidarity to which the Church calls us and which she tirelessly promotes" (SRS 40). Benedict XVI affirms that only a humanism open to the Absolute can guide us in promoting the building of structures, institutions, culture and ethos in service of the universal common good (CV 78).

Concupiscence

Concupiscence or the inclination to evil is the tendency in each human being to oppose the action of grace, or the life of the Spirit. It reflects two situations we stand in as human beings in respect to our salvation: "As 'spirit', man, the Christ-like Christ himself, who is 'the spirit' (2 Cor. 3.7) — is filled with the power of God; of the Holy Spirit. As 'flesh', on the other hand, man is delivered to his own weakness as a creature, nay, especially in Paul, delivered to sin."[46] Here flesh does not mean sexuality, rather human assertion and human ways as opposed to the life of the spirit, the new birth and new creation of grace. Love integrates human tendencies, while non-integrated striving of all human tendencies occurs because of the predisposition to lack love after the Fall. Concupiscence in this sense is the human tendency which opposes the collaborative relationship with God, which is the grounding of love and the meaning of human existence. It is the tendency to egotism, the choice of a false self as one's identity which causes one to see themselves and others as mere things and to lose their sense of personhood.

Concupiscence can also be the weakness of freedom, which enters into human desires for the good and orients them in a contrary direction. St. Paul remarks, "For I do not do the good I want, but the evil I do not want is what I do." (Rom. 7.19) Concupiscence also points to the experience of sin as bondage, a sense of the pervasiveness of a sinful attitude and one's powerlessness before it. Bondage implies that when one acts, they exercise their freedom serving God or sin, i.e. one serves God or mammon.

In the setting of Jesus' Sermon on the Mount, Matthew offers the Christian community a warning about a divided heart. "No one can serve two masters; either he will hate the one and love the other, or he will be devoted to the one and despise the others. You cannot serve God and mammon" (Mt. 6.24). In Christian preaching on this text, mammon is often equated to money or possessions. But technically mammon literally means "that in which one puts trust and faith." Putting one's trust in mammon suggests a type of covetousness, or over-investment in possessions, power, ideas, or anything one might use to replace God in one's life.[47] Service of mammon instead of God reflects a weakness of faith. Insufficient faith leads people to trust in uncertain riches. It is not surprising that the next lines in Matthew's gospel urge people not to be anxious. If one places trust in what cannot save, it follows one will be prone to anxiety. It is not that Jesus is telling people not to enjoy the good things of life. He is warning them not to invest in them to the degree that they expect them to deliver ultimate values and their satisfactions. Then they are expecting of them what they cannot deliver.

Mt. 6.24 presupposes the possibility of a slave having two owners with equal shares to him and therefore with equal claims to his services. This situation did exist in the ancient world. A slave could be freed by one master but not the other, so that they were half free and half slave. In such a relationship it was impossible for a slave to display the same devotion to both masters, especially if their wishes and interests might vary widely. Jesus draws the obvious conclusion, a slave would have to love the one master and hate the other.

The meaning of the master–slave relationship is key to unlocking this text.[48] The mixed quality of the relationship captures the mixed nature of human life which the term concupiscence refers. Yet the power of concupiscence does not ultimately define human existence. Redemption always remains the strong force in human life. When applied to the relationship between God and human beings, the master–slave relationship suggests the exclusivity of discipleship, the way ultimately to address concupiscence. Jesus in this parable does not question the position of a slave under two masters, but the person who suffers from the illusion that he or she can serve both God, and things in life to which they impart the faith and trust one should only put in God. Possessions easily fill this need.[49]

The contemporary psychologist and Christian thinker, Gerald May, gives further insight into the nature of concupiscence in modern life. He claims that all addictions are replacements for God. In his words:

> . . . addiction attaches desire, bonds and enslaves the energy of desire to certain specific behaviors, things or people . . . These objects of attachment then become preoccupations and obsessions; they come to rule our lives. And again, addiction is the most powerful psychic enemy of humanity's desire for God.[50]

Concupiscence is a fingerprint of original sin. It can take over human life unless it is checked by recognition of God. Because of the presence of concupiscence, the split condition of human life, the person never becomes wholly absorbed in good or evil.[51] Faithfulness implies not moral perfection, but rather the effort of men and women to bring the whole of themselves to their moral decisions, in biblical terms, to love God "with one's whole heart and with all one's strength." "It ultimately takes a whole lifetime for our love to come not only from our whole heart but also from our whole vitality and from all our powers, and the same is true for our wickedness."[52] Yet, it is only in the experience of concupiscence and its ambiguity that we know Christ, ". . . it is also the form in which the Christian experiences Christ's sufferings and suffers them himself to the end."[53] Through entering into Christ's dying and rising human beings have the potential to "overcome sin" as it is experienced in concupiscence because of the graced nature of human life.[54]

Personal Sin

Personal sin is free cooperation with the forces of sin of the world and concupiscence. It is an act which reflects the quality of one's relationship to God. In the classical tradition, original sin is joined to consideration about the personal sin of the individual, but today there is more emphasis on the history of sin, as in sin of the world, as also a stimulus to personal sin. Biblically, the heart of sin in the Hebrew Scriptures is the failure to live in a covenantal relationship with Yahweh. This relationship is made clear in the laws of the covenant (Exod. 19.4-5) The essence of sin is not the breaking of some external code of conduct. It is a free decision of the heart in which one rejects God. Men and women express this inner rejection in sinful actions. However, given the tradition of the Church that God's eternal law is expressed in the human conscience, and human beings have the capacity, given to them by God, to know the demands of this law, sin is also acting against this "truth." Rejection of God is expressed in rejection of right reason, which in turn is against the good of one's neighbor and oneself.[55] Hence sin involves the inward decision to evil, evil with regard to God and others. It is ultimately an offense against oneself.

Sin offends God because it is a refusal to know God, to accept God, and to recognize God's reality and the right relationships it directs (Isa. 58.6-7). Since the right relationship that covenant with Yahweh directs is for the good of the person and the community, sin is also an act of self-destruction. Sin is the violation of norms which are expressions of God's will in our nature. Nature, however, does not contain any ready-made norms, but it does contain the possibility of being meaningfully assumed in the personal relationships which exist between people and which become expressions of their relationship with God. These laws, however, are not always self-evident. Human beings are also called to establish norms, not just accept them.[56] Sin therefore is not just in the unwillingness to accept norms, but in the refusal to establish them. The link between our inner spirit and our external action can be established as "hardness of heart" in both cases (Mark 10).

The Catholic Church holds that there are graduations in our moral-religious activity as a confirmation or rejection of our covenant with God, our response of faithfulness. The traditional terms "mortal sin" and "venial sin" in the Catholic tradition reflect this insight. Sin is in the true sense of a personal decision and utterance against God. The distinction therefore between the two can be made in the first place in terms of the split in human person in regard to their knowledge and will before this stance. Human beings are always in some form of transition between less and more capability to unify the powers of their lives toward the good or toward evil. One can speak of adopting a life direction, toward the good, or away from it, where individual decisions after a while add up to a stance toward life and God as well. Human life is such that our expressions toward people and the surrounding world ultimately are ones toward God. Good choices take a lifetime to become a good life, hence the need of the grace of perseverance. One bad choice does not mean moral destruction, unless the grace of conversion from it is resisted, and often resisted over a long period of time.

Some decisions therefore are more serious than others in that they are done with more consciousness and deliberateness of will. Others are more conditioned, like a common fault. These actions are good or bad in themselves, but we are often less conscious of their relationship to God. Since we do not live wholly within the Covenant or outside the life of grace, these acts are not central enough really to renew that life or to destroy it. They are not responses or rejections to a new offer of grace. Daily faults, or venial sin, are actions which stem less from our center of personality, and more from influences outside the person and the person's nonintegrated tendencies. We assume these actions are free, but in the deepest sense, as some good actions, the depth of our person is not expressed. These are not so central to our will that they symbolize a rejection of the life of grace. A decision in a grave matter, a mortal sin, has the quality of emptying our heart of love. Stealing usually does not place us before such a central decision, whereas infidelity in marriage is a more serious failing.[57] All actions, however, accumulate in our lives; they either prepare us at death for a final good action in which we commit our lives to God, or they express a progression which in the last resort expresses that opposition to grace which has grown to full strength. Sin, in the Christian understanding, is a voluntary breaking of the covenant with God, whereas the good actions are a free accepting of it.

The determining factor in mortal sin lies in the personal turning away from God. Still the determination of action itself is not completely irrelevant, for normally it is only in serious actions that one is fully involved as a person and commits oneself in his or her basic stand to God. Here we try to avoid two extremes. On the one hand, only looking at the gravity of the matter and thereby materializing sin; on the other, neglecting the importance of the matter involved and thereby spiritualizing sin excessively.

There are three ways the tradition speaks of sin. Sin is a *fact*, like original sin. It is a fact of human life. Sin is an *act* in our free cooperation with the forces of sin and evil. Sin is a *state*, like the direction we cause in our own lives through our choices. We move from good to better, or from bad to worse, either in the acceptance of grace or in its rejection. Sin is also the state of being situated in a world where the rejection of God's initiative of grace effects the life situation of all people. Relevant to our discussion of context is the awareness that in First World cultures, where unbelief is a culture, lack of consciousness of moral responsibility is in itself a reflection of the presence of sin in the world. Sin in the manner in which we have discussed it is essentially a theological relationship. It assumes a relationship with God or with the truth which lies at the heart of each person's conscience.

Grace and Context

It is not our sin alone which affects others. We mediate for one another for the good when we witness ethical values, when we love. We choose to shed light for another on a path of grace, or we can keep others in the dark through our malice or destructive acts. While we do not determine the free decision of another, we can open or bar for one another the way of love. We mediate or obstruct the offer of grace.[58] Just as we can speak of sinful structures in the world, in an analogous way we can speak of frameworks which we create in this world, as graced. Works of our hands, like our families and the institutions in which we take part, can share in Christ's restoration of all things in himself. Christians assume grace is a stronger force than sin, for Christ not only restores but fulfills all things in himself (Colossians 1).

For instance, the quality of an institution depends on the quality of service of each person who contributes to them. Yet there is a way we can refer to an institution, by analogy, as graced. Institutions can embody grace in ways that are patterned and stable, that can be counted on, that can express love in effective ways beyond the capacity of a single person to show love to someone, or to care for a person's or group's needs or rights, or to foster the common good. We can identify as a structure of grace any cultural or social institution that enables people to express their love effectively, that fosters the common good.[59] One that counteracts selfishness, consumerism, individualism, or any other characteristic of society that works against the common good can be considered a vehicle of grace in this world.

We can also speak by analogy of situations or events of grace. Peter Hodgson in his book, *God in History*, suggests that God is not present in the world as an agent performing acts, or as inspiration alone, nor as an ideal, or even only as a companion and friend. Rather God is also present in specific shapes or patterns of action that are a shaping and transformative power within our history.[60] They move the processes of modern life in a certain direction, that of a creative unification, or bring multiple elements into new wholes without compromising or negating diversity. Or that of building a synthesis which bonds human solidarity, enhances freedom, breaks systemic oppression, heals the injured and broken and cares for the natural. God also acts this way within our families and communities, our civic organizations and our schools and is the horizon of all our efforts to do the same in our small ways. These moments are moments of grace, and can be called graced events in our world today. As we are aware that sin grows in this world and can characterize the situation in which we must live, we also need to acknowledge that knowledge and freedom grows also, not just in the life of the individual, but in the world at large. We need to see the world as a place where God is active in positive ways through human beings. Just as the energy of God's presence in our individual lives enables us to overcome sin and live a graced life, so also we must trust in God's action in our world, as enabling and trusting us with its transformation. A core belief of a faithful life is that God takes us seriously and invites us to collaborate.

Discernment of Good and Evil in the World

The moral-spiritual tradition emphasizes how an individual lives a life of virtue, avoids sin and its occasions, and learns to integrate and control the upsetting and disorienting aspects of concupiscence in their lives. Often this tradition advises to withdraw from the world, in order to become a good person. However, in light of the modern awareness of the responsibility of the person to transform the world, to take responsibility for the world and its direction, discernment of good and evil in this world also has to take account of how to actively transform the world for the good.

Because we are situated in this world, new tools of discernment become important. The first is ideological criticism. This is the process by which we examine the ideas in place which define relationships in a society and ask, in the light of the gospel, whether they are true or define life in a manner which simply blocks change and establishes the status quo.

A second tool of discernment is an attitude which takes human responsibility seriously. The most common reaction before the problems of our complex society today is "flight," the sentiment that there is nothing that can be done. People may actually desire to bring change but do not know where to begin. They may resolve to live a personally good life, follow the law, be modest in one's lifestyle, but not tackle problems beyond an immediate circle of relationships. If human beings must assume responsibility for the quality of life of their neighbors, moral discernment involves more than following a moral law.[61] Human beings are called to a synergistic relationship with a God who is concerned about the world. Moral discernment is about more than one's own personal perfection. It concerns responsibility for the creation of values in the world which will guide moral behavior, the fostering of institutions in the world which will protect those values and the framing of roles in this new world which will enable new generations to become fulfilled as human beings as well as take their place in the world.

To do this requires a third tool of moral discernment, social analysis. To be effective agents of God's own concern for human history, people must acknowledge the possibilities and constraints in any concrete situation and seek "fitting" ways to carry out these values. Moral discernment is the ability to perceive how the values of God's Kingdom are active in human history and are able to guide the action of human beings.[62] In the next chapters we will pursue these questions.

Notes

1 Edward Schillebeeckx, *Church: The Human Story of God* (New York: Crossroad, 1990), 22.

2 Karl Rahner, "The Experience of Self and the Experience of God," *Theological Investigations* XIII (New York: Crossroad, 1983), 123–24.

3 Augustine of Hippo, *Confessions of St. Augustine*, trans. F. J. Sheed (New York: Sheed and Ward, 1943), 3 (Book One, I).

4 Karl Lehmann, "Transcendence," in *Sacramentum Mundi: An Encyclopedia of Theology*, Vol. 6 (New York: Herder and Herder, 1970), 281.

5 Bernard Haring, *Sin in the Secular Age* (New York: Doubleday, 1974), 27.

6 Karl Rahner, "The Certainty of Faith," in *The Practice of Faith* (New York: Crossroad, 1983), 32.

7 Roger Haight, *The Experience and Language of Grace* (New York: Paulist Press, 1979), 129.

8 Susan Neiman, *Evil in Modern Thought: An Alternative History of Philosophy* (Princeton, NJ and Oxford: Princeton University Press, 2002), 322.

9 Alistar McFayden, *Bound to Sin: Abuse, Holocaust and the Christian Doctrine of Sin* (Cambridge: Cambridge University Press, 2000), 8.

10 Ibid., 10.

11 Ibid., 11.

12 See: M. Scott Peck, *People of the Lie: The Hope for Healing Human Evil* (New York: Simon and Schuster Inc., 1985).

13 Neiman, *Evil in Modern Thought*, 7–8.

14 Ibid., 325–26.

15 Ibid., 322.

16 Josef Fuchs, S.J., *Personal Responsibility and Christian Morality* (Washington, D.C.: Georgetown University Press, 1983), 129.

17 However, nature as we find it is relevant to ethical reflection. "A moral judgment about right ethical conduct cannot be deduced from what is given in nature, but can be found through human, rational, evaluative reflection within human reality as a whole." Josef Fuchs, S.J., *Moral Demands and Personal Obligations* (Washington, D.C.: Georgetown University Press, 1993), 33.

18 Ibid., 130–31. Fuchs asserts that all the values involved in a situation remain pre-moral, that is, not yet moral precepts, until a total appraisal is made of their determining influence of what is right. "What must be determined is the significance of the action as value or non-value for the individual, for interpersonal relations and for human society, in connection, of course, with the total reality of man and his society and in view of his whole culture. Furthermore, the priority and urgency of the different values implied must be weighed" (131).

19 Fuchs, *Personal Responsibility and Christian Morality*, 133. Fuchs quotes Chiavacci here, ". . . the objectivity of morality is not necessarily based on an unchangeable being (in other words, on a 'perceptive' understanding of natural law), but on the indispensable correspondence of act to being."

20 John T. Noonan traces shifts in the understanding of the moral significance of slavery, usury and divorce in the Church. See: *A Church That Can and Cannot Change: The Development of Catholic Moral Theology* (Notre Dame, IN: The University of Notre Dame Press, 2005).

21 See: Philip J. Rossi, S.J., "Theology from a Fractured Vista: Susan Neiman's Evil in Modern Thought," *Modern Theology*, 23, no. 1 (January 2007), 47–51 (48). I am

indebted to Rossi's insights on Neiman and the theological reflection he suggests that she opens.

22 Neiman, *Evil in Modern Thought*, 257.

23 Ibid., 254.

24 See: John Perry, S.J., *Torture: Religious Ethics and National Security* (Maryknoll, NY: Orbis Books, 2005).

25 Juan Luis Segundo, *The Historical Jesus of the Synoptics*, trans. John Drury (Maryknoll, N.Y.: Orbis Books, 1985), 104; see also 71–85, 178–88. The use of a "political key" is necessary to render the Christian message truthful in a situation of conflict and massive structural oppression. If it is to be helpful in unlocking Jesus' significance for people struggling against the powers of evil today (and against discouragement at evil's success), the political key must be completed and balanced by the anthropological key of Paul (Romans 1–8) and by interpretive keys coming from the signs of our own times. Both express the single-minded concern for delivering people from the evils which keep their humanity in check. See: Frances Stefano, *The Absolute Value of Human Action in the Theology of Juan Luis Segundo* (New York: University Press of America, 1992), xxi.

26 *Catechism of the Catholic Church*, Apostolic Constitution *Fidei Depositum*, John Paul, Bishop (Liguori, MO: Liguori Publications, 1994), 1889:462.

27 Protestant theology understands grace in the face of the problem of sin. Catholic theology through Aquinas understands grace before the problem of human finitude; as finite people we cannot bring about the fulfillment of our being. Both perspectives help to illumine how the doctrines of grace and sin explain our experience of the world.

28 Roger Haight, *The Experience and Language of Grace* (Dublin: Gill and Macmillan, 1979), 124.

29 Karl Rahner, *Foundations of the Christian Faith* (New York: Seabury Press, 1978), 31–32.

30 Karl Rahner, *Hearers of the Word* (New York: Continuum, 1994), 115.

31 Karl Rahner, "Reflections on the Unity of the Love of Neighbor and the Love of God," *Theological Investigations* VI (London: Darton, Longman and Todd, 1969), 231–49.

32 Karl Rahner, "The Experience of Self and the Experience of God," *Theological Investigations* XIII (New York: Crossroad, 1983), 123–24.

33 Karl Rahner, "Experience of the Holy Spirit," *Theological Investigations* XVIII (New York: Crossroad, 1983), 200.

34 William Dych, S.J., *Karl Rahner* (London: Continuum, 2000), 38.

35 Stephen Duffy, *The Graced Horizon* (Collegeville, MN: The Liturgical Press, 1992), 209.

36 Piet Schoonenberg, S.J., *Man and Sin*, trans. Joseph Donceel, S.J. (South Bend, IN: University of Notre Dame Press, 1965), 124–68.

37 Schoonenberg, *Man and Sin*, 20.

38 Judith A. Merkle, "Sin," in *The New Dictionary of Catholic Social Thought*, ed. Judith A. Dwyer (Collegeville, IN: The Liturgical Press, 1994), 883–88.

39 Patrick McCormick, *Sin as Addiction* (New York: Paulist Press, 1989), 171. "By understanding the addictive character of sin we gain a more realistic grasp of human freedom. An awareness of the addictive behavioral and belief systems which permeate our social structures helps us to see how sin operates on various levels and situates personal freedom before it is engaged in conscious decisions. In this way we come to recognize that such freedom is not the either/or, guilty/innocent of the crime model but exists on a continuum in which persons are more or less free" (ibid.).

40 Fuchs, *Personal Responsibility and Christian Morality*, 154–56.

41 "Medellin Documents," in *The Gospel of Peace and Justice: Catholic Social Teaching Since Pope John XXIII*, ed. Joseph Gremillion (New York: Orbis Books, 1976).

42 Helder Camara, "CELAM: History is Implacable," *Cross Currents* (Spring 1978), 55–58.

43 This dramatic change on the part of the Church of Latin America meant the renunciation of centuries of state patronage and steps toward the transformation of the Church into a servant of the poor. See: *The Church and Culture since Vatican II*, ed. Joseph Gremillion (Notre Dame, IN: The University of Notre Dame Press, 1985). For the Puebla Document see: *Puebla and Beyond*, ed. John Eagleson and Philip Scharper (New York: Orbis Books, 1979).

44 John Paul II, apostolic exhortation. *Reconciliation and Penance* (Washington, D.C. United States Catholic Conference, 1984), no. 16.

45 See: Mark O' Keefe, *What Are They Saying about Social Sin?* (New York: Paulist Press, 1990).

46 Schoonenberg, *Man and Sin*, 81.

47 *The New Jerome Biblical Commentary* (New Jersey: Prentice Hall, 1990), 708.

48 *Theological Dictionary of the New Testament*, ed. Gerhard Kittel, trans. Geoffrey W. Bromiley. Vol. II (Grand Rapids, MI: Eerdmans, 1964), 270–71.

49 *The Interpreter's Bible*. Vol. 7 (New York: Abingdon Press, 1951), 320.

50 Gerald G. May, *Addiction and Grace* (New York: Harper, 1988), 3.

51 Rahner remarks, ". . . the essence of concupiscentia as we conceive it as such that it prevents man's personal decision from achieving total and definitive mastery over his nature on account of the inertia of the nature contrary to that decision." "The Theological Concept of *Concupiscentia*," *Theological Investigations*. Vol. 1 (Baltimore, MA: Helicon Press, 1961, 1965), 372.

52 Schoonenberg, *Man and Sin*, 33.

53 Ibid., 382.

54 Concupiscence is not sin, as personal sin. Rather, it is a manifestation of the fallen nature of human life.

55 William E. May, "Sin," in *The New Dictionary of Theology*, ed. Joseph A. Komonchak, Mary Collins and Dermot A. Lane (Wilmington, DE: Michael Glazier, 1987), 957–61.

56 Schoonenberg, *Man and Sin*, 23.

57 Ibid., 25–37. The major negative prohibitions of the Hebrew Scriptures and New Testament capture the essence of those actions considered very serious.

58 Ibid., 196.

59 Mary Evelyn Jegen, SNDdeN, *Just Peacemakers* (New York: Paulist Press, 2006), 106.

60 Peter C. Hodgson, *God in History: Shapes of Freedom* (Minneapolis, MN: Fortress Press, 2007).

61 The significance of human responsibility in this regard is derived from the doctrine of cooperative grace. Human beings are co-creators with God. Moral discernment thus is the capacity to see the call of this relationship in a concrete way in history. It is the capacity to perceive the relationship between the visible or historical and the invisible or the transcendent or eschatological. See: Juan Luis Segundo, *El hombre de hoy y Jesus de Nazareth*. Vol. 2, *Historia y Actuadidad: Sinopticos y Pablo*, 502.

62 Segundo comments that Christianity is a summons to liberty. In its basic principles it does not possess any moral panaceas or science of behavior that will give one the permanent possession of the truth that is necessary to solve moral problems. See: *Evolution and Guilt*, 93ff. There is a need for adult responsibility in moral discernment since Christianity does define the paschal mystery as the overall orientation of one's existence, yet the paschal mystery itself is not a science of detailed behavior.

Chapter 4

ACTING IN THE WORLD: FINDING A WAY

As people attempt to integrate the cultural, social, or personal elements of context with a sense of personal freedom and its attendant moral responsibility they can slip into two extremes. Some claim the situation so shapes us; that our choice is severely limited or non-existent. Others imagine moral choice in a vacuum, without any account given to the real world factors that shape one's freedom and perspective. Both approaches only hold a piece of the truth, and each avoids the perspective on moral experience the other holds. To get a more complete picture of moral experience today we need to form a broad picture of how interactions in the world can affect the exercise of our freedom, as well as recall principles which guide assessment of moral responsibility from a personal perspective. We will begin by considering some key dimensions of contemporary Christian anthropology.

Forming a Broad Picture

While the personal freedom upheld by the tradition is essential to understanding any moral responsibility, in practice *all freedom is freedom in relationship*. All freedom is subject to conditions imposed by concrete historical existence. The world in which we live is so connected to the exercise of our freedom that it forms a "second nature" to our existence. The social dimension of our freedom is not something we accept or reject. Rather it forms the structure of freedom itself.

In this world, *human freedom only exists in a total structure of relational existence which involves God, self and the world*. We act not only in the world but within the context of our knowledge of this world. This knowledge involves the values we have learned in society and the technical knowledge we have of our environment. In practice *human freedom always involves a structured relationship of knowledge of the world that involves human values and technical knowledge*.[1]

Human freedom is not just a state or an expression of selfhood, it is also meant to be creative. *Human freedom is fully human when it fashions out of the concrete possible of human living a world which is more human.* The world in which we find ourselves can be experienced as a "given" in life. We are born in a certain situation, with certain talents, coupled with particular opportunities or their absence. This situation is a "given." However, as our life proceeds, its shape is our task. As in the parable of the talents, we are given the task to use our gifts and transform our situation not only for ourselves but for others.

John Paul II's concept of work reflects this truth about freedom, that it is meant to be constructive and creative. Work proceeds from the vocation to be human. Work is more than something that produces articles to be bought and sold. It is part of the process by which a person becomes a human being, raises a family, fosters education, and participates in the wider culture and society (LE 9.3).

We do not exercise our freedom to transform our lives and our situations alone. We need others to do this. This forms the fourth understanding of how our freedom interacts with the world. *Personal freedom only reaches its fulfillment within the context of community.* In community we bond together and integrate the freedom achievements and gifts of human beings. The measure of freedom is its capacity to go out of itself in love rather than into itself in egotism. Characteristic of the trajectory of its growth in the Christian life is its increasing universality. Freedom always involves a freedom before and with real people, and an increasing freedom to love in effective ways. Freedom is expansive, involving the ability to provide better conditions for human development for a wider group of people.

A fifth understanding of how our freedom interacts with the world is *freedom's exercise is always linked to concrete people and their historical reality.* Christian freedom before the world is not an abstract vision or plan for a better social order. Rather its content is always defined in terms of a concrete society with its possibilities and limitations. In this sense, we do not think of society as the juxtaposing of already "finished" individuals. Rather society and its respective cultures is a system of human reaction and interrelationships which constitute and form part of the total human condition of every individual.[2] We become fully human by engaging in the process of creating our world.

For this reason we cannot totally separate our experience of freedom itself and freedom in this world. It is obvious that sometimes we do not choose to make our world a better place, nor do we choose to work on our own lives, to improve bad habits, to get free from addictions. The transformation of our "second nature" therefore has two dimensions. In the first place "second nature" means that total social condition into which a human being is born. This social context is so inherent to human life that it forms a "second nature." It is integral to a total understanding of the human person. A second meaning is that one's second nature is formed by human agency. In this sense one's first nature is what has been given through birth and living conditions. One's second nature is the result of human freedom acting on the complex of "givens" in each human life.

However, for some people, the above processes are more difficult than for others. Structures of society can militate against their desire to transform their lives, or can block their participation in changing society. A social system is a specific way of conceiving inter-human relationships. Any social system tends to be embodied in institutions which perpetuate it. This leads to the sixth understanding of our freedom before the world. *The fulfillment of human freedom always includes the changing of human relationships which are dehumanizing through the changing of institutions which perpetuate and structure these relationships.*

Lastly, every social system has cultural beliefs or ideology which sustain its functioning. This structure of beliefs, laws and values legitimates the existing relationships in a given society. All societies have these ideas, thus a seventh understanding of our freedom before the world is that we are called to think critically. *Since all societies are based on ideologies, it is a task of human freedom to identify and examine them.*

How then does our freedom, as an essential dimension of human nature, and freedom, as functioning before the world, interact? What is the end result? We can imagine this more like a circuit than like a balancing act. The goal is to establish factors on a social level so that personal and societal growth can mutually "set off" or stimulate one another.[3] While freedom is conditioned by society, freedom in itself still exists. Its goal is to create the conditions where humankind can flourish, and the person also can come to fulfillment. However, in this interaction between the personal and social levels of life different "laws" operate. When freedom operates at a social level other factors condition its operation, which are not operative purely on the individual level. Let us explore those issues now.

Acting in Society

We assume that when we act vis-à-vis the world we are in a paradoxical situation. On the one hand the world always exerts a type of limitation on human freedom. On the other hand we are called to transform our existence. Our freedom is influenced by society, inheritance, culture and environment. Yet freedom constitutes what it means to be a human being in this world. The results of these factors are "received" and "given" in life. Yet, human beings can direct to some degree the shape of these influences and their response to them. This is a result of their essential freedom.

Therefore, the "world" has both positive and negative influence on our freedom. The structures of family and society are necessary to develop humanly. Participation in both is integral to human development. Yet, these structures naturally bring a limitation to human freedom, a repression of possibilities of human living. When these repressions become unnecessary, that is, they have no positive function in the total fabric of society or in the life of the individual, they are part of the "sin of the world," as St. Paul understood it (Romans 5–8). These are repressions generated not by the needs of human association but from the additional interests of domination. They are societal limitations which must be changed.[4] The Latin American bishops at Medellin recognized the sinful influence of structures as situations of "institutionalized violence" against the poor in their country. Here structures not only induce individuals to sin but discourage and seek to defeat the human spirit from seeking its full humanity.

We recognize that these societal limitations can be of varying natures. For instance, creation of culture results only when people have time and energy left beyond mere survival. One can only make changes in the second nature of human life from a posture of a type of "abundance." Conditions of food, clothing and shelter and the proper means for insuring their use and maintenance have been set. We need a type of "freedom from" want in order to engage our freedom in the "freedom to" transform our lives and our world. We set goals and take initiatives only after we have a basic minimum from which to start. Therefore to deny others this minimum is not only to deny them what they need for survival, but it is to deny them the minimum needed for their freedom to operate in this constructive way. These are institutional structures whose organization prevents the minimum needed for human life. This is a form of structural sin.

Another type of societal limitation exists at the level of access to the means to enhance one's life and community. Human freedom is not just meant to survive, but also to develop. Here societal structures limit the means to build the world of the future;[5] the means to express and develop cultural identity, to generate and sustain life, to be educated, to express one's opinion, to worship, to work, to have equality of gender, race and national identity. Yet political and social needs are not absolutes in themselves. They must be considered within the framework of acting in society. Their importance is judged in light of how they impact the next step in a person's life or their role in the life of a community to move toward improvement and change. Their hierarchy is set by how effective they will be in a concrete way in building the future in a concrete way. The right to dissent is important, but if there is nothing to eat, then this core need takes precedence. The right to liberty is key, but if no one knows the alphabet its meaning is qualified. Yet, on the other hand, even if a perfectly benevolent dictator were to provide all the fundamental human freedoms so that no member of that political community were lacking food, shelter, health, and education, an important aspect of human well-being would be violated if the members of the community were deprived of their say in the organization of that community.[6]

Therefore, while acting in society requires attention to the historical and contextual situation in order to know what decision is to be made, general principles of what is due human life are also important. All decisions are not made simply on their consequences, with no sense of general principles or visions of the human good. In order to know what is good within a situation, one must know what is good beyond what is specific to a particular situation. Hence, acting in society, while dependent on one's assessment of the concrete historical situation of a particular context, also requires a vision of the good life in society, and a vision of the human good. At the same time it must acknowledge that life in society is always imperfect and at times influenced by human wrongdoings and sin. The challenge is to guide its action, not just to enhance the freedom of an individual, but also to strengthen the structures which support other individuals in having access to that freedom and ensuring it in the future.

A third type of societal limitation is at the level of ideology. People recognize today the problem of getting to the truth of a situation. Can we trust the information we are given from public officials? Do the media really inform us, or just entertain us? More subtle, however, is the problem of a false ideology in any society. This is the complex of values and behavior patterns communicated by a society to an individual which are prejudiced in favor of the vested interests within the society. Those who are powerful and have influential connections often frame the public debate in terms of a worldview which suggests that their experience is normative. This blinds us. We find that we are unwilling to fund public services which we do not use, and thus consign the poor to isolation and degradation. We expect people without automobiles to have mobility in a car-dependent society. We expect people without decent schools to thrive in an educational system that favors the wealthy. We expect people without money to accept without question the values of free market liberalism.[7] This limits the moral imagination of the community and its vision of the range of possibilities of integrating disenfranchised members into the prosperity of the country. This kind of ideology has to be criticized to the degree that it serves as a promoter of the status quo, and feeds the assessment that "there is nothing that can be done." Ideology here is more than a set of tools to understand the world; in this sense it is a self-serving mental system. It blocks the moral vision necessary for all members of a society to assume responsibility for access to decent public goods for everyone as one of the obligations of living in the community.

How do we measure the range of possibilities for all members of a society? One way is to ask how this action might move people from a situation of "freedom from" want or necessities in order to live in a fuller situation of "freedom to" build a future. Ideals and visions of the human good are essential to this, but they cannot replace the concreteness of enabling freedom as a norm in all relationships between individual growth and social reality. Naming institutional limitations in society as necessary or excessive separates the givens or impersonal foundation of order that grounds all freedom from the elements in society which must be changed.

Finally, when we act in society we have different types of relationships open to us. We have strong and weak affiliations. Strong affiliations like family, Church and to some degree nationality are grounding relationships which often specify how we are related, to whom we are responsible and where we stand in a network of authority. Weak affiliations are more transitory where these obligations are not specified, yet we "feel" connected in some ways. In our global culture, we feel connected to people across the world because of our common humanity, even though our obligations to others are not spelled out legally or even morally. Within our own societies, we may feel divided by race, class and gender; however, these divisions can be overcome by expanding our sense of affiliation with others with whom we do not have strong bonds.[8] Weak affiliations are often created through outreach and creativity. Internet circles and movements for change are all more transitory than affiliations of family and Church, yet they give us stepping stones to move from a "good intention" to do something about a situation, to the means for a concrete action. The Church urges us to do this through a sense of solidarity, which expands our sense of justice through the recognition of situations and injustice and taking the means to respond to them.

We do this by two means. First, we seek to be faithful to the needs and responsibilities of our strong affiliations. Building the bonds which tie together our family, churches, civic societies and national life are primary means to express and develop our own freedom and to establish the means for others to flourish. Second, we enter into transforming relationships with those with whom we have weaker affiliations, bringing a wider circle of concern into our lives, and helping to integrate emergent peoples and marginalized concerns into the dominant and established centers of our social life. This vision of acting in society differs from a cultural vision of society as that which facilitates the least amount of restriction on the operation of individual freedom. Rather, acting in society in an authentic manner means that the limitations of social constraint are accepted as part of the true functioning of our freedom. In a Christian vision of life, only love has the power to motivate freedom in this manner and to build a society where more and more people can find a satisfying life.

Looking at Moral Action through the Tradition

While we are more aware today of the impact of the world on our actions, we still rely on the first language of morality in the Church to judge specific actions in moral terms. The classical tradition contributes a picture of moral action in the world through its act analysis approach to morality. This approach to ethics remains a best practice of the Church in assessment of "classes of actions," that is actions considered as human behaviors which either are constructive of human dignity or destructive of it, actions which we choose or reject on a personal level. The tradition upholds that the action itself, our intention, and the circumstances must be related in such a way that we produce a right action. It is important therefore to understand this focus in moral thinking, so that attention to context does not become distraction from acknowledging the significance of concrete actions to moral integrity or faithfulness.

Morality in the strict sense is not situated in the society, it belongs to the person, to the self and to his or her internal attitudes. Only the free person can be moral or immoral in the strict sense of the word.[9] While we recognize that no person is totally free from limiting factors on their freedom, we assume a moral assessment of our actions always involves a core modicum of freedom which makes our actions truly our own.

Acts are generally not termed morally good or evil; rather acts are *right or wrong* insofar as they can be judged as suited or unsuited to the reality of the human person and his or her world. They are right or wrong because they lead to or away from the good of the human individual, or of right relationships in the world. While we call such acts morally good or evil, strictly speaking it is only a person with his or her free attitudes and decisions who can be morally good or evil, a sinner, in the strict sense.

Many today make a distinction between the moral good or moral wickedness of the *person* and the moral rightness or moral wrongness of *acts*. Since only the interior morality of the person is morality in the proper sense of the word, the morality of acts is more morality in an analogous sense. It is measured not by the attitudes of the person but by the fittingness of the acts to the good of the person and of his or her world. The rightness or wrongness of the acts is, by analogy, moral, since the person, in order to be morally good, must try to become a person only in right acts in the world. The tradition has taught that a person's moral goodness is basically an interior reality, an attitude and disposition of not being closed in on oneself but of being open to what one knows of God, the human person, and of right behavior in the world of humankind.[10]

The tradition affirms that each person has a core freedom or the capacity to exercise a control over their own actions, to choose right from wrong. In addition, they have an operational freedom, a freedom which has restrictions, both internally and externally.[11] Many decisions of conscience can be made through the help of moral norms which point to fundamental moral obligations in relationships with God, others, the world and self. These "gold standards" mark moral progress or decline in the lives of Christians.[12] However, to understand how these norms apply in concrete situations, or which norms apply, or to decide what to do concerning a particular problem that does not exactly fit the norm, the person has to put together a number of components of a moral decision through the capacities of their conscience.

Conscience

Richard Gula explains conscience as a capacity, a process and a judgment:[13]

> The *capacity* of conscience is part of being human. It makes it possible to know and do the good; however exercise of this capacity requires we take the responsibility for developing ourselves as moral persons. Character formation, the development of the virtues and standing in a Christian community all develop this capacity.[14]

Conscience as a *process* is the task of gathering the necessary information which morally has bearing on direction of the decision. We attend to specific norms which pertain to the judgment at hand. We seek the moral truth by making use of sources of moral wisdom wherever they may be found. We look at the situation for all the morally relevant factors, and think honestly about them, whether they concur with our preferences regarding the outcome of our decision or not. We try to understand the facts of the situation. We might consult the social or behavioral sciences for clarity. We cannot know whether something is contrary to reason unless we know what it is. We seek the advice of others who have experience with the matter, and who also are people of conscience, and known to be good. The goal of this process is to seek what is right to the best of our ability and to come to a personal evaluation of the matter.

Some think that if a person follows a known norm in the situation, they are not following their conscience. The error is in thinking that "following my conscience" is always something other than actions guided by the norm. This is not true. Through conscience, the person freely chooses to allow the norm to have bearing on their decision, even if it requires an action which is morally challenging. The outcome of this process is the arrival at moral truth, to the degree it can be known by this person or community at this time. What is key is that following one's conscience requires an honest seeking of what is right.

Conscience as a *judgment* is the concrete assessment of what I must do in the situation based on my perception and grasp of the values involved. At this moment of the decision I am the most personally engaged, because I decide more than what to do, I decide also in this moment, in this decision, what kind of person I am going to be. When we decide to make a concrete decision, our action has both a concrete dimension and a personal one. I first decide whether I am going to go out of myself in love, or into myself in egotism. Am I going to look at the truth of the situation sincerely as I find it, or am I going to create my "own truth" which serves my personal desires and wants? The prior search in conscience as a process also expresses this internal attitude. Second, I decide what to do in the concrete order of this world. What gives a moral decision its personal dimension is that the moral action is expressive of "me" and in it I realize a deeper attitude toward God, others, the world, and self. This last dimension of conscience is what I must follow to be true to myself. This is the "core sanctuary" of the person, which cannot be violated (GS 16). The Church affirms that each person is bound to follow his conscience faithfully in all activity so that they may come to God, before whom she or he will give an account of their life (2 Cor. 5.10; GS 17). Therefore, a person must not be forced to act contrary to his or her conscience (DH 12). Conscience alerts us not just to right decisions which involve boundary actions — those actions which involve an explicit moral law, like stealing. Conscience also alerts us to what is better or best for us. It sensitizes us to "existential calls," the sense that this action needs to be done by me. These other calls of the moral life involve taking responsibility for ourselves and our world and have bearing on our sense of faithfulness.

When we try to determine whether an action is right or wrong, we find ourselves perhaps automatically or by upbringing assessing the relations among the elements of the deed, the intention and the circumstances. Words such as theft and murder are actually summary terms which assume a *moral object/the deed* itself, i.e. taking something that does not belong to me; an *intention*, to keep for myself or some other profit; and morally relevant *circumstances*. I take these things against the will of the owner. This includes the consequences of what is done. The tradition understands that for an action to be good, it must be good in its object, circumstances and end or intention. The end does not justify the means.[15]

Debates in the Church

While these rules of thumb seem helpful, they have also generated much debate in the Church as to which of the three elements in moral decisions is the most important in determining right from wrong. The deed itself refers to a more objective morality, while the motive refers to what the action means to the person, a tendency toward subjective morality. Mixing the two, objective and subjective considerations are necessary; however, it can also lead to confusion. Giving primary consideration to the consequences to the exclusion of the others leans toward situation ethics.

The debate between contemporary moralists in the Church comes down to one between those who hold that "we must look at all dimensions (morally relevant circumstances) before we know what the action is and whether it should be said to be (morally wrong)."[16] Others argue that it is always morally wrong to act against basic human goods, such as life and knowledge, which are self-evidently such to all mature persons. Destruction of these basic goods is never morally permissible.[17]

The difficulty lies in the question of whether we can describe an action as right or wrong, prior to evaluating it. Words which we generally use to describe wrong actions — stealing, murder, etc. — contain this evaluation in them. These terms avoid mixing subjective and objective elements to muddle the moral evaluation, because they assume subjective considerations in their definition. For instance, stealing means a businessman or -woman takes money to which they are not entitled. One's motive might not be the stealing itself, but the lifestyle which the money can make possible. However, motive does not change the fact that it is stealing. Jean Porter argues that Aquinas assumes it is first necessary to arrive at a correct description of the act from a moral point of view before we know its object.[18] The tradition teaches that the deed we do qualifies the will. If I will to steal, I will a morally wrong action, and when I do so I am using my will for evil rather than for good. In general, actions are wrong because they are inconsistent with the good of the human person.

However, simply saying the deed or what is done is the moral object is possibly too simple. Many actions allow for indefinitely many possible true descriptions of "what is done." If a doctor removes a patient's limb to save her life, the intention "to save her life" is not a reason added onto the deed (the object), it enters into the object itself.[19] We cannot derive a judgment about the moral value of an action from a determination of the object of the act as simply the deed itself, because we cannot determine what the object of the act is without some prior consideration of the action, taken as a whole. Aquinas judged that in most cases the correct assessment of a particular action will be obvious (I–II 100.3). Conventional norms of morality attend to most precepts of the natural law. Certain actions like murder, theft, adultery, and the like are basic and hold irreducible moral significance. However, it is possible that we will encounter an action that is so complex that we cannot say immediately whether it is right or wrong. This is especially true when dealing with new moral issues or situations. Some actions look like murder or theft but perhaps are justified because they do not fulfill what is prohibited. Others are not justified because they do violate the point of the relevant prohibition.[20] For instance, the use of torture for the sake of national security is an issue which requires this kind of moral discernment. Whether it is right or wrong is not obvious to all people, and the practice requires moral scrutiny for its full significance to be realized.[21]

In these cases, we must consider the different factors of an action as considered above and in terms of the moral wisdom which the individual and the community possesses at that time, and assess the particular action.[22] The fact that the Church can be limited as a human community does not negate belief in the guidance of the Holy Spirit in the Church or in the magisterium.[23] The natural law leads all people to know right from wrong, however, knowledge of what these actions are, beyond those of the "gold standards" of conventional morality, is the outcome of a process of moral evaluation, not its presupposition. Being faithful as Christians involves the willingness to enter into this process of assessment personally and in the community.

Authorities and Stabilizers

If one aspect of freedom is the ability to bond increasingly diversified elements into a unified whole — we bond because we want to — we have to ask, how do we deal with selfishness and the tendency of human nature to look out only for its own concerns. People are individuals, centers of worth, but they are also self-centered. One role of authorities and stabilizers is to facilitate the conditions which adapt our conduct to the conduct of others. When we accept authority in our lives we affirm the role they as individuals or structures play in facilitating the broader personal goal of moving out of ourselves toward others in life.

To some degree, each person is his or her own authority. We control our own behavior and set goals which are worthy of our lives. Yet on the social level we also need authorities.[24] Authority comes in the form of stabilizers, forms of social organization such as the family and the state, laws and government which are necessary for corporate life.[25]

These structures provide the means which "loosen" us up from the concerns of our own lives in order to address the needs of others. They also provide the external control to check the human tendency of great power which makes people disregard the needs and identity of others as persons.

These and others structures of corporate or social existence provide the conditions which also support and influence us. Social structures offer an important contribution of human flourishing by offering a quality of life which transcends the accumulated efforts of individuals. Structures accumulate in history as a condition which orients the operation of our freedom. They can build us a facility for a life of freedom or love, or a life of dehumanization and sin. In this sense they are both the legacy and the hurdle by which we have to work out our lives.

However, there is nothing in human nature that, on its own, will take the risks to build a better world. Nor will any social structure automatically make a person into a good or a bad person. Culture at times suggests otherwise. Some thinkers posit to the human race as a species an inherent structure or drive by which human beings will progressively become more fulfilled. That is, by following the instinctual drive of the species human perfection will be reached.

This rests on the assumption that the goal or happiness of human existence is given by the species and interest in the species is powerful enough to motivate the carrying out of this goal.

However, Christian theology holds that the human individual is not structured so that its fulfillment is to serve the function of the species.[26] While being a member of the human race gives one the experiences of language and culture and in this sense a framework of meaning, they cannot provide meaning in the fullest sense of the term. Meaning as a sense of purpose and direction does not come into human life simply through association with others. Rather each human being has to construct a meaningful life structure through human risk, by constructing his or her own path. Principally, this comes from the risk to move out of oneself in love rather into oneself in egotism. As Christians we see this as fundamentally a response to the gift of salvation.[27] People are motivated to love from within, not from any other force. They must see the sacrifice involved in love as a way to realize themselves, and choose to make a gift of themselves to others, to life, and as Christians to God. This must come freely. It is in this light that we understand the corporate or social existences of human living. It provides the conditions which influence this free choice, but it can never provide a mechanical path which, if followed, will lead to human development.

The importance of corporate life never replaces the fact that common works and efforts derive their significance from the fact they are expressions and enablement of human freedom. It is here that our awareness of context and belief in the moral responsibility inherent to freedom intersect. It is never the case that human freedom derives its significance from carrying out any mechanical vision of the unfolding of history or human development. The flourishing of the human person, his or her humanization, is always the "end" of any corporate action (GS 35). The good of the person, within the limits and possibilities of his or her communal context, is the norm by which all is valued.[28] The human person thus is the only subject, agent, and goal of freedom in that history itself is the history of human freedom.[29] Despite the supports and limitations of the condition of our "second nature," it is the person himself or herself who must use these means responsibly. Furthermore, it is the struggle to direct and utilize these means which is the situation in which all human freedom comes to fulfillment. At core, it is the context in which the Christian asks, am I faithful? and seeks an answer.

Moral Agency and Context

When we try to move our inquiry to include more systematically the situations of modern living, we must turn to a framework which does not negate the core understanding of the tradition, nor philosophical and theological constants of living in society, yet goes further to give us a practical lens into modern life. For instance, in *Managing as If Faith Mattered* the author claims, ". . . often we act as one person, following one set of goals and standards in our private lives, while we become a strikingly different person — someone molded by expediency and necessary compromise — at work."[30] How do we retain our belief that people are ultimately responsible for what they do, yet also recognize that factors such as culture, social place, profession, and gender impact not only moral action but our moral perceptions, as well as our ability to carry out what we judge to be right?

Christians have several means at their disposal for this task: among them are cultural analysis, use of narrative (especially Scripture), and using models to summarize re-occurring experiences in modern living. We sharpen our understanding by naming situations that point to re-occurring forces that shape our moral experience and imagination in a manner which is morally significant. This is the work of cultural analysis. John Paul II did this when he referred to a "culture of life" and a "culture of death" competing for allegiance in modern society (EV 28). We ask how these cultures and life situations shape our thinking about common problems in life and society today.

Another way to get insight is through narrative. Through story we create a moral paradigm which illustrates virtue or vice in a parallel universe to the one we are in. The Christian story also encounters counter-narratives that ground the meaning of life in values against the gospel. The key narrative in the Christian life is Scripture, where we look to the values and deeds of Jesus as normative for moral choice today. We ask what bearing his gift of salvation and the very gift of our lives has on our daily lives. The lives of the saints are another type of narrative. It is not surprising that Pope John Paul II canonized many saints during his pontificate, especially saints who lived in "modern" times, and in situations of war, family life, imprisonment, and poverty which were unique to the modern experience. The life of the Church provides a continuing narrative through the example of others.

A third way to imagine how values are realized in concrete situations is through the creation of models of modern living to summarize common experiences we all have. Models are not mirrors of reality "out there." Rather they are ideal types, or abstractions formed either from theoretical positions on a topic or similar experiences in living. They give us a mental construct or heuristic device to examine selected aspects of thinking on a subject or patterns of behavior in response to living in complex systems. No one thinks exactly like the patterns defined in a model. No one person's life is exactly like the life in a model. Models are to be taken symbolically, not literally.[31] However, models are not useless because they are not exact. Rather they can disclose features in a situation which impact lives, yet might remain hidden without some way to bring them to light.

Models are useful because they can shed light on reality. Using models is a compromise between only speaking of isolated situation and making generalizations which are so unspecific they are not helpful. A model is also a metaphor. A metaphor both tells us what something is and what something is not. We know some realities better because of metaphorical language. In the New Testament Christ is depicted under many images and metaphors — as shepherd, bridegroom, vine, door, light, king and judge, to name a few.[32] Models provide a language that is always partial and inadequate, but never false or merely subjective.[33] They are organizing images that give a particular emphasis and enable one to notice and interpret certain aspects of experience. Often we need more than one model to understand a reality. Avery Dulles remarks that we often overcome the limitations of one model by combining models. "Phenomena not intelligible in terms of one model may be readily explicable when another model is used."[34] All models are limited and while one may explain most adequately the situation under consideration, we cannot deny the reality the others represent. What makes the models different is they often have different "root metaphors" or they speak out of different concerns, or starting points. They employ different conceptual categories and different vocabularies.[35] A model is not focused on understanding the moral experience of an individual in the Church, as we might do in a situation of spiritual direction. Rather a model points to how the experience of an individual fits today into that of the wider Christian community.

The search to be faithful, to deepen in understanding of the Christian life in modern society, plunges us into mystery. As Karl Rahner points out, while the human person seeks to respond in freedom to the calls of his or her everyday life, at the level of reflection he or she always remains ambiguous at some level regarding the answer. All we can do is respond to God in faith and trust that we have responded well to this fundamental question of our existence.[36] As we choose a lens for this next step in our inquiry we keep the words of Rahner in mind.

Choosing a Lens

In our search to be faithful in terms of our context, we wonder how to think about context in some orderly manner. We cannot consider every context of modern living; this is impossible. But we can set up some models of thinking about select contexts which can give us insight into the plurality of situations in which we find ourselves. Using this heuristic device, we hope to move toward a model of thinking that helps us consider more concretely life in society and our moral responsibilities today.

We will draw on the work of Mary Douglas to examine four contexts which make up the day to day experience of the Christian living in the world today.

Mary Douglas, a cultural anthropologist, is known for her reflection on cultural differences. Her four-fold typology of cultures will be used to help us to recognize the presence of Christians in new situations and to reflect on the differing challenges they face.[37]

Differences between cultures, according to Douglas, are rooted in how people learn to perceive their social relationships with one another. Four factors enter into the different patterns of relationship found in any community. These four are mutually reinforcing: the acquired ways of perceiving one's place in society; the social context and its dominant patterns of interaction; individual behavior choices; and the forms of religious vision.

Douglas claims that variations between different social contexts can be understood in terms of what she calls "grid" and "group" experience. "Group" refers to a situation in which forms of authority and the pressure on the individual exercised by a closed society are central. Allegiance to the group leadership is pivotal. Where "group" is strong, conformity and obedience are key influences. People tend to be classified as members or not, as either insiders or outsiders.

"Grid" refers to a form of organization that is less controlling and less explicit. It is constituted by the network of roles, rules, and relationships that build people up with one another. "Grid" focuses on self rather than on the collectivity, thus it is both more informal and more complex. However, it is not always a more "free" situation than group life. There is a different form of social control. "Grid" is less a question of codified social control from above than of assumptions that guide how individuals behave with one another in different situations. To function according to the codes of one's profession is to experience what Douglas means by "grid expectations."

Douglas puts these two forms of social organization together to show how society can move from highly structured to highly unstructured situations, not only in terms of social obedience (group) but also in terms of interpersonal expectations (grid). Painting in broad strokes, less nuanced than Douglas' own work, we can glean some different cultural forms in which members of the Church live today. In the following chapters we will reflect on these contexts in order to situate how the desire to be faithful and these contexts intersect in Church life today.

Douglas claims there is a dependence of the form of religion in a society on its form of organization. We assume there is dependence of the form of ethical experience on the form of cultural organization in which a member is acting. A context does not erase the realities of a traditional understanding of Christian ethical responsibility as we have described it. But context does impact how one lives, hears, thinks about and implements an expression of fidelity as a Christian.

We will suggest each context has a unique contribution to the Church and its mission to the world, as well as limitations and tensions. Each context also presents its own characteristic trajectory of conversion, which arises not just from moral calls of being human in general, but from the call to both work within and reach beyond the context itself. Here we will develop these points only in outline form. In subsequent chapters we will develop them.

Grid and Group Experience

Grid and group interface to form different patterns of fields of relationships that represent a range of experiences of members of the Church.

Types of Cultures

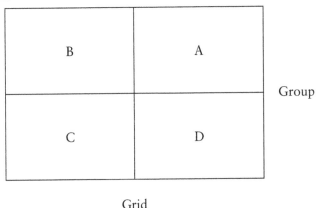

Grid

We can imagine that the vertical line dividing the above square in half represents the range of "grid" influence, from zero presence at the bottom to strongest at the top. The corresponding horizontal line, forming a cross, represents the range of "group" control, from zero at the left to the strongest at the right. In this way four smaller squares emerge from the different combinations of grid and group, offering a model for identifying four quite different cultural forms for being a Christian today, as they represent different patterns of relationship. Marking each quarter in sequence B, A, C, D, we can proceed to visualize differences in context on the form of cultural organization in which someone lives.

Context A is the traditional community, one that we easily recognize. Both grid and group are strong. This culture has clear authority, which commands group life, and a network of implicit norms that structure interaction between individuals. Context A is the classical image of the Church in action and also family life in its formal form.

At Context B the sense of belonging to a definite group is lessened in this culture, but behavioral expectations are at a maximum. The grid expectations of one's peers exceed the social responsibility pressures of the group. Role definition does not come only from some collective authority but rather from gaining recognition from one's profession or group whose power to credential is essential for functioning.

It is not hard to recognize the situation of postmodern life in what Douglas describes as low-group and low-grid situation, or Context C. There one finds a more extreme lack of structures and supports. Role definition is at a minimum. Douglas claims that modern industrial society affords people more opportunities than ever to live as an isolate.

Context D represents a radically different response to the complexity of today: community formed on withdrawal from others. People respond to the chaos of our times through a search for identity in a group. This is a weak-grid/strong-group community culture, or an enclave. The grid is weak because the members only relate to each other, not to people outside the group. Group membership is, however, accompanied by "rules" about non-conformity of any kind. We will see later that this is a very different type of group experience than that in Context A.

It is likely that we live in several of these contexts at the same time. Each "world" so to say has its own logical base and enters into the worldview of the member. The great advantage of Douglas' grid-group model is its capacity to clarify diverse cultural climates for Christians living today, to begin to speculate on their mutual resistance and conflict, and their divergent assumptions and priorities. The models help us to visualize differences in situations, not differences in people based on race, class, age, health, ethnic background, temperament, gifts, emotional strength, or fragility, etc. Douglas shows how underlying visions and beliefs, rooted in various forms of social expectation and control, produce four completely different forms of culture. Although she identified these conflicting forms of cultural environment in "primitive" tribes as well as complex societies, her insights are relevant for understanding our present cultural shifts, and the different situations in which members are called to be faithful today. In the next chapters we will explore these different cultural contexts in greater detail.

Notes

1 Juan Luis Segundo, *Faith and Ideologies*, trans. John Drury (New York: Orbis Books, 1984), 90ff.
2 Juan Luis Segundo, *Grace and the Human Condition*, trans. John Drury (New York: Orbis Books, 1973), 26, 37.
3 Juan Luis Segundo, *El hombre de hoy y Jesus de Nazareth*, Vol 3. (Madrid: Chistianidad, 1982), 914.
4 See: Judith A. Merkle, "Sin," in *The New Dictionary of Catholic Social Thought*, ed. Judith A. Dwyer (Collegeville, MN: The Liturgical Press, 1994), 883–88.
5 Segundo, *El hombre de hoy y Jesus de Nazareth*, Vol 3., 915.

6 Severine Deneulin, "Necessary Thickening," in *Transforming Unjust Structures: The Capability Approach*, ed. Severine Deneulin, Mathias Nebel and Nicholas Sagaocsky (Dordrecht, the Netherlands, 2006), 39.

7 Vincent D. Rougeau, "Enter the Poor: American Welfare Reform, Solidarity and the Capability of Human Flourishing," in *Transforming Unjust Structures: The Capability Approach*, op. cit., 171.

8 See for instance: Sabina Alkire, "Structural Injustice and Democratic Practice," in *Transforming Unjust Structures*, op. cit., 55.

9 Josef Fuchs, *Christian Morality: The Word Becomes Flesh* (Dublin: Gill and Macmillan, 1987), 19–27.

10 Ibid., 105–8.

11 For a discussion of these differences in the thought of Lonergan, see: Kenneth R. Melchin, *Living with Other People* (Collegeville, MN: The Liturgical Press, 1998), 75.

12 See: Josef Fuchs, "The Absoluteness of Moral Terms," in *Readings, No. 1: Moral Norms and the Catholic Tradition*, ed. Charles Curran and Richard McCormick (New York: Paulist Press, 1979), 94–137.

13 Richard Gula, *Reason Informed by Faith* (New York: Paulist Press, 1989), 123–35.

14 Here we refer to a Christian conscience, acknowledging that all people form their conscience through their respective associations.

15 Francis J. Connell, "Human Acts," in *The Historical Development of Fundamental Moral Theology in the United States*, ed. Charles E. Curran and Richard A. McCormick, S.J. (New York, Paulist, 1999), 135–49.

16 Richard A. McCormick, "*Veritatis Splendor* and Moral Theology," *America* 1969: 13 (October 30, 1993), 8–11 (10). See also: Bernard Hoose, *Proportionalism: The American Debate and Its European Roots* (Washington, D.C.: Georgetown University Press, 1987).

17 John Finnis, *Moral Absolutes: Tradition, Revision and Truth* (Washington, D.C.: Catholic University of America Press, 1991). Germain Grisez, *The Way of the Lord Jesus*, Vol. 1, *Christian Moral Principles* (Chicago: Franciscan Herald Press, 1983).

18 Jean Porter, "The Moral Act in *Veritatis Splendor*," in *The Historical Development of Fundamental Moral Theology in the United States*, op. cit., 225.

19 Richard A. McCormick, S.J., "Proportionalism: Clarification through Dialogue," in *The Historical Development of Fundamental Moral Theology in the United States*, op. cit., 182.

20 Porter, "The Moral Act," 238.

21 See: John Perry, *Torture, Religious Ethics and National Security* (New York: Orbis Books, 2005).

22 "All that is received in someone is received in him through the medium of the receiver." Thomas Aquinas, *Summa theologiae* I. Q. 75.art. 5. Noonan suggests, at the end of his reflection on the development of moral theology in the Church, that revelation is always given, however, "Whatever revelation was given could not, at least in its enunciation, application, and development, exceed the capacities of those who received it." Those capacities involve being limited by their education, their social conventions, their language, their own experience of life. John T. Noonan, *A Church That Can and Cannot Change: The Development of Catholic Moral Teaching* (Notre Dame, IN: University of Notre Dame Press, 2005), 216.

23 Josef Fuchs, S.J., *Christian Ethics in a Secular Arena* (Washington, D.C.: Georgetown University Press, 1984), 110–12. See also: *Moral Demands and Personal Obligations* (Washington, D.C.: Georgetown University Press, 1993), 138–47.

24 Some base a theological foundation for authority in a theology of creation. See: Fuchs, *Christian Ethics in a Secular Society*, 105ff.

25 Delegated authority within these groups, or the shared authority of a marriage, derive their identities from the nature of the group in which they are situated.

26 Segundo, *El hombre de hoy y Jesus de Nazareth*, Vol. 3, 946.

27 "The personal decision for the God of salvation therefore does not directly concern the innerworldly behavior or man, but man himself as a person. He lets himself be reshaped, and reshapes himself in inner freedom: thus he is not a sinner, but redeemed — whether this be in categorical knowledge of God's salvific action (GS 11–13) or without such knowledge (cf. GS 22)." Fuchs, *Christian Morality*, 21.

28 We say this noting that in a particular context it can be judged that the good of the institution, or the good of society itself needs to be the focus of ethical inquiry and has priority. See: John W. Glaser, *Three Realms of Ethics* (Kansas City: Sheed and Ward, 1994).

29 Karl Rahner, "History of the World and Salvation-History," *Theological Investigations V* (New York: Seabury, 1975), 98ff.

30 Helen J. Alford, O.P. and Michael J. Naughton, *Managing as if Faith Mattered: Christian Social Principles in the Modern Organization* (Notre Dame, IN: University of Notre Dame Press, 2001).

31 I.G. Barbour, *Myths, Models and Paradigms: A Comparative Study in Science and Religion* (New York: Harper and Row, 1974), 7.

32 Avery Dulles, *The Craft of Theology: From Symbol to System* (New York: Crossroad, 1992), 48.

33 See: Stephen B. Bevans, *Models of Contextual Theology* (New York: Orbis Books, 1992), 25.

34 Avery Dulles, *Models of the Church* (Garden City, N.Y.: Doubleday Image Books, 1978), 32.

35 Dulles, *The Craft of Theology*, 49.

36 Karl Rahner, *Foundations of the Christian Faith*, trans. by William V. Dych (New York: Seabury Press, 1978), 133.

37 Michael Paul Gallagher draws on the grid-group analysis by Mary Douglas to understand the silent pressures of different cultural contexts in terms of their significance for arriving at religious commitment. See: *Clashing Symbols: An Introduction to Faith and Culture* (New York: Paulist Press, 2003), 27–34. Here I adapt Gallagher's insights and Douglas' model to ask the significance of the grid-group model for understanding context in moral experience. Mary Douglas elaborates on the grid-group model in *Natural Symbols* (New York: Vintage Books, 1973), chapter 4. Douglas draws on this model to argue that secularism is a product of a definable social experience.

PART II

DEVELOPING THE TALENTS OF A NEW AGE

Chapter 5

CHURCH AND FAMILY: A SPIRITUALITY OF ENGAGEMENT

Context A in Mary Douglas's "Types of Cultures" model at the end of the previous chapter is the traditional community, one that we easily recognize. Both grid and group are strong. This culture has clear authority, a sense of group life, and norms which regulate relationships between individuals. Context A can represent the traditional image of the Church, as well as the traditional family in society. Both cultures combine clear authority, a hierarchy that commands group life, with a network of implicit norms that structure interaction between individuals.

Obviously, the meaning of Church and family goes beyond this classification. Yet Douglas's analysis indicates they share as institutions the capacity to provide a mixture of stability and dependency which few others can offer. Students, when asked for their image of Church, echo Douglas's analysis when they reply, "a sense of home." It is noteworthy that they make the link between Church and family. Gallagher indicates that life in the "A" square need not be domineering or unhappy.[1] There can be flexible and humane forms of authority and secure social roles which offer a set of supports for the individual. This is the natural climate that has provided a sense of home for human beings, either as family or spiritual home.

The Changing Nature of Ecclesial and Family Life

We live in a time marked by unprecedented change.[2] A new state of the world has emerged from the combination of social, economic and political forces with changed technology, ideology, and cultural redefinition. These changes cause a shift in society's equilibrium, as these elements do not match. Social and ethical systems no longer control our technology; identities as peoples are no longer defined by the same boundaries; and time-held ideas no longer carry meaning nor provide insight into solutions to problems. People and nations jostle for identity and position in a world of shifting ground, often by means which challenge the fabric of our families, communities, and Church.

Church and family are affected by these seismic changes, which have occurred in most dramatic form since the Second World War. Theologian Don Browning charges that while processes of modernization and globalization provide new possibilities for the prosperity and health of the modern family, they are also a threat to the stability and quality of marriage and family life. Christianity transformed family relations in antiquity.[3] However, families today are disrupted by divorce, out-of-wedlock births, the emerging culture of non-marriage, and the increasing absence of fathers from their children. The collapse of marriage is also a contributing factor to world poverty.[4]

The Church, as well as all institutional religions, is challenged by these new times. Many today are interested in spiritual matters, but they have doubts regarding the role of the Church in this search. Dissatisfaction within the Catholic Church can be over the unsettling effect of Vatican II or rapid change with insufficient catechesis. Those accustomed to a more traditional Church feel it has changed beyond recognition. Others are affected by the impression that the hierarchy is reluctant to utilize more consultative/democratic practices in the Church. Women are concerned that their ecclesial responsibilities are seen as complementary, and by the same token subordinate, to those of men.[5] Disagreement over moral issues evokes mixed feelings toward the necessity of Church identity in personal life. Scandals — financial, sexual, and those relating to the use of power — cause people to question the integrity of the Church in many of its ecclesial communions. The search for spiritual inspiration can be displaced from the Church to music, art, poetry, or fiction, together with the new picture of the universe emerging from contemporary astronomy.

Robert Bellah maintains that both Church and family are questioned in American society, because in general people do not like institutions.[6] Institutions are seen as something from the past, filled with unexamined customs and codes which no longer fit modern society. People find them oppressive. The limitations institutions place on them are judged to be not worth the benefits they provide. Institutions do limit free choice, especially if autonomy is one's highest value. However, many moderns take the benefits of institutions for granted, without taking account of the investment required to provide these important stabilizers in life.

The state of affairs today is that people need institutions yet feel ambivalent about them.[7] Mary Douglas finds this same ambivalence regarding people's attitude toward home. Individuals long for it as a place yet fear its restrictions and implicit commitments. She remarks that when people reflect on the tyranny of home, it is not surprising that young people long to leave home to be free from its scrutiny and control.[8]

Do We Need Institutions?

Douglas claims people mature through two dominant life patterns which offer different forms of social control. In the first, individuals see themselves in relationship to a structure: i.e. hierarchy, sex role, and seniority or age status among others all enter into self-understanding. Habit and ritual contribute to a coherent symbol system and organized way of life.

In the second system, self-understanding is rooted more in the sense of self as an individual. Here control comes through becoming more sensitive to the feelings of others, as one becomes aware of one's feelings. The first, a condensed code (Douglas' term is "restricted code"), is institutionally rooted. The second, an elaborated code, floats free from institutions and is embedded more in the feelings of the individual.[9] The difference between the two can be illustrated in the distinction between two directives from parent to child to pick up his or her toys. After unsuccessful attempts at answering the child's plea, "Why?" the parent might say, "Because I say so!" That reflects a condensed code. In another case, the parent remarks, "How do you think mom will feel when she comes home and this place is a mess?" This reflects an elaborated code, one that relies on sensitivity to the other. As we mature, elaborated codes are used to criticize institutions. However, elaborated codes can never float entirely free of institutions, for we take them for granted as the very basis from which criticism is possible.[10] If people tried to live their lives through elaborated codes alone, they would have to make up their lives as they go along. Nothing could be taken for granted, because there would be no institutional context to tell them where they are.

How Does God Reach Us?

It is not uncommon today to identify a spiritual connection to God with the interior life or the inner dimension of life dissociated from groups, a community or a tradition. Formally though, religion is considered a door to the sacred through texts, creeds, codes and ceremonies. It is a condensed code, and as one, many find it unnecessary. They find a personal posture toward God or elaborated code sufficient. Religious research in the U.S. indicates the extent that religion is individualized. In Robert Bellah's *Habits of the Heart*, religion for one woman named Shelia was called Sheilaism. Shelia saw herself as her central "ultimate concern." Bellah remarks, "Sheilaism is rooted in the effort to transform external authority into internal meaning."[11] Religion shifts to being a cosmic selfhood, which magnifies the self to the point that it becomes identical with the world. This allows one to be religious while at the same time transcend family, ethnic

culture and formal religion to define a self free of external constraint. He found
Shelia typical of many whom he interviewed. At the other extreme, others image
religion solely as an external authority and regulation. Neither form of religion
adequately offers a language able to mediate between self, others, nature and
God in our society today.[12]

A common remark today is, "I believe in God, but do not go to church."[13]
Roof's recent study of religion among baby-boomers finds that 95 percent of
church dropouts believe it is possible to be a good Christian without attending
church, and nearly two-thirds of the dropouts consider themselves to be good
Christians. As moderns we often fail to ask, not how does one reach God, but
how does God reach us?

Karl Rahner takes a different approach to the question of the necessity of the
Church. For Rahner, the human person is not just a "being," but rather a "being
in the world." A consequence is that the human person must seek God, or pursue
mystery in life through ritual, rites, dogmas, prayers, etc. Faith in God, as personal
and mysterious as it is, is always entered into historically, in a time and place.[14]
Rahner explains that religion is necessary, not just because it arises from a felt
human need, and thus can be dismissed as a need if not felt. If this were true, in
our terms, an elaborated code would be sufficient. Rather the only way to enter
into one's own transformation to fulfillment, or follow a spiritual path, is in time,
in history. If God shares God's Self through revelation, Scripture, then we must
ask where is the group in time which lives by this revelation.[15]

J.M.R. Tillard takes this argument one step farther. The letters of St. Paul
imply that reconciliation with God is inseparable from entrance into the unity of
sisters and brothers in the body of Christ. The self in this way is absorbed into
Christ. The new way of life "exists in the space opened by Christ on the cross,"
and this space is the ecclesial body.[16] The Christian way of life is a way of life in
which others are essential. Others are radically essential because life "in Christ"
is that of a body, the body of reconciled humankind vivified by the Spirit of the
living God.[17] Faith is not a personal reality which one constructs. Rather faith
is lived in a tradition, a history of relationships, in an institution in a religious
form. As institutional, it is doctrinal, moral, ritual, and so on.

It is obvious that there is value in the personal construction of religious identity
and its implied elaborated code. The document on religious freedom of Vatican II
expresses that no one should be coerced into a religious posture (DH 4). However,
it is not accurate to imagine religious belief as a choice between the condensed
code of religion and its commitments, and the elaborated code of personal faith.
Rather the two are interdependent in the mature Christian.[18]

Context A life, reflected in Church and family as institutions, is not life in
unilateral institutions that cancel out personal expression, criticism and diver-
gence. As institutions, they have a mixed quality between the institutional and

the personal which is essential to their health. To make this clear, let us examine how a view of culture grounds a stance on family and Church.

The Relevance of Culture in Understanding Christian Life

Understanding of Church and family is based typically on a conception of culture as a coherent set of meanings that inform social practices. Catholicism, as well as Christian life in general, is often expected to be a unique transformative subculture within society. Today the meaning of Catholic and Christian identity is in question. Standards to measure personal fidelity, beyond those of basic morality, are unclear, and a typical Catholic or Christian is difficult to describe. People ask, how can one be Catholic, immersed in society, and faithful at the same time? How we understand the relationship of the Church to the world affects this answer.

For Catholics, prior to Vatican II a key pastoral strategy for the Church to carry out its mission and to support its members was the creation of parallel institutions within industrial society. This strategy set a climate for Catholic identity where it was practiced. Catholic hospitals, schools, newspapers, political parties and the like were organized around the broad term "Catholic Action." Pius XI wanted Catholics to be involved as Catholics to foster a better society.[19] Catholic Action attempted to apply principles of the Church to counteract the poverty, insecurity, and material misery of the laboring population.[20]

From Leo XIII to Vatican II this Catholic Action movement formed a paradigm through which Catholics lived in the world. People generally perceived that secular society had fallen away from the Church.[21] Greed and irreligion had led to over-investment in secular matters and lack of attention to the spiritual life. Through spirituality a person could make an alternate response in and toward a society that was no longer Christian.

Catholic Action recognized the autonomy of secular life. However, Catholic theology prior to Vatican II envisioned a split between the material order and the supernatural. This theological understanding of the world depicted the world in terms of the Church, rather than the Church in terms of the world.[22] In the United States, a good Catholic not only attended the sacraments but engaged socially in a round of activities that immersed them in a parallel society, a social entity that sheltered them from an alien and hostile world.[23] Everyone knew their place in this model of Catholic life. Catholic Action was participation of the laity in the apostolate of the hierarchy.[24] The Church here was clearly the hierarchy.[25] Most Catholics held that social problems could be solved by personal morality, a Christian upbringing, private charity and close association with the Church.[26]

This institutional framework for the Church's presence in society reflected not only an approach to its mission, but a sense of Church, spirituality, and vision of moral responsibility in the world for its members.[27] The Church clearly had a condensed code of presenting itself. People understood their place and their responsibilities in the Church. However, the style of Church, society, and theology which supported it has changed.

Search for a New Catholic Identity

Today cultural theorists suggest that a Catholic culture is less likely to be a unified whole of beliefs simply transmitted to every Catholic and is closer to a common engagement around key beliefs of the tradition centered on human dignity. Kathryn Tanner, in *Theories of Culture: A New Agenda for Theology*, criticizes a more traditional cultural approach.[28] Tanner claims that earlier concepts of culture allowed the anthropologist to describe a culture as static, and find a coherent order in a given culture. Today, theorists take more notice of how historical processes such as conflicts and pressures from the outside influence change in culture. In other words, Tanner argues that culture is more complex than unified models of culture suggest.

Cultural theorists once held that cultures formed a distinctive unit of life and could be identified with a characteristic set of norms, values, beliefs, concepts, dispositions, or preoccupations of a particular people. The elements of a culture were seen as interrelated, providing a form of meaning and order. Since each culture possessed an internal organization, social scientists held that by studying a specific context of living, this "snapshot" provided a key to understanding culture in a wider whole.

Tanner criticizes this more traditional sense of culture. In her words:

> It seems less and less plausible to presume that cultures are self-contained and clearly bounded units, internally consistent and unified wholes of beliefs and values simply transmitted to every member of their respective groups as principles of social order.[29]

Early cultural theory assumed that a culture is an entire way of life in that everything about a group distinguishes it from others. It associated cultures with a social consensus in which every member of the group more or less shares.[30] Theorists today question whether there is the high degree of coherence and consistency among elements of a culture which earlier theories claimed. The broad spectrum of outlook within any religious group testifies to the regularity of pluralism, rather than to the inevitability of unity.

Today we ask how the pluralism among members of the Church can reconcile with their identity as Catholics, or how the condensed code of the Church interacts with the elaborated code of its members. Currently the minimal quality of unity necessary to act "in the name of the Church" in the public arena is a highly contested question. Because Catholics hold social power in society not only as citizens with voting power but as individuals through elected office, power which is not absolute but simply one factor in a democratic process, the question remains how one is Catholic and socially effective. How is one free to prudentially affirm Catholic principles to the degree they can be effective given the constraints of a real context and yet also responsible to the counter-cultural call of the gospel? What criteria enable us to deal with the culture wars between groups in the Church and sort out what actions and positions are consistent with the Church's mission to the world?

Tanner sheds light on these questions as she addresses the quality of consensus in a shared culture. Cultures are not upheld by every member of a social group. In her words:

> Every member of a society may declare the same beliefs, prominently display in their discourse the same fundamental categories, hold high the same values; it is highly unlikely, however, that they will all mean the same thing by them.[31]

A reconstructed social theory, as Tanner espouses, retains the belief that culture is an essentially consensus-building feature of group living, however, it is more limited in its vision of the extent of this consensus. It can be minimal in its content and can form the basis for conflict as well as for shared beliefs and sentiments. Even if culture is not a common focus of agreement, a shared culture does connote a common *engagement*. Tanner asserts that culture in this sense is a sense of sharing "common stakes." All parties at least agree on the importance of the pursuit of a value, even if they don't share a common understanding of what they mean in all cases.

Does reconstructed cultural theory nullify the traditional belief that a Catholic moral outlook is a foundational vision, a condensed code? Brian Johnstone claims that coherent systems of thought and belief are foundational for the moral life. All moral methods are processes by which a community adopts, founds, validates and communicates a moral way of life.[32] Methods cannot be so diverse as to be ineffective to direct human behavior. On the contrary, they must be clear and coherent enough to be understood and followed in a way of life. Reconstructed social theory would not negate this affirmation but would locate this coherence not just in shared teaching, but also in the quality of community life in which Catholics are formed. The coherence Johnstone marks is a practical harmony, not just a formal one. While the teaching office of the Church has a unique responsibility in this coherence, all members of the Church are responsible to hand on its values.

A reconstructed view of culture is less likely to view norms for action as the main principles of action in society. Norms as cultural forms do not produce action unless one factors in how historical agents make use of those cultural forms in particular situations. Again, reconstructed theory draws us to the real contexts in which people live and function. The call to form one's conscience made by *Gaudium et Spes* and the call for local discernment encouraged by Paul VI in *Octogesima Adveniens* 4 seem inseparable from the vision of coherence suggested by Johnstone and reinterpretation of a Catholic identity in society called for by reconstructed theory. Interpretation of a principle of Catholic life in one's context, or the call to "read the signs of the times" in this light is less an application of theory already known and more an activity of constantly reconstituting Catholic belief itself in practice. According to Tanner, "Cultural forms have the force of social directives only by way of human agents struggling over their meaning and social import."[33]

A reconstructed view of culture affirms the importance of a wide range of people participating in the expression of Catholic life in society. Rather than something already established, culture is brought into the present only by the active efforts of people interpreting it and using it anew. Tanner explains that this new approach stresses how interactive process and negotiation, indeterminacy, fragmentation, conflict, and influences beyond one's normal boundaries are part of real life experience, and part of any vision of Catholic culture. In this light, debates over what constitutes Catholic identity in the public realm are actually constitutive of a new Catholic culture.

A reconstructed view of culture is able to view change, like the impact of globalization on the Church, not as an anomaly but as an ongoing process in the life of the Church. Culture has its own internal principles of change that arise out of challenges to dominant cultural forms and arrangements which co-exist at any given time. These internal strains and conflicts produce change. Tanner asserts that what appears as stability is simply a temporary moment in an ongoing process. Change, conflict and contradiction are viewed as within culture rather than as a threat to it.

How we envision Christianity in this more complex cultural map is a major factor in the question of what it means to be faithful. If we see the core moral call of the natural law as the God-given task of more fully humanizing the human person and the world, then Catholics, Christians of other communions, members of other world religions, all people of good will join together in this common effort. Yet questions remain. In carrying out her life and mission are there social boundaries necessary for the Church? Do Christians as a social group have their own culture? Is there a distinctiveness that relies on their separation from other groups in society? Tanner's response is that the cohesiveness of Christian life is not that it creates a separate culture, but that it provides an abiding reference point for the direction of one's life, whether in or out of the Christian community.[34]

Tanner suggests that unlike the days of ghetto Catholicism, Christian communities do not function as complete cultures. Rather Christian communities share an overlapping of tradition and horizons with the culture surrounding them. What is Christian or Catholic is difficult to isolate. While some claim that the Christian does the same things as his or her neighbor, just with a different outlook, this solution is too simple.[35] Christianity means more than living with a different set of motivations. Tanner argues that the believer forms an unusual type of voluntary association within a wider society, instead of a separate society in and of themselves. This association shapes members for altered social relations beyond the interactions within the Church itself. Christians live in their respective culture with a distinctive set of operations which is more significant in her view than only with a unified social vision based on Christian faith. A type of common vision arises from such praxis, and from the need to debate the direction and content of future investment. Tanner emphasizes praxis and the real communities in which Christians function, together with the quality of the interactions, standards and values to which they conform to as members when she assesses a shared culture. Such an association shapes one's whole way of life, without being a separate society.

If we follow Tanner's line of thought, the goal of faithful action of the Church and her members is to shape the practices of those outside it, to penetrate fields where social decisions are made, to "bring forth charity for the life of the world." The Church is to inculturate the values of the faith within the systems of daily life. While we will show there is a time and place for clear institutional identity with the Church in the public realm, ultimately reconstructed cultural theory locates the social dimension of Catholicity primarily outside the boundaries of the Church.[36] However, the total activity of life in the Church is essential to it.[37]

Common experience shows that a variety of factors "carry" the Catholic social tradition in society. Institutions, legislation, the arts, media, politics and social sciences, movements, and good works, while not directly Catholic-inspired, function to carry the Church's values. However, if we follow a reconstructed cultural theory it would be wrong to conclude that Catholic identity in this process is without content. Marks of Catholic identity mix with other values of a socially oriented life or institution or movement in society.[38] Richard McBrien names three characteristics of Catholicism: mediation, sacramentality, and communion. These characteristics have a place in the mix with more broadly held values of human dignity that identify the faithful Catholic in society today.[39]

How then can one be faithful and Catholic in a modern cultural situation of fluid boundaries? Tanner claims that cultural identity is more a hybrid, where cultural ideals are lived out in relationships of resistance, appropriation, subversion, and compromise.[40] These four operations certainly set a direction to ongoing reflection on the avenues by which Catholics function in a more complex cultural model. Let us explore the insights of McBrien into the uniqueness of Catholic identity.

Mediation, Catholic Life, and Faithfulness

Among the three characteristics of Catholicism, mediation is the most counter-cultural. The concept of mediation goes against the cultural ideal of American society which suggests that the core realities of life are mainly self-constructed. If I have sufficient income, it is because I work hard, Americans hold. Stephen Carter notes in his text, *Civility*, that Americans tend to see their freedom as the ability to do what they like, rather than the capacity to do what is right.[41] Our freedom is measured by its exercise rather than by the quality of its direction and the effects of its choices. We imagine we travel through life individually, creating our fortunes through our own efforts. Those who promote seeking the common good find it difficult to convince their neighbors. How does one convince others they should self-select to abandon their preferences, in order to care about the needs of another? If civility is the sum of sacrifices we make because we live with others, Carter argues that religion is one of the few things in our society that calls us to this higher standard.

The Church sees life very differently than our culture. The Eucharist celebrates this difference. Faith is not a personal reality which I construct. Rather faith is lived in a tradition, a history of relationships, in an institution in a religious form. As institutional, it is doctrinal, moral, ritual and so on. Even the "Word of God" is mediated in a body of Scriptures, ones formed through a tradition of preaching and belief and interpreted by a community. The Eucharist itself is only understood within the matrix of Scripture, sacraments, and ethical testimony which keeps alive the memory of what Jesus lived for and why God raised him from the dead. An understanding of mediation gives us a fuller understanding of the meaning of the Church.

Louis-Marie Chauvet tells us in *The Sacraments: The Word of God at the Mercy of the Body* that the Church is not Christ, it is his symbolic witness in the world. Faith in Christ, however, involves the renunciation of seeing, hearing, and touching Christ immediately. Rather, "Faith begins precisely with such a renunciation of the immediacy of the see/know and with the assent to the mediation of the church."[42] There is no such thing as an original Christian. We are all Christian because of the long tradition of the witness of others in the faith community. When we understand this, we grasp the meaning of mediation.

Chauvet cautions that one becomes Christian only by entering an institution, and the modes of Christian behavior which may appear the most "personal" (meditative prayer) or the most "authentic" (concern for others) are always the expression of an apprenticeship interiorized for a long time and of habits inculcated by institutional and highly ritualized processes.[43] This is the meaning of mediation. What is most spiritual always takes place in what is most corporeal. We understand ourselves as Christians, speak of ourselves as Christians and lead our lives as Christians only because of the Church, and through the mediation of the body, within the body of a society or particular context of life.

The Church too experiences mediation. The fundamental dependence of the Church on its Lord is expressed in the Eucharist. The sacramental offering of the body and blood of Christ is the ritual mediation which symbolically shows what the return gift of the Church is: the existential offering of its own life, and the life of all its members. We pray that the Holy Spirit may come over us so that, through the Church's participation in the Eucharistic body, it may become the ecclesial body of Christ.[44] Through love and justice, we seek to make Christ in the middle of the world, as the ultimate goal of the Eucharist is charity among members, and within the whole of humanity.

Johann Baptist Metz reminds us in *The Emergent Church* that when this sense of mediation is collapsed we get a kind of "bourgeois theology" that actually conceals the Christian call to faithfulness. Religion loses its capacity to call us beyond our self-interest and makes it easy to compartmentalize one's living and one's religion. Metz calls this the religion of the middle class. It appears to espouse belief in conversion but its religious vision rests more in the unquestioned status of the middle class in the world, and its religious practice establishes not the reign of God but middle class self-interests and future.[45] In contrast, the following of Christ involves a "searching freedom" where relationship with Christ in community is essential to the discernment of one's direction and purpose.[46]

People see concrete institutions, or other sensible mediations like language, traditions, and boundaries of belonging, as obstacles to truth today. Truth is created. We have your truth and my truth. The Church, by contrast, sees mediation as the very milieu within which human beings attain their truth, and thus respond to the Truth which calls them. Here mediation is the milieu in which the subject becomes subject by responding to a reality beyond their own desires. The Eucharist marks this sense of mediation. The character of the love it evokes comes not from the degree of one's generosity but from its nature of response to the prior gift and commitment of God which it celebrates. The fidelity it marks comes from the belief in the Christian community that we seek to become what we have first received.

Sacramentality, Catholic Life, and Faithfulness

Sacramental order is the symbolic order. It is different than the cultural order. A symbol places side by side all the elements of a whole. In the Christian life, our symbols bridge the gap between God, ourselves and the world. A symbol requires the subjection of partners to the other, and because of this the symbol can provide an order in which I find my meaning by finding my place within it, a meaning bigger than myself. Christians interpret life in relationship to the life, death, and resurrection of Jesus Christ. The Church testifies to this. When we as Church hear the Scriptures as Jesus' very word, Jesus is present in His word. Each time the Church takes the bread, pronounces the blessing, breaks it and gives it, it is in memory of the Lord Jesus, it is He who gives it through the Church. Chauvet reminds us that the Church considers the sacramental gestures and words it expresses are His gestures, and His words. In the fullest sense of the word the Church is the "sacrament."[47] Essential to a sense of faithfulness in the Christian life is the priority of the ecclesial we; the Church precedes the individual. We do not baptize ourselves. Christian identity is bestowed only within an ecclesial pattern common to all Christians. Our faith is not one only of personal immediacy with God; rather it functions through the signs and symbols of the Church. This is what sacramentality confirms.

The tension between personal faith and its institutional framework is highlighted in the sacramental life. The sacraments remind us that we do not move from non-faith to faith without obtaining from Jesus the competence to make this leap. The Eucharist invites us to search for faithfulness in a matrix of belief. We seek to know God's mystery as revealed in Jesus Christ through Scripture. We live through the sacramental celebrations the Church performs in memory of Jesus' death and resurrection both in our initiation into the mystery of Christ in baptism and being members of his living body in the Eucharist. Finally, we act in the name of the gospel through our action, seeking to be faithful. John Paul II cautioned us against both an overvaluation of the sacraments as the sole mark of a "practicing Christian" and an overvaluation of ethics — political or emotional or charismatic — as our "wedding garment" of salvation. In *Dives in Misericordia* John Paul II calls people to open their lives to the order of mercy. It is the Mercy of the Father, Son and Holy Spirit that must be revealed now in our modern world. Only it is more powerful than evil: more powerful than sin and death. Therefore God's love and mercy as made manifest in the Eucharist reminds us that even our notions of what justice is in our world today need to be continually revised. Mercy constantly reframes what we understand, calling us to forgive, calling us to invest, conferring "a new content" on justice through the introduction of that creative power of love "which is more powerful than sin" (DM 14).

A Christian ethic of faithfulness, therefore, has love as its form. It is a response to the priority of God's love. We have said that Christian identity is a structure, not a self-creation. A structure is a whole of which each component is an integral part and in which each component finds it value only by references to the others. The Eucharist is the structure of Christian identity as it seeks to be faithful. There is the gift, its reception and the returning gift of concrete action in society which forms the ongoing process of Christian identity, not only in the Christian but in the world. Instead of justifying ourselves through our actions alone, we welcome daily the Spirit of the Risen One into our lives and join ourselves to His presence in the world.

Communion, Catholic Life and Faithfulness

Communion marks the reality of Catholic life that the grace received in the sacrament is given also as a task to accomplish in our lives together. We pray to become what we have celebrated and received. However, the communion to which we refer is not the "us" of a cultural religion, where belonging simply comes from convention and upbringing. It is a communion formed from a faith which is personally appropriated. This is paradoxical. In the Spirit, what is most individual is not obliterated in communion. We acknowledge in the Eucharist the creation of a new "we" created by baptism and expressed in the Eucharist: "we pray to you." Yet, this "we" is not the self-selected "us" of the lifestyle enclave of modern society.[48] It is not even the "we" of primary relationships of family and friends. Rather it is the "we" of the identity given to us by Christ, and reciprocally of the fragile unity capable of being achieved in our pluralistic and global society amid all which threatens communion in our world. In the Eucharist we celebrate that Christ is being raised and continues to raise a body of humanity of which the Church is the primary locus only because he is first raised by God.[49] We celebrate that the Church then is the servant of humanity to achieve this unity in the concrete in all the myriad ways its members live and walk. We do this with Christ our savior, not just as a moral example, but as a gratuitous gift. Chauvet reminds us that the Mass is not just useful or real to the extent it mobilizes energies in order to transform the world. Rather its primary significance is the communication of the gratuitous gift of God. The liturgy calls us constantly to build the communion we receive by calling us to a liturgical reading of our ethical action as a life of faith and love, a "spiritual offering" in its successes and failures. As well as summoning us to an ethical reading of liturgy, the grace received in the sacrament is given as a task to accomplish. The sacraments are not the whole Christian life; they acquire their significance in relation to Scripture and ethical life.[50]

The call to communion is to strive for the unity where differences are not obscured, yet not definitive of living. The call to dialogue with difference assumes an identity from which to start. It is a call to engagement. However, the sacramental offering of the Body and Blood of Christ is the ritual mediation which symbolically shows the nature always of the return gift: the letting go of something which breaks down unity. In Carter's words, this is the sacrifice for neighbor, often the stranger, essential to civility. With St. Paul, we are cautioned with the Corinthians against receiving the Eucharistic body while distaining the ecclesial body. Amid the culture wars within the Church, the pastoral challenge of blending new parishes, the national call to immigration and health care reform, the need for better working relations between clergy and laity, the Eucharistic community hears the call to communion. At the same time we believe there can be more than our current world marked with global poverty, terrorism, human trafficking, war, genocide, and ecological destruction. We believe as a Eucharistic community that the darkness of our world remains secretly inhabited by the strength of an active presence of the Body of Christ. In turn we seek to be that presence in the world, amid its darkness and the opacity of our vision.

The Family Transformed

Families too are Context A structures. Expectations of family life derive not from personal tastes but from the "continual building up of a sense of social pattern."[51] Family, like community, is a call to manifold engagement.[52] Families in a formal sense provide a framework to guide behavior, indicating rights, responsibilities and obligations. Families are meant to ground us. As children grow they learn right and wrong in terms of a given structure. However, not all families are the same. Each cultural group has expectations for what a family unit is and does.[53] The degree to which a set of family relations comprises a distinct social unit and the range of activities that are carried out by this unit varies from nation to nation, culture to culture, and even family to family. Family life, however, is a major locus of personal engagement in the life of most adults. Engagement in these commitments marks faithfulness in most adult lives.

Today, however, young adults see a diminished role for marriage in its institutional aspects.[54] David Matzko McCarthy maintains that for many, marriage is not seen anymore as an institutional context of a life course. People instead focus on certain individual life goals: finishing school, financial independence, living independently from the family, or achieving full time employment. All take a priority over marriage as a key step toward achieving adulthood.[55] There is a tension between marriage in the traditional sense of embracing the social idea of the establishment of a household and the interpersonal meanings of marriage and family. Some refer to this as a conflict between marriage as "pure relationship" and the solidarity, communication, and life disciplines required to maintain a home.[56]

Mary Douglas centers family life in a Context A paradigm. A traditional family (Douglas uses the term "positional"), family shapes behavior by building up a sense of social patterns and enforcing ascribed role categories. Personal expression is restricted by faithfulness to one's ascribed role, one's place in relation to others.[57] Family in this sense follows a condensed or "restricted" (Douglas's term) code. However, Douglas recognizes that modern society has called forth a corresponding pattern of family life which is personal. The "modern family" is oriented to social mobility and changing social pressures as work demands a more verbally articulate individual. Here the successful entrepreneur must have a different formation than simply taking on a social role. The emphasis in the personal family is on autonomy, personal growth, and internal ethical sensibilities. The personal family fosters self-expression. There is still social control, but, according to Douglas, "behavior (in the personal home) is controlled by being made sensitive to the personal feelings of others, by inspecting (one's) own feelings."[58] This is an elaborated code. Today modern professional and upwardly mobile working class families are in a state of an elaborated code and personal family systems.[59]

Douglas claims still that the family is a Context A phenomena. A personal family system alone cannot meet its tasks because it has little place for the necessity of the commons and the common good, essential to family life. How do we blend the values of a traditional family and its capacity to foster deep and abiding solidarity necessary for human happiness and the personal system, which is sustained by the current linkages of work and family?[60]

Theologian Don Browning claims that modern cultural values such as expressive and utilitarian individualism cannot sustain marriage without a public theology of covenant and subsidiarity which defines marriage not only as a deeply meaningful personal and spiritual relationship but as a public institution.[61] Browning reflects on what kind of institutional supports marriage needs. The nineteenth-century antidote to the negative impact of the market on family life was the family model of the breadwinning father and domestic and economically dependent mothers. A strong antithesis to an unmitigated market economy today, however, cannot be sustained by this family model alone. The women's movement questions the subordination of women which this arrangement implies. Furthermore, American culture accepts the disruptions that market employment and market-driven consumption have visited on families. Increased divorce, later marriages, more single parenthood, and stepfamilies are seen simply as "family change," and fitting tradeoffs for the benefits of modern life.[62] Browning calls for sustained cultural work to support marriage as it faces the tensions between work and family brought about by the forces of modernization. This is not a technical or economic fix alone, rather one which requires religion. Christianity is called upon to offer its own symbols to help reconstruct a broader vision of marriage and family.

McCarthy maintains that modern families are not going to revert back to a traditional family and condensed code alone, nor will they be able to sustain themselves utilizing only the values of the personal system. Rather they will blend modern personal systems with traditional systems in creation of family life. Families will live in the tension of being both traditional ("positional") and personal at the same time. They will blend the traditional social functions of the family with the personal and emotive values of modernity. Personal families will need a positional or traditional reference point.[63] The style of this engagement will reflect a search for an alternate way of life that assumes pluralism, rather than seeking to fight against it.[64]

Lisa Sowle Cahill sees a new generation already in the process of this *engagement*. They appreciate the traditional values regarding marriage and family, but do so with an eye on their contemporary experience of family fragmentation and consumerism, as well as the stress and strain of contemporary life, especially when both parents work, and/or enter public and professional roles. Operating beyond the confines of the old conservative-liberal paradigm, they value traditional elements of family life as they build their lives today. However, those lives are inserted in a context of "increased but still incomplete gender equality," more economic stress, more promotion of consumerism, and a stronger critique of American culture as capable of delivering justice for all.[65] They seek to integrate common Catholic values of commitment and monogamy, openness to procreation and parental responsibility, the cultivation of religious identity in the home, and the family's dedication to service for the common good with the pressures of living contemporary life.[66] However, they do so less with theoretical concerns and more with a focus on the practicality of living a balanced married life today. They engage the challenge to reinvent married life today in its new context.

Browning suggests that the need to revive marriage is worldwide. Core beliefs of all world religions need to be taken beyond their confessional relevance toward a common vision of the sacredness life, how men should treat women, and the role and limitations of state over family life.[67] Douglas sees the answer as the creation of a vision of a traditional (positional) family which operates with elaborated speech where people are sensitive to the claims of the whole and respond to their social roles.[68]

We have seen that both Church and family exist in a matrix where the stability of a constricted code exists in tension with the meaningfulness of an elaborated code. The relationship between the two has to be renegotiated in society today so that the gift of these important institutions can contribute to this new millennium. However, as a Context A phenomenon, the authors cited claim that their synthesis cannot be accomplished without the directional role of the positional or constricted pole. This is counter-intuitive to the way moderns think. What significance might this have for a sense of faithfulness today?

The Church, Conscience, and Faithfulness

The tension between the values of an elaborated and positional code comes into focus in a key way when people in the Church refer to conscience. On the one hand, we have said earlier that conscience is a deep center of knowing right from wrong in each person. On the other hand, conscience requires an *engagement* in a broader context of meaning and values than one's own intuitions. All people have a conscience, so why is forming one's conscience in the Church important in the Christian life? We see today that ambivalent feelings regarding the role of the Church spill over into questions regarding its role in morality. People recognize that the formulation of some moral norms in the Church are conditioned by time and culture, and even by erroneous judgments. Yet, the Church claims the authority of a tradition, a positional authority in the lives of Christians. How are these things reconciled?

Some Christians assume that Christian ethics means making norms from the pronouncements of Jesus in the gospel. A better understanding is Christian ethics involves reflection on what Jesus has done for us, and therefore on who we are as human beings, and what obligations flow from this. Awareness of who we are before God highlights conscience at its first level, as a capacity. Core beliefs of faith such as: we are made in God's image; Christ gives a new meaning to existence; and creation is for the good of all, to shed light on how the Christian is to proceed in the search for a good decision.[69] Faith seeking understanding is the core meaning of theological reflection. Faith takes us beyond just the facts and issues, to their meaning in the wider scheme of things. Conscience therefore attends to this responsibility. James Gustafson says that to do ethics with theological awareness is to reflect on how things really and ultimately are.[70] We ask how things are ultimately, in God's eyes. In the words of Vatican II, "Faith throws a new light on everything, manifests God's designs for man's total vocation, and thus directs the mind to solutions which are fully human" (GS 11). Reason is informed by faith. This does not mean reason is replaced by faith, nor reason without faith. Reason is shaped by faith.

Perception of a situation and one's responsibilities in it also depend on character, and faith has a role in its formation. Norms and values are important, but character — our moral qualities — shapes decisions and action. Character is formed in community.[71] While the Christian lives the same daily existence as everyone else, they are also presented with the Christian mysteries as a framework in which to interpret their experience. Creation, sin, incarnation, and the paschal mystery join with the symbols and narratives offered by the Christian community to explain their relationships to God, others, creation and themselves. Faith, hope and love are given to us to overcome the anxiety, futility, and selfishness which overpower our vision of what is possible in daily life.[72] The Eucharist confirms that our acceptance of God's salvation expresses itself in the ethical responses of our lives. The Scriptures, sacraments, and ethics of the Church form an inseparable matrix of Christian living. What influence might this have on our conscience?

This vision of the ultimate meaning of life can be protective and dispositive.[73] It provides a condensed code when life's meaning is distorted by an elaborated code of a modern culture which can define human worth simply by what one can produce, by power, or by the amount of technological gadgets possessed. The Christian can measure whether cultural values, while desirable and attractive in themselves, are really the only standards by which a situation can be judged. Faith perspective can be a dispositive influence. Faith prepares one to approach a life issue with a set of attitudes, ones formed by the practices formed by faith. The Church in this way forms our moral imagination. In conscience formation, the Church helps us to order what is ultimate and what is subordinate in our lives.[74]

At the second moment of conscience, conscience as process, we gather the necessary information to make a decision in the concrete. While all people are called to follow the natural law, do good and avoid evil, it is another matter to know what this means in the concrete. In the technical areas of the sciences, economics, politics, and the like, the Church has no special expertise. Here the Church, like all people of good will, has to study the facts of the situation, and discern in it what serves the meaning of human life. But as a community of moral discernment, the Church does have moral wisdom. Its status as a religious body does not erode its relevance to the public discussions of modern life.[75]

The Church has a role in the formation of our conscience as a community of moral wisdom accumulated, passed on, challenged, and rethought.[76] The wisdom arises from the experience of the Church community and its work in passing on the moral tradition. This is an experience where people not only face life decisions, but do so in the context of faith. Its pastoral experience, its prophetic actions, and its scholarship are all ways the Church deals with new issues and engages in internal and public debate. At times, because of the complexity of some issues, there is pluralism in the Church regarding a particular issue. Even in the Church the answer to all questions is not known, and alternative solutions by conscientious Christians are possible (GS 43).[77]

The special ministry of the hierarchy, or magisterium, is to provide a structure which helps to unite the Church in its search for the truth and discovery of it (LG 23). The whole college of bishops succeeds in the authority of the college of the apostles (LG 18). They instruct through formal definitions of the faith, decrees of ecumenical councils, encyclicals, letters, and the like.[78] These different pronouncements of the magisterium often carry different weight.[79] Finally, they work to foster in the Church a community of moral deliberation. They are to foster dialogue around moral issues, listen to the moral experience of the people of the Church, and be open to the world.

The Church is this way offers a positional code. The Church's official word on moral issues in the search of conscience holds a key place. Yet, when dealing with the moral pluralism in the Church and in society, we find people of a strict interpretation, as well as those who find alternative opinions valid and having good reasons. The insight and word of the Church are supported by the Spirit of God, yet are also human. Church teaching can change on certain matters when new information and experience challenge the norm in place. Given this historical situation, some moral teaching in place is "the best possible at the time," given the ambiguities surrounding the issue. Yet, the Church holds that its moral doctrine is not merely a suggestion; rather it is obligatory.[80] In other words, acting beyond it is an unusual experience, not an ordinary one.[81] When an individual Christian does this they accept this responsibility in conscience.

While all baptized people are responsible for passing on the Christian faith, only the Pope and the bishops can designate a teaching as official.[82] The primary task of the bishops is to proclaim the apostolic faith and to foster in the Church the assimilation of the values of the tradition so that these may be creatively present in word and deed in the world. This task of the bishops is grounded in the mission of the Church to preach salvation in Christ. The tradition of the Church is to hand on what it has received, that Jesus Christ is the one and saving event in which we are to believe. The bishops do not add onto this revelation, which ended with the last apostle. Rather they seek to make this revelation relevant in each age. In this sense the teaching of the Church develops or deepens, as the Church understands the significance of the gospel in each age.

The role of the magisterium in the Church is to see that the saving word of Christ will really be addressed to the concrete situation of each age. Theologians in the Church work with the magisterium in this task. Since the Holy Spirit guides the Church, all believers share in this revelation. Yet the magisterium is the concrete way the Church discerns and maintains its historical links to Jesus Christ in face of new developments.[83] The magisterium does have a role in giving an authentic interpretation and exposition of the natural law, however, the natural law is not revealed. Josef Fuchs comments, "It is the proper task of the magisterium to watch over everything that belongs to the divine *deposit of faith* and also over everything without which this deposit cannot be defended. But it is certain that the detailed totality of the natural law does not belong to this."[84] While the bishops and all the people in the Church are to reflect on problems "in the light of the gospel" (GS 48), this does not mean that the Christian faith itself generates the solution to these problems. Rather the Church brings to the dialogue the values of the gospel and the moral wisdom of its tradition.

In terms of Douglas's analysis, it is clear that the Church provides a condensed code of morals to live by.[85] The Church and its teachings have the characteristics of a Context A reality. They are authoritative and "provide a religious cosmology with which to confront the dilemmas of existence."[86] The Church offers a "way" to live, not just a message. However, as with the family, the condensed reality of the Church is stretched in an elaborative direction through the personal culture of the times and through taking seriously the situations in which people live their faith. As members live in diverse situations and cultures, they face multiple tensions of modern living. The "Church of the commons," of solidarity, typical of Context A life, faces the strain of integrating this diverse reality.

For instance, few today would venture to define material and social welfare in the same way for all societies, however our common humanity requires it. Yet its diverse needs could lose the fight for identity in our shifting world without the "positional" reference point of religion, and the Church's stance on human dignity in all its forms. Here the Church, as in the past, engages in a type of "compenetration" with each culture. As a religious entity which transcends one culture, it becomes engaged in the daily life of every socio-political reality to inculturate the gospel. This mission changes the culture, as well as changing the Church.

The third expression of conscience is the decision to act one way or another. Here also the community of the Church impacts our conscience. When we speak of Church, we refer not only to its official leaders, but also to its members. Its mystics, saints, and sinners, as well as its popes, parishioners, followers, and critics all are its "faithful." From this witness of the Church we receive the example of what is worth our effort and the range of possibility that life can offer. The moral example of the Church therefore shapes our lives.

The Church as "home" is a place where we work out problems of the commons, as well as a center through which we engage the world as Christians. To foster a home in this world both the Church and its members are called to a new type of engagement. Some members might again need to "opt for the Church," in new ways. The Church itself is challenged to engage with voices, competencies, questions and peoples that to date have not held a significant place at its table. It is such engagement which will foster new communities of meaning within the Church and its faithfulness to its call. Only such engagement can translate the values fostered by the believing community into action for the good of the world.

Notes

1 Michael Paul Gallagher, *Clashing Symbols: An Introduction to Faith and Culture* (New York: Paulist Press, 2003), 30.
2 Lester Thurow, *The Future of Capitalism* (New York: William Morrow and Co., 1996), chapter 1.
3 Don S. Browning, *Marriage and Modernization: How Globalization Threatens Marriage and What to Do About It* (Grand Rapids, MI: Eerdmans, 2003), 75.
4 Ibid., 17, 227.
5 George Tavard, "The Ecclesial Dimension of Spirituality," *The Gift of the Church*, ed. Peter Phan (Collegeville, MN: The Liturgical Press, 2000), 228.
6 While Bellah's research is primarily with American society, it seems fair to assume that other First World societies share this cultural attitude. See: Robert Bellah, Richard Madsen and William M. Sullivan, *The Good Society* (New York: Vintage, 1992), 3–18.
7 Robert Bellah, "Marriage in the Matrix of Habit and History," in *Family Transformed: Religion, Values and Society in American Life*, ed. Steven M. Tipton and John Witte, Jr. (Washington, D.C.: Georgetown University Press, 2005), 21.
8 Mary Douglas, "The Idea of Home: A Kind of Space," in *Home: A Place in the World*, ed. Arien Mack (New York: New York University Press, 1993), 261.
9 Mary Douglas, *Natural Symbols: Explorations in Cosmology* (New York: Pantheon Books, 1982), 24, 26.
10 Bellah, "Marriage in the Matrix of Habit and History," 24.
11 Robert Bellah, *Habits of the Heart: Individualism and Commitment in American Life* (Berkeley, CA: University of California Press), 235.
12 Michael H. Crosby, "Spirituality," in *The New Dictionary of Catholic Social Thought*, ed. Judith A. Dwyer (Collegeville, MN: The Liturgical Press, 1994), 917–20.
13 Wade Clark Roof, *A Generation of Seekers: The Spiritual Journeys of the Baby Boom Generation* (San Francisco: Harper San Francisco, 1993).
14 Declan Marmion, *A Spirituality of Everyday Faith: A Theological Investigation of the Notion of Spirituality in Karl Rahner* (Louvain: Peeters Press, 1998), 57.
15 "Faith," in *Sacramentum Mundi*. Vol. 2, ed. by Karl Rahner (London: Burns and Oates, l968), 313.
16 J.M.R. Tillard, *Flesh of the Church, Flesh of Christ: At the Source of the Ecclesiology of Communion* (Collegeville, MN: The Liturgical Press, 2001), 11.
17 Ibid., 12.
18 In the strictest sense, the personal response to faith which occurs in the heart of the person is an enabled response. Contemporary biblical scholarship suggests that Jesus understood the nearness of the Kingdom to be an empowering event, one that enabled the acts of the Kingdom which transcended even those which were socially understood (Mt. 5.39). The ecclesial community is the primary locus where one comes to understand the origin of this core religious experience.
19 Hubert Jedin, "Popes Benedict XV, Pius XI, and Pius XII," in *History of the Church: Vol. X: The Church in the Modern Age*, ed. Hubert Jedin (London: Burns and Oates, 1981), 26.
20 Edward J. Cahill, S.J., "The Catholic Social Movement: Historical Aspects," in *Readings in Moral Theology, No. 5 Official Catholic Social Teaching* (New York: Paulist Press, 1986), 5.
21 David J. O'Brien, *American Catholics and Social Reform: The New Deal Years* (New York: Oxford University Press, 1975), 22ff.

22 For a discussion of the "distinction of the planes," see Gustavo Gutierrez, *A Theology of Liberation* (Maryknoll, NY: Orbis Books, 1997), 43ff.

23 O'Brien, *American Catholics and Social Reform*, 30.

24 W.A. Purdy, *The Church on the Move: The Characters and Policies of Pius XII and John XXIII* (New York: John Day, 1965), 176. See also: Pius XI, *Quadragesimo Anno*, 96.

25 Richard P. McBrien, "An Ecclesiological Analysis of Catholic Social Teaching," in *Catholic Social Thought and the New World Order*, ed. Oliver F. Williams, C.S.C. and John W. Houck (Notre Dame, IN: University of Notre Dame Press, 1993), 153.

26 Aaron I. Abell, *American Catholicism and Social Action* (Garden City, N.J.: Doubleday, 1960), chapter 2.

27 This model also provided a context within the Church for active congregations of religious to function.

28 Clifford Geertz, *Interpretation of Cultures: Selected Essays* (New York, Basic Books, 1973).

29 Kathryn Tanner, *Theories of Culture: A New Agenda for Theology* (Minneapolis, MN: Fortress Press, 1997), 38.

30 Ibid., 25–29.

31 Ibid., 46.

32 Brian Johnstone, "Moral Methodology," in *The New Dictionary of Catholic Social Thought*, ed. Judith Dwyer (Collegeville, MN: The Liturgical Press, 1994), 597.

33 Tanner, *Theories of Culture*, 50.

34 Tanner, *Theories of Culture*, 98.

35 Ibid., 122.

36 Ibid., 103.

37 For a fuller development of this topic see: Judith A. Merkle, *From the Heart of the Church: The Catholic Social Tradition* (Collegeville, MN: The Liturgical Press, 2004).

38 Jonathan Boswell sees these located in core values of solidarity, power-sharing diversity and justice for the poor. "Solidarity, Justice and Power Sharing: Patterns and Policies," in *Catholic Social Thought: Twilight or Renaissance?*, ed. J.S. Boswell, F.P. McHugh and J. Verstraeten (Leuven: Peeters, 2000), 95.

39 Merkle, *From the Heart of the Church*, 41–59, 241–65.

40 Tanner, *Theories of Culture*, 58.

41 Stephen Carter, *Civility: Manners, Morals and the Etiquette of Democracy* (New York: Basic Books, 1998), 78.

42 Louis-Marie Chauvet, *The Sacraments: The Word of God at the Mercy of the Body* (Collegeville, MN: The Liturgical Press, 2001), 25. I draw from Chauvet's insights in this section.

43 Christopher Steck, S.J., refers to, ". . . background values and moral beliefs that are shaped by a combination of unreflected experience, cultural conditioning, and explicit moral reflection. These values and beliefs often form an unacknowledged lens through which agents perceive their moral world." "Saintly Voyeurism: A Methodological Necessity for the Christian Ethicist?," in *New Wine, New Wineskins*, ed. William C. Mattison III (Lanham, MD: Rowman and Littlefield, 2005), 41, note 10.

44 Chauvet, *The Sacraments*, 135.

45 Johann Baptist Metz, *The Emergent Church* trans. Peter Mann (New York: Crossroad, 1986), 5.

46 Johann Baptist Metz, *Followers of Christ* (New York: Paulist Press, 1977), 40. See also his *Faith in History and Society* (New York: Seabury Press, 1980), 51–54.

47 Chauvet, *The Sacraments*, 167.

48 Robert Bellah, *Habits of the Heart: Individualism and Commitment in American Life* (Berkeley, CA: University of California Press, 1985), 71–75. A lifestyle enclave is focused on private life in which we share only a segment of life, usually leisure and consumption. In contrast "a community tends to be an inclusive whole, celebrating the interdependence of public and private life and the different callings of all" (72).

49 Chauvet, *The Sacraments*, 135–45.

50 Chauvet, *The Sacraments*, 40.

51 Douglas, *Natural Symbols*, 24.

52 Larry Rasmussen, *Moral Fragments, Moral Community* (Minneapolis, MN: Fortress Press, 1993), 139.

53 *Families in a Global Context*, ed. Charles B. Hennon and Stephan M. Wilson (New York: Routledge, 2008). *Families in Transition: The Case for Counseling in Context*, ed. Masamba ma Mpolo and Cecile De Sweener (Geneva: WCC Publications, 1987).

54 Barbara Defoe Whitehead, "The Changing Pathway to Marriage: Trends in Dating, First Unions, and Marriage Among Young Adults," in *Family Transformed*, op. cit., 175.

55 David Matzko McCarthy, "An Overwhelming Desire for Home," *Proceedings of the Catholic Theological Society of America*, Vol. 63 (June 2008), 60. McCarthy cites the research of Andrew J. Cherlin, "The Deinstitutionalization of American Marriage," *Journal of Marriage and Family*, 66, no. 4 (2004), 848–61. I am indebted to McCarthy for his reflection on Mary Douglas and the relevance of her analysis to this issue.

56 McCarthy, "An Overwhelming Desire for Home," 63.

57 Douglas, *Natural Symbols*, 44–45.

58 Ibid., 47. As cited in McCarthy at 64.

59 McCarthy, "An Overwhelming Desire for Home," 65.

60 Christopher Lasch, *Haven in a Heartless World* (New York: Basic Books, 1977; Norton, 1995), 37. Lasch describes marriage as a refuge from modern society.

61 Browning, *Marriage and Modernization*, 26.

62 Ibid., 38

63 McCarthy, "An Overwhelming Desire for Home," 67. He cites Douglas: "The personal family system and elaborated language contain 'seeds of alienation'." *Natural Symbols*, 47.

64 Julie Hanlon Rubio, "A Familial Vocation beyond the Home," *Proceedings of the Catholic Theological Society of America*, Vol. 63 (June 2008), 71–83.

65 Lisa Sowle Cahill, "Notes on Moral Theology, Marriage: Developments in Catholic Theology and Ethics," *Theological Studies* 64 (2003), 97.

66 Ibid., 80.

67 Browning, *Marriage and Modernization*, 230–32.

68 Douglas, *Natural Symbols*, 50–51. As cited in McCarthy at 67.

69 Richard McCormick, "Theology and Bioethics," *Hasting Center Report*, 19, no. 3 (May/June 1989), 5–10, as quoted in *On Moral Medicine: Theological Perspectives in Medical Ethics*, ed. Stephen E. Lammers and Allen Verhey (Grand Rapids, MI: Eerdmans, 1998), 63–71.

70 James Gustafson, *Ethics from a Theocentric Perspective. II: Ethics and Theology* (Chicago: University of Chicago Press, 1984), 98.

71 Values and ethical ideas about what is good, just, and right, and the sense of obligation and ways of thinking on which they are based, are socially embodied in particular social traditions and communities. In other words, there is no way of thinking independent of a tradition, no "view from nowhere." Jean Bethke Elshtain, "Really

Existing Communities," *Review of International Studies*, 25, 1 (1999), 141–46.

72 Richard Gula, *Reason Informed by Faith* (New York: Paulist Press, 1989), 53.

73 McCormick, "Theology and Bioethics," 68–69.

74 "For it is the proper task of the magisterium (the teaching authority of the church) to watch over everything that belongs to the deposit of faith; and also over everything without which this deposit cannot be defended." Josef Fuchs, "Natural Law," in *The Dictionary of Catholic Social Thought*, ed. Judith A. Dwyer (Collegeville, MN: The Liturgical Press, 1994), 674.

75 Lisa Sowle Cahill remarks, ". . . it is best to construe 'public discourse' not as a separate realm into which we can and ought to enter tradition-free, but as embodying a commitment to civil exchanges among traditions, many of which have an overlapping membership, and which, meet on the basis of common concerns." "Can Theology Have a Role in 'Public' Bioethical Discourse," in *On Moral Medicine: Theological Perspectives in Medical Ethics*, op. cit., 59. Stephen Carter, *The Culture of Disbelief* (New York: Basic Books, 1993).

76 James Tunstead Burtchaell, "Community Experience as a Source of Christian Ethics," in *From Christ to the World*, ed. Wayne G. Boulton, *et al.* (Grand Rapids, MI: Eerdmans, 1994), 64–79.

77 See: Josef Fuchs, S.J., *Christian Morality: The Word Becomes Flesh* (Dublin: Gill and Macmillan, 1987), 138–40.

78 Gula, *Reason Informed by Faith*, 206.

79 Francis A. Sullivan, S.J., *Creative Fidelity: Weighing and Interpreting Documents of the Magisterium* (Dublin: Gill and Macmillan, 1996).

80 This obligatory nature is most evident in negative moral commands, those moral commandments expressed in negative form in the Hebrew Scriptures and New Testament (GS 27; VS 52.3, 67.2, 115.3).

81 Josef Fuchs, S.J., *Christian Ethics in a Secular Arena* (Washington, D.C.: Georgetown University Press, 1984), 57–67.

82 Gula, *Reason Informed by Faith*, 205.

83 Karl Rahner, "Magisterium," in *Sacramentum Mundi*. Vol. III (New York: Herder and Herder, 1968), 354.

84 Fuchs, "Natural Law," 674.

85 We are not attempting here to offer a complete theology of the Church.

86 Gallagher, *Clashing Symbols*, 28.

Chapter 6

Groups of Particularity and Profession: Speaking and Hearing the Truth

The shift from the top right-hand to the top left-hand square in the model presented in Chapter Four is one way to understand the characteristic Context B style of life. Grid rather than group forms the main locus of social control. The sense of belonging to a definite group is lessened in this culture, but behavioral expectations are at a maximum. The grid expectations of peers exceed the social responsibility pressures of the group. Role definition does not come only from some collective authority, but rather from gaining recognition from one's profession or group whose power to credential is essential for functioning.[1]

In Douglas's words:

> This is the second of the main types of social environment . . . For convenience I shall call it small group . . . Its members know one another and can count their ranks and prospects of promotion. They are not conscious of remote control by leaders located far to the left. Hemmed in and face to face, their destiny is in their own hands and they meet it with intrigue and jealousy . . . high classification requires a well-defined category of rejects and anomalous persons. But small group broadens the category of potential rejects to include the whole range of acquaintance, male, female, kinsman and unrelated.[2]

Small group life is a characteristic of modern culture. Alexis de Tocqueville, a French sociologist who visited America in the 1830s, wanted to understand the nature of a democratic society. In *Democracy in America* he commented on the nature of American individualism. "Individualism . . . disposes each citizen to isolate himself from the mass of his fellows and withdraw into the circle of family and friends; with this little society formed to his taste, he gladly leaves the greater society to look after itself."[3] Tocqueville noted that Americans joined associations to overcome the relative isolation and powerlessness that results from the insecurities which arise from living in an increasingly commercial society. Associations, along with decentralized local administration, mediated between the individual and the centralized state. They provided forums in which opinion could be publically and intelligently shaped and the habits of public initiative and responsibility passed on.[4]

Context B can be used to understand professional life, as it shares some characteristics of small group life in Douglas's analysis. A culture without "group" allegiance but with high "grid" interaction is competitive. There is a decline of group identity and sense of belonging. Relationships are more fluid and mobile, as one finds in a modern business and professional environment. However, the pluralism, pragmatism and material measures of success of the Context B world also convey expectations. Conforming to these expectations forms a different type of belonging. Life is defined by multiple belonging and struggle to resolve the conflicting pressures of the different contexts of life; i.e. work and family, political position and religion; professional expectations and life goals.[5] Group life, in its various forms, fosters a resolution of these tensions.

Small groups have also had a rebirth in the Church.[6] People find in small faith-sharing groups what seems unreachable in the large institution. Face to face contact sparks a sense of shared commitment to religious ideals, and help with dealing with the pressures of a secular society. The group helps people recover deeply felt convictions and a sense of the obligations that accompany religious or ethical behavior. Sharing in these groups can counteract the competitive and achievement orientation of the workplace. Focus on matters of faith helps members move beyond only achievement concerns and gives them new perspective as to how to be faithful in their life situation.

The modern workplace fosters competition, individualism and impersonality, values that intensify the problems of modern society and sharply contrast with the kinds of trust conducive to community and family life — love, intimacy, sensitivity, and cooperation — which are fostered in faith-sharing groups.[7] The integration of work and family is a major concern brought to these groups. Faith commitment today requires more than church membership, it entails an adult appropriation of one's baptism, and the identity it confers. Many find that the small group within the wider faith community is the place where this best comes about. Small groups are a way that traditional churches can combine the benefits of their institutional strength with the more dynamic and intimate groupings that nurture faith.

Groups of Identity and Particularity

A third type of small group experience is a group of identity and particularity. These groups attend to personal concerns left unmet in the wider society, often ones based on race, class, gender, or a particular life situation. When people gather in small groups it affects their religious outlook. Douglas claims that Context B culture fosters a different kind of religious practice than we find in Context A culture. Context B is more individualized. God is less a revelation to be obeyed than a source of peace and comfort for the self. When the public dimensions of life are separated from the private, and religion is left to the personal sphere, the institutional dimension of Christianity is given secondary importance. As privatized, religion is called upon primarily to meet people's need for self-fulfillment. While groups of particularity function in the wider society, they also function within the Church and bring to the Church new issues.

Small groups, based on race, class, gender, and ethnic identity within the Church, help people relate their personal identity to their Christian faith. They challenge the faith community to adopt a conceptual framework that does not foreclose multiple perceptions and varied interpretations of life. Attention to the reality of pluralism of culture in the Church honors that "faith" and "reason" cannot be removed from their embedded contexts and acknowledges that context contributes to important difference in their manifestation across cultural boundaries.

This awareness began at Vatican II with a new impetus. At the Vatican Council the Church learned that it was not just Western and Eastern, but also Asian, Latin American, and African.[8] The small group life which grew up after the Council enabled this awareness on a local level. People could reflect on their personal identity and give voice to expressions of Christian identity and mission first distinguished by regions — Latin American, African, Asian, European — and then by social groups as the poor, women, blacks, Hispanics, and indigenous peoples. Life situation also gathered people looking for a deeper quality of life.

We find Context B life expressed not only in groups based on common place or region, but also in how one's position in society marked by life situation — race, class, and gender — is a starting point for consideration of relationship to God. Small group settings foster the awareness that while sharing a common identity and dignity, people also have personal and unique experiences of God, self, and world conditioned by their social place. Biography, geography, gender, race, and class can affect how people perceive key goods in their lives, what is worth their effort, and how they prioritize them. The Vatican document *The Church in the Modern World* recognizes the mission of the Church to these diverse people in new contexts (GS 41–44).

After Vatican II, it became apparent that none of these social or geographical identities could be understood in isolation. Contexts and identities are multiple and overlapping. Many people, especially those involved in modern migrations, describe their identity as a hybrid, one made up from a new synthesis of two or more cultures. The realities of class, caste, race, gender, and ethnicity, and local, regional, and global economy and polity are intertwined in this era of globalization. Local Church, a new focus after Vatican II, was challenged to integrate these new global realities as peoples from around the world became parishioners living side by side, reflecting the new life situations of modern living. In turn, these new groups "gave voice" to concerns which could only be spoken by them. Instead of defining the problems of others, the Church began to allow those problems to be defined by those experiencing them. The Church increasingly looked at culture as an important factor in living out its mission.[9]

It seems fair to say there is no uniform meaning of culture in the Church; rather the term is used in different ways. First, culture refers to a constant in being human, to the collective efforts by which a people build a style of living together, and in turn create themselves. Second, culture refers to differences and variety among peoples, as people have various ways of living which developed uniquely through response to historical and other events. Third, culture is an identity used as a defense against oppression. Culture is a sense of identity called upon to respond to acts of domination by another. What did this new awareness of culture, articulated by groups of particularity, bring to the Church, and what did the Church bring to them? Did they refocus an understanding of faithfulness in any way?

New Sense of God

Black, feminist, and Hispanic thought in the Church arose from the secular movements of emancipation in society. In the second half of the twentieth century, the evils of colonization, and its role in the process of the modernization and development of parts of the global community, came into full awareness. These groups questioned whether one's place in colonization affected which God one unconsciously worshipped.

Was there relationship between the imperial identity of the colonizers and the universalizing style of theology they supported? Was what was handed on as Christian identity simply a model of life which supported the cultural identity and place in the world of those who oppressed continents of people in order to advance their own purposes, or who oppressed women? If the identities given by this process are stripped away, who is a faithful Christian? Did those who had the painful memories of economic and cultural enslavement have a different "faith" and sense of faithfulness, than those who enslaved?[10] The critical thinking raised by these groups helped the Church recognize how it participates in the historical consciousness of the world. It led the Church to be more open and inclusive of diversity in its practice.

In addition, these diverse groups questioned whether the explanation of salvation which the faith community upheld addressed their life experience. Black and feminist theologies, and to some degree pacifist theologians, questioned how the Kingdom of God is God's will for everyone, yet it is communicated in the Christian tradition in a manner in which the evils of racism, chattel slavery, abuse of women, patriarchy, violence, and war can co-exist with the salvation offered by Jesus Christ. They countered that acceptance of the salvation offered by Christ demands a call to transforming union with him in the work of liberation of human suffering, or resistance to evil as it is socially embedded. When there is a separation between the proclamation of salvation in Jesus Christ and the ethics or the converted life to which the Christian is called, it does not speak to human experience. As those suffering from these evils, they reflected that the following of Christ can appear to call them to a passive acceptance of their cross rather than emancipation from this concrete evil.

On the most part, new theological reflection arose from small faith-sharing groups. The new theologies in Latin America, Asia, and Africa, along with black, feminist, and Hispanic theologies entered into Catholic life. Primarily they articulated the experience of being human in modern society, which went beyond the traditional perspectives. Being human was influenced by social location, race, class, gender. Human becoming depends on one's response not only to the traditional moral restrictions of the various forms of egotism, but also to the social conditions which mark one's own or another's possibility of human flourishing.

Because they are centered in movements which begin outside the Church, their starting point is a human problem shared by believer and non-believer alike. They put flesh on the Church's call for all people to be faithful, as these groups experienced in very personal ways the meaning of their call to holiness and its costs. They experienced the basic human faith through which people form relationships, create values and respond to the problems of their lives as they responded to and articulated their situation.[11] As the Church acknowledged these groups, they fostered their religious faith, which builds on this more fundamental type of faith. Religious faith included but moved beyond the starting point of their issue. Christian faith is an identification of the ultimate possibilities and limits of human life and the universe with the revelation of Jesus Christ. Faith is the surrender of one's whole being to the person, community, and teaching of God, who "saves men and women with his grace from the evils which, here and now in this life, point toward absolute paralysis, absolute enslavement, absolute death."[12] These groups witnessed to the reality that the transcendent quality of religious faith is marked by its concern for issues in this world and the tasks of love.[13] Lastly, they reminded the Church that religious faith is the source of a new meaning structure, as it constantly calls us to change our erroneous perceptions and biases in our search for the truth.[14]

A Questioning of Norms

The reflection and theologies which arose from the particularities rather than the generalities of people's lives also threw light on the search for norms of living faithfully in modern times. As we have said, in post-Vatican II times, Catholic moral theology made steps to move from a sole consideration of acts within the horizon of personal and Church life to concerns of how to transform culture and society. Attention to moral acts and their effect on the state of one's soul shifted toward a new consciousness of Christian responsibility for the state of the world, and the situation and circumstances in which "the other" lived. Important directives from the Church on issues like bioethical matters and sexual morality continued, however, they went hand in hand with an effort to envision a more contextual understanding of the Christian life. Josef Fuchs comments:

> The council tends to refer human behavior less to set, formulated laws and norms than to the God-given task of more fully humanizing the human person and the world . . . The concern here is to understand the contemporary mode of reality of the world of the human person and to analyze and draw up projects with a view to the possibility of a fuller humanization of this world.[15]

The voices of small groups in the Church greatly influenced this shift. Latin American theologians argued that the fact that a majority of Christians and humanity live in conditions of inhuman poverty is significant to the definition of the Christian life in modern times.[16] Indifference to this reality is out of the question in any authentic rendering of a faithful Christian life. Norbert Rigali commented that a "world-consciousness" was now needed when constructing the norms of the Christian life. If the moral agent lives in the global society increasingly linked to everyone else, then the Kingdom more and more becomes the gap between what is and what is possible in a particular situation:

> The historical form of the moral law that governs our world today, for example, mandates efforts to create international, worldwide community, attempts to reverse the arms race and to reduce stockpiles, and endeavors to bring about the transformation of social structures . . . These are basic moral imperatives, representing vital human needs in today's world.[17]

The context of living in a global society needed to be more formally integrated into the normative values of the Christian life.

In Douglas's terms, pluralism in theology contributed to a more elaborated code of the Christian life. As small faith groups helped people make sense out of modern experience, and give meaning to it, they helped people live and act in coherent ways. Through the small group movement many people began to approach the Christian tradition from the vantage point of a central concern or set of concerns which represents for him or her the human situation. Christian theology became pluralistic.

James Gustafson reflects on this shift more formally as to its impact on ethics. When one responds to a vision of the Christian life which begins with a life issue, a theologian will interpret and order the tenets of the Christian faith in such a way that they are brought to bear on a life question. It is the theologian's interpretation of human existence by means of a central life question which forms distinctive approaches to the Christian life and to the description of what constitutes Christian living. Different theological ethics arise from various organizing perspectives, which are starting points for thinking about the Christian life.[18] Practically, Christians experience this diversity of approach as concerns regarding racism, sexism, militarism, ecology, holistic living, and option for the poor entered into the discourse of what it meant to be faithful.

Ways of Being Christian

Matthew Lamb clarifies in more detail just how various starting points for theology impact a normative vision of the Christian life.[19] Lamb claims that different approaches render different emphasis in how one sets norms in Christian ethics. Tension between different groups within the Church and their visions of faithfulness in the Christian life reflect these differences. Lamb provides a typology of visions of the Christian life which sheds light on these tensions.

Lamb's first category, a *classical approach*, focuses on absolutes in its depiction of norms.[20] Since truths in this framework are eternal and necessary, the Christian life consists in living these truths in the ways they apply to practical life. Prudence guides one in knowing how to apply these truths to a particular situation. A *praxis orientation*, Lamb's second type, equates what is normative with what is modern and secular, where the term "secular" means liberal sociopolitical, cultural, or Marxist praxis (practices). What promotes the modern and secular is good and what hinders it is bad.[21] In Lamb's third type norms are approached in such a way that only God is normative. Obedience to the Word is more prominent than a normativity which is "empirically" available. Thus norms tend to be related to the decision of faith-love responding to the Word of God.[22] In Lamb's fourth category norms are treated in a way that militate against the absolutes of the first category; the identification of the Christian life with liberal or Marxist praxis of the second; and the simple faith-love response of the third. Norms for this type are acquired through a mutual interaction between reason and faith, an interaction which seeks to avoid the tendencies of the first three types.[23] Lamb's fifth category sees norms involving a conversion of consciousness which is both personal and which involves a concern for social structures. This conversion is intrinsic to the Christian life. In this framework, norms flow from praxis.[24] This fifth basic theory-praxis relationship is characteristic of groups of particularity, as mentioned above.[25] Their interpretation of God, significance of human experience, understanding of moral agents and their acts, and how persons ought to make moral decisions is based on a type of hermeneutical process. There one discovers what is most fitting only through the use of social analysis and a faith commitment expressed through engagement with a specific oppressive situation. Subsequently one comes to knowledge of and union with God, coupled with the willingness to engage in creating norms which are fruits of this new practice, and not entrenched in former patterns of domination, oppression, and margination.

In this category, response to salvation happens on the level of human values practiced in history. Faith, love, following of Christ, and openness to God remain ways of behavior made possible by Christ. In themselves, they are mysteries which cannot be acted upon by human beings.[26] Yet, men and women actualize their human and Christian existence through acts which express these potentials of salvation in concrete ways. These acts are not only necessary to express a salvation already given but also to enter into the process by which the meaning of this salvation can be learned. They are acts by which a human being actualizes his or her own existence and ultimately does God's will. Since groups embody all five visions of the Christian life, it is not surprising there are difficulties which arise when there is conflict as to what it means to be faithful.

A Trajectory of Conversion

In what Douglas calls a "distinctive culture of competitive individualism," small group identity provides an important lens on the meaning of faithfulness, but also has some inherent tensions. The competitive nature of Context B life is easily observed in the business world and in interaction in society among groups based on race, class, and gender. However, it also exists in the Church, as shown in the culture wars regarding different interpretations of Christian faithfulness. Small group focus on a particular alienation needs the call of the wider Church to address concerns beyond their starting point. In Douglas's language, a small group tends to articulate an elaborated code, with less attention to a restricted one.

These groups typically charge that the ethic or practice in place is false, and the unconsciousness it represents simply perpetuates a particular alienation by explaining it away. For the small group, it is a priority that the practice, rule or attitude is changed. A danger is though that Christian faithfulness can become collapsed into addressing this single concern. A restricted code addresses the "life of the commons," and its multiple concerns, and does not have the small group concern as its starting point. Yet, because small groups represent voices which are often excluded from the vision of the "common good," at a particular time they can be rightfully suspicious about addressing a more inclusive good. For example, feminist theologians measure the good as that which promotes the well-being of women, blacks that which corrects racism. However, when there are conflicts, how are these various alienations and human goods evaluated hierarchically and prioritized? As each performs as an organizing horizon for the construction of an ethic, new light is shed on the reconciliation and universality of the moral demands placed on all, and the notion of the common good enlarged. Each vision is necessary for this fuller vision. However, the universal call of Christ to unity summons a reconciliation of these priorities in the concrete. If this is not done, there is impasse.

At times competing groups resolve this impasse by tolerating one another. David Hollenbach claims though that tolerance alone is often not adequate. As a matter of personal virtue, tolerance promotes accepting differences between people; yet this seldom generates positive action to address the institutional causes of problems like urban poverty.[27] Practicing tolerance alone is not the ultimate marker of faithfulness. Small group life can easily fall into this vision.

The implicit anti-institutional culture of small group life leads these groups to stay focused on the group, and not, for instance, build coalitions with others. Association with mainstream institutions, members of Context A life, might be seen as taboo, as they are perceived as the enemy. There is an implicit challenge in Context B life to move beyond these inherent tensions in order to be successful. In civic affairs, without collaboration with large associations who are capable of promoting legislation and government action for significant public investments in areas such health care, nutrition, education, and housing, any action by small groups often proves to be ineffective for social change.[28] Yet in the Church, if official representatives practice a restrictive stance inhospitable to the pluralism and voices generated by the small group mode of operation, then the dialogue necessary for small group concerns to enrich the whole can be lost.

The interplay between Context A life and Context B life in the Church illustrates that both have an essential role in clarifying what it means to be faithful today. Small group life can situate the moral person not only as an individual in their essential moral capacities, but also in terms of their place in a cycle of oppression. Through this lens, one is either a victim or an oppressor. The tradition upholds, however, that through his cross Christ liberates both the perpetuator and the victim from this situation. Morally, Christ calls each to be faithful, but differently. The victim is called to stand up to this falsehood. A perpetrator is called to stop the behavior and change the structures that perpetuate it.[29]

Attention to context, however, can define a person more narrowly than the wider tradition would affirm. One is always more than a racist while acting like one and more than a victim even though one appears paralyzed by fear. The Church upholds that the moral potentials of this deeper self, defined through its more essential and universal categories, are necessary for the transformation of the person to occur. While race, class, gender and poverty are at the heart of much human suffering, so are communication failure, greed, lust for power and possessiveness. In other words, the religious vision which flows from small groups needs a developed sense of sin, one which accounts for the capacity and range of human destructiveness beyond the particular alienation which is the group's starting point. Context A life in the Church reaffirms this through its creed, code, and rituals. Context B life in the Church puts flesh on a particular expression of alienation and healing, often one aligned with modern movements of emancipation.

Context B life in the Church can also be a locus of unbelief. Unbelief can arise from the scandal of social evil, as goodness appears powerlessness before massive human suffering. However, unbelief can also arise from a matrix of life in which grid expectations so fill the day that attention to suffering beyond personal suffering is dulled and no real need of God is expressed. People simply believe in rational society or technological power, and religion is never embraced beyond its function to be a balm to problems. Religion becomes solely therapeutic. Such religion is humanly created, to fill a social need, but does not embrace a religious posture. Context B life can become an elective universe where humans can fill all needs without a deity. Such a humanly constructed "religion" is an illusion. Metz charges that in such a culture the Church is unnecessary, or weak, and a convenient and culturally correct one is preferred. Yet, such a Church is incapable of representing the gospel or challenging its members. Its visions of human flourishing are often limited to those within its own circle and not that of every human being.[30]

When contextuality is more important than tradition, more important than any ideal or essential unity the faith may possess, this also occurs.[31] Context B life serves the Church in its capacity to put flesh on the human situation in its struggle to be whole. The call in Context B is for people and groups to move beyond their own unseen ethnocentrism. The Church in Context A life and Context B life is called to maintain the tension that the universal is embedded in the particular, and the particular features of a culture can be judged in the light of the universal.

Effective ministry marked by mediation, sacramentality, and communion in this context is challenged to lead people beyond these contextual limits, without dismissing them. James Cone captures this tension when he states that religion must be able to point to something in its living that is not simply a religious legitimation of the values of the society in which it lives.[32]

The Church seeks to hold on to a sense of transcendence and human dignity which religion protects and an account of history and realism which social engagement requires. Small groups, Context B life, contribute uniquely to this process. Stories which show evil and survival through faith testify to the truth of life which the Church seeks to foster. That is, the truth of the incarnation shows itself in the incarnation of the truth in face of human suffering in the world. If the concern of ethics is the authentic life and the development of persons and societies toward the *humanum* within history and ultimately to a future with God, the Christian community, through its narrative of human suffering and the hope in the face of it expressed in small groups, certainly narrates the truth which the life of Jesus Christ affirms and establishes. This is another expression of taking context seriously in the Christian life. As long as the moral agent is understood only non-historically as the rational animal, moral law is conceived simply as a system of universal or general rational laws. If the person is now understood as a person acting within the development of history and having a life whose destiny is linked integrally with the destiny of everyone else, an understanding of the moral law and ultimately of the Christian life is affected and shaped by historicity.[33] Included is the call to take responsibility for the creative possibilities that are brought forth and emerge only in the course of history to change the conditions in which suffering is endured, as well as the need to establish enduring human values in the structures of life which impact human flourishing. The development of self is linked to the development of the conditions in which others can flourish. The challenge we see in Context B life is the promise and pitfalls of putting these two truths, of the *humanum* and *in history*, together. As Christians pray "Thy Kingdom Come," Context B life puts flesh on the significance of this imperative in the lives of every Christian and community, and has its own place in the tensions implicit in its pursuit.

Catholicity and Culture in Global Society

Today catholicity has to be considered not just abstractly but in light of the current context of modernization and globalization. While globalization frames social activity with new powers of communication, it also offers the limited vision of a single market economy, and political tensions of a post-Cold War era.[34] Globally, the constant interface between cultures contends also with a dominant culture of capitalism which provides its own "religious sense" of what is ultimate, and offers a competing logic which grounds practice in matters far beyond the economic life.[35] Modernization mentalities can reduce the solution to problems of the world to the right set of technical and economic fixes. Christians exist in this matrix of relationships, and share the same cultural complexity as the Church in an evolving world. At a minimum, the search to be faithful in modern society requires that these challenges are taken into consideration.

Robert Schreiter offers some directions for consideration of this problem. He claims that both integrated and globalized views of culture are necessary social scientific backdrops to understand catholicity and the mission of the Church today.[36] An integrated approach to culture views the Church in light of its patterned systems in which all the parts create a unified whole. For instance, official social teaching of the Church contributes to this integrated sense of Catholic culture in its social mission across the world. Michael Shuck remarks that to the degree that social teaching "coheres around a theologically inspired communitarian social ethic which has yielded a cluster of shared, integrated insights concerning religious, political, familial, economic and cultural relations in society," it provides this sense of a unified whole.[37]

Globalized approaches to culture, on the other hand, point to the tensions and pressures of a mobile world. They take into account that culture is also something to be constructed, and involves struggle between members of different groups to be recognized and heard. This alternative sense of culture recognizes differences within a local culture, and the impact of global realities on everyday living in an unequal world. In an analogous manner, integrated and globalized language parallels the restricted and elaborated code metaphor used by Douglas.

Globalized approaches also take into account how symbols and patterns which affect visions of human flourishing are communicated around the globe. "Freedom," "prosperity," "whole earth," "war on terrorism," all focus energies and hold out a vision of human purpose. These "cultural flows" are insufficient to create a culture, and are not received uniformly. They circulate ideas that have limited power in one culture, but in a global context provide meaning to the experience of many, even though people have different interpretations of their meaning. Notions of human rights, women's equality, liberation, war and peace, and ecological responsibility are not interpreted uniformly across the world or always within the church community. Yet they impact the Church's social mission through their influence on its members. They call the Church to contribute its own message to these extra-ecclesial movements, which involves the Church's capacity to challenge those with differing interpretations to examine their coherence to the gospel in that context. Cultural flows are not a shared philosophical system, yet they are operational ideas which mobilize human energies in conflicting directions. They are the results of the new forces of globalization and the interconnected character of life in the world today. Schreiter's attention to these globalized realities alerts us to the pluralism, conflict, and extra-ecclesial influences in envisioning faithful practice in the Church which earlier approaches were slower to recognize. They illumine how small groups in the Church can integrate global concerns into its daily life and set the stage to comment on another facet of Context B living — business and the professions.

Business and Profession

The cultural analysis which Douglas espouses highlights patterns in which individuals respond to the surrounding world. Context B life reflects common dynamics as to how people perceive their place in society, share dominant patterns of interaction, make individual behavior choices, and share a religious vision. Context B life is one where grid relationships are key. This makes sense when we think today of what is termed "business culture" or "professional life." Professional life conveys a built-in interpretative scheme of how to act in relation to others. The horizontal network of professional roles, rules and relationships does not come down from above, rather it is built up over time through people relating to one another. Grid is less structured than group, but it does convey expectations.

Ruth Chadwick defines a profession as work which has been linked to a body of knowledge, mastery of which regulates entrance to its ranks, and as work characterized by an ideal of service. Professions are also characterized by a certain amount of autonomy in their self-regulation. All people work, while members of a profession "practice." Hidden in this definition is an assumption that the group defines what "competence" means in their own terms. What separates work and profession? In part, a worker becomes a professional by being able to give reasons for doing their work in a certain way.[38]

If a plumber comes to fix a leak in your house and you pay the plumber for a competent job, does that make the plumber a professional? In a broad sense, we can say yes. The term professional is used for any job well done, as we refer to the professionalization of a task. However, we usually distinguish between any job well done, a type of professionalism and a profession *per se* by giving weight to a number of considerations. Professions provide an important public service; they provide both theoretically grounded and practically grounded expertise; they have a code of practice; they are organized and regulated for purposes of recruitment and discipline; professionals are allowed a high degree of independence of judgment for effective practice.[39] We can intuit how various grid relationships have conveyed a professional status on some types of services through reflection on how we form judgment regarding misconduct. If someone who installs cable service does a good job and is honest in keeping his time card, we would not regard him as a bad cable servicer if we found out he abused his wife or altered his expense account. We might if the person were a doctor or a lawyer. The latter situation would sully the reputation of the profession, whereas the former likely would not. The lines between the two get muddled in today's society, especially in the area of finance and politics.

As David Carr notes, "In the understanding of Mary Douglas, a culture 'without' group allegiance but with high 'grid' interaction is essentially a competitive society rooted in exchange relationships of a quasi-commercial kind."[40] Role definition does not come from a collective authority as in Context A life, rather from gaining recognition in a competitive market with other individuals. According to Robert Bellah, success is measured in American society in rather ambiguous ways, as American standards of success are often limited to income level and comparison to the consumption levels of their neighbors.[41] The American version of success also impacts how professional life is understood. Traditionally, professional life is supposed to serve the greater good. But when income level and consumption become markers of success and the intrinsic worth of the work in society is lost, profession wilts to careerism. A non-professional worker experiences this shift of meaning also. If little attention is given to the intrinsic worth of the job, the worker feels simply like a cog in the industrial or entrepreneurial processes of the service industry.[42] A sense of instrumentalism creeps in. Bellah reflects on this problem: "We have repeatedly had to notice that during the nineteenth century, the social world changed from being a community, a cosmos of callings, into an industrial-corporate society organized around competing professional careers."[43] Context B life renders a high value to being successful in the eyes of one's peers, which is often in tension with the more objective world of traditional virtues in Context A life.

Structures and Faithfulness

In Context B life, the search to be faithful is dramatically impacted by globalization. John Paul II addresses this change in his social encyclical *Laborem Exercens*. After the Second World War, the free market philosophy and the corresponding public policies encouraged the reorganization of the economy around privately owned, internally diversified, giant corporations, operating on the global level without ties of loyalty to the societies to which they belong. This created a widening gap between rich and poor nations, and between rich and poor within these nations (LE 7). It fostered the surrender of decision-making power affecting the well-being of society to a small economic elite. Governments helped this process through privatization and deregulation and by removing institutions designed to constrain the market to protect the common welfare.[44] Labor under these conditions has been restructured on an international level, and the fallout of this structural change is felt at every level of society.

Sociologist Richard Sennett indicates that shifts in U.S. economy and law have oriented work and business and business practices to a more transitory and utilitarian form of teamwork. Institutional memory and loyalty is seen as a hindrance to progress, and the demands of the common good a barrier to success. Institutional practices with its checks and balances and a sense of mission beyond profitability are weakened. Focus on craftsmanship or management skills shifts to the ability to move quickly from one task to another and engage co-workers without any long term commitment.[45] Social participation and politics also take on the culture of the market, and the exchange-model of the market even slips into definitions of interpersonal life, and marriage.[46]

In the face of these new institutional developments, John Paul II offered several principles about the meaning of work and human dignity in this new situation of the internationalization of labor. First, he states, "the basis for determining the value of human work is not primarily the kind of work being done but the fact that the one who is doing it is a person" (LE 6). Next, work cannot be treated simply as a tool, or factor, in the process of production. It cannot be just bought or sold like any other element in the production cycle. Most important, the Pope charges that labor is not respected in itself but is under the control of those who control the means of production (LE 7, 8). There has to be "the priority of labor over capital" (LE 12). Labor is more than a special kind of merchandise; rather the human element in the production process should be treated differently than things. Work is part of a process by which a person becomes a human being, raises a family, fosters education, and participates in the wider culture and society. To deprive someone of work or to create conditions in which work is not secure or is monotonous and dehumanizing is against the fundamental meaning and purpose of the role work is meant to have in life. Therefore labor and capital are "inseparably linked" (LE 13). Capital considered apart from labor is an illusion, since capital comes from labor. What then does the world of work and professional life have to do with the search to be faithful? We will look at the impact of Context B life on the quest of an individual to be faithful, as well as point to the opportunities Context B professional life offers to the individual or group which are not available to others.

Mixing the Languages

What happens when the worlds of Context B life and the values and expectations of Context A life are in tension? We see evidence of the tensions between these two worlds in society today. Catholic politicians are challenged to express Catholic positions on abortion in the public realm, and can face Church censorship if they do not. We hear physicians rejecting assisted suicide laws by arguing that participating in death rather than healing undermines the trust people should be able to place in their profession. In the first example, there is a tension with the limited authority held in a political role in a democratic process (a grid position) with the value judgment of a particular issue of one's religion (a group position). In the second, there is a strain between who dictates a professional practice and its role in maintaining a professional identity (a grid position), and the deep values which ground a profession in its service to humanity, in this sense handed down through the healing tradition (a group position).

The array of problems before us demands that people of faith construct a public theology, and Context B life can contribute to this task. A public theology is a way of speaking about the reality of God and God's will for the world that is intellectually valid in the marketplace, offers insight into real problems, and is morally effective in the world of goods and services. Key is the search for the common good, the moral truth, in the public realm. Voices from Context A (group) life and Context B (grid) life can contribute to this search. John Coleman puts it succinctly: the common good "looks to both some objectivity of the good and a concomitant societal consensus about public goods and the institutional relationships necessary for human flourishing."[47] Without such a consensus nothing happens in the real world. While experience and place in society impact one's sense of the truth, the common good, and even perceptions of what is good, this pluralism does not place us in an impossible situation. Context B life gives voice to many of these goods which would remain hidden without representative bodies in society to voice them. Context B life also fosters the set of skills, and how the society monitors them, which are necessary to name problems and create solutions. Context B life is a key way the Church expresses the contribution of faith and reason in society.

Practical reason addresses the truth in contingent matters, and moral truth is a practical truth, what is good in this situation.[48] The challenge of Context B life is to accept that people have different perceptions of truth and what is right, without sinking into a relativism or hopelessness that "truth" can never be found. James Gustafson reminds us:

> The task of theological and ethical work becomes that of finding justification both for religious belief and for moral decisions, which do not deny the relativities of history, but which provide a objectivity short of absolute claims . . . If the absolutist has morality conforming to an immutable order and thus has difficulty in coping with historical change, the relativist has an openness to change but a difficulty in developing the criteria of purpose and action to guide choices and given direction to moral activities.[49]

Context B life involves a unique call of faithfulness. To pursue truth and good in the public order requires that members of the Church listen to voices that challenge and bring into public dialogue the core values of human flourishing fed by their faith tradition.

Opportunities for the Good

There are opportunities in Context B life to do good that are not available in other contexts. Through Context B life the Church can express its mission in ways that go beyond the traditional strategy of owning or controlling some major "instruments of culture" such as schools, hospitals, newspapers, and other media.[50] Small groups are often socially critical, and not as invested in maintaining the main structures of society in which they live. They can be more innovative. Small groups are also the backbone of society, as the associations, groups, movements, and trade unions. From non-profit organizations to volunteer groups, the transformative relevance of these groups lies in the style they adopt, the work they do, and the formational opportunities they offer. Groups within professions work to improve the quality of their practice, yet also respond to gaps within the profession that are recognized by all. Such activity serves to enhance the cognitive range and effectiveness of the science or profession itself, whether this is in economics, law, education, medicine, biotechnology or politics.[51] Professional expertise is key to these conversations in areas where the institutional Church is not an official or competent voice. Context B life elicits the need for professional ethics where the horizon and expectations of the profession itself merges with the goals of the common good.[52] Within the Church this involves taking seriously the racial, ethnic, gender, and class reflections of the Catholic people as well as others with whom it is in dialogue. The Church can foster development of the spirituality of work and the professions, as well as insist on better systems to incorporate the professional competence of the people of the Church into the articulation of its life and mission.

Church-sponsored groups and those supported informally by Catholics and people of good will can mutually support and enrich one another. Faith-based organizations are another face of small group initiatives which involve Catholic participation but might not be under the formal direction of the Church.[53] The Christian understanding of God's revelation includes the promise of the Spirit to introduce us to and help us to reinterpret the truth of Jesus within our own cultural condition. The call to be faithful in Context B life is the call to name yet go beyond our own particularities, to speak and hear the truth, which contributes to the search for the truth for all.

Notes

1 Michael Paul Gallagher, *Clashing Symbols: An Introduction to Faith and Culture* (New York: Paulist Press, 2003), 27–34. Mary Douglas, *Natural Symbols* (New York: Vintage Books, 1973), 84–88.

2 Douglas, *Natural Symbols*, 88.

3 Alexis de Tocqueville, *Democracy in America*, trans. George Lawrence and ed. J.P. Mayer (New York: Doubleday, Anchor books, 1969), 506. As cited in Robert Bellah, *Habits of the Heart* (Berkeley, CA: University of California Press, 1985), 37.

4 Ibid., 38.

5 See Bellah on "therapeutic contractualism" and the instability it brings to commitments. Ibid., 128–30.

6 Stuart A. Wright, "Religious Innovation in the Mainline Church: House Churches, Home Cells, and Small Groups," in *Work, Family and Religion in Contemporary Society*, ed. Nancy Tatom Ammerman and Wade Clark Roof (New York: Routledge, 1995), 261–81.

7 Ibid., 275.

8 Donal Dorr, *Option for the Poor* (New York: Orbis, 1992), 151.

9 Gallagher, *Clashing Symbols*, chapter 4.

10 See: Susan Abraham, "What Does Mumbai Have to Do with Rome? Postcolonial Perspectives on Globalization and Theology," in *Theological Studies*, 69 (June 2008), 377. These major cultural disruptions of oppression are not separate from the internal disruptions in the human heart. See: GS 10: "The truth is that the imbalances under which the modern world labors are linked with that more basic imbalance which is rooted in the heart of human beings . . . [where] many elements wrestle with one another." For this reason it is important to address the structural elements which maintain and foster them. The integration of context more directly in Catholic moral theology helps to foster this discernment.

11 Here the author understands faith in a more general manner than the *initium fidei* of the act of Christian faith. Anthropological faith itself is an expression of the supernatural and has a place in morality, even though the supernatural is not consciously acknowledged. This faith has its origin in the universal call to salvation, and is expressed in part in taking responsibility for one's life situation. As anthropological faith it defines the common moral road of all men and women. The project of human freedom is synonymous to the obligation of love against which all human beings will be judged. Juan Luis Segundo, *Grace and the Human Condition* (New York: Orbis Books, 1973), 111. This type of faith, albeit in different language, is also suggested in the encyclical tradition. See: John Paul II, *Sollicitudo Rei Socialis*, 38.

12 Segundo, *Grace and the Human Condition*, 156.

13 Commitment to the oppressed is an intrinsic element to Christian faith. Juan Luis Segundo, *The Liberation of Theology* (New York: Orbis Books), 87.

14 Juan Luis Segundo, *Faith and Ideologies* (New York: Orbis Books, 1984), 71.

15 Josef Fuchs, "Natural Law," in *The New Dictionary of Catholic Social Thought*, ed. Judith A. Dwyer (Collegeville, MN: The Liturgical Press, 1994), 673.

16 Francisco Moreno Rejon, "Fundamental Moral Theory in the Theology of Liberation," in *Mysterium Liberationis*, ed. Ignacio Ellacuria, S.J., and Jon Sobrino, S.J. (New York: Orbis, 1993), 215.

17 Norbert J. Rigali, "The Future of Christian Morality," in *Chicago Studies* (Fall 1981), 288.

18 James Gustafson, *Ethics from a Theocentric Perspective* (Chicago: The University of Chicago Press, 1981), 139ff., 157–63.

19 Matthew Lamb, "The Theory-Praxis Relationship in Contemporary Christian Theologies," in *Proceedings of the Thirty-First Annual Convention* (The Catholic Theological Society of America, 1976), 149–78. See also: Matthew Lamb, *Solidarity with Victims* (New York: Crossroad, 1982), chapter 3.

20 Lamb comments that "Normativity is in the eternal and necessary, not in the flux of the universe of existence." "The Theory-Praxis Relationship in Contemporary Christian Theologies," 157.

21 "The normativity tends toward an identification of Christianity with modern, secular (liberal or Marxist) processes. What promotes the identification is good: what hinders it is wrong, such as the identification of Christianity with classical cultural practices in the first type" (ibid., 162). Or, in another place, "These variants have in common a more or less thorough rejection of classical-traditionalist metaphysics. Theory is not given a necessary domain of external truths but is seen as no more than ever revisable approximations to the flux of contingent events in history" (ibid., 158). Colin E. Greene comments that an Enlightenment vision of emancipation offers a normative vision of freedom which banishes religion and ethics from the public square, and holds out a notion of freedom which is conceived of almost entirely as freedom from external constraint. See: *Christology in Cultural Perspective: Marking Out the Horizons* (Grand Rapids, MI: Eerdmans, 2003), 197. Latin American theologians and others claim that is its precisely this Enlightenment ideology which has given rise to systematic injustice, oppression and racism, which are perpetuated in the divisions which separate the first world from the rest of the world's inhabitants.

22 "The normativity is not 'empirically' available (in the sense of critically provable by appeals to external data) but is rooted in the decision of Christian faith-love responding to the Word of God. The normativity, then, is radically gift and grace in a non-identical relation to human experience" (ibid., 164). Lamb classifies Barth and von Balthasar as central theologians of this type (ibid., 162–65).

23 "Normativity is determined by this theoretic (mostly metaphysical) union of identity and non-identity insofar as it enables them to avoid the tendencies toward reductionist identity in the first two types, or toward a revelationary positivism in the third type" (ibid., 171). Lamb classifies Bultmann, Tillich, Niebuhr, Rahner, Pannenberg and Tracy in this type (ibid., 165–71).

24 "Both the reflex-character and the normativity question in the theory-praxis relationship involve a concomitant change (conversion) of social structures and consciousness" (ibid., 177).

25 For another interpretation of the differences among these theological "schools" and their impact on normative issues, see: Robert Gascoigne, *The Public Forum and Christian Ethics* (Cambridge: Cambridge University Press, 2001), 96–106.

26 Juan Luis Segundo, "La condicion humana," *Perspectives de Dialogo*, II, no. 12 (March–April, 1967), 56.

27 David Hollenbach, *The Common Good and Christian Ethics* (Cambridge: Cambridge University Press, 2002), 178; see also his chapter 2.

28 Ibid., 207.

29 A moral theology sensitive to context indicates that the corporate or social existence of men and women provide the conditions which influence free choice. The important contribution of social structures to quality of life transcends the accumulated efforts of individuals. The structure itself accumulates in history as a condition which orients the operation of freedom. These structures can build up a facility for a life of freedom or love or a life of dehumanization and sin. However, the social existence of human beings can never provide a mechanical path which, if followed, will lead to human development. Free choice is always done within a matrix of possibility and constraint.

See: Juan Luis Segundo, *Evolution and Guilt*, trans. John Drury (New York: Orbis, 1974), 3–8.

30 Johann Baptist Metz, *Faith in History and Society* (New York: Seabury Press, 1980), 53, and see also p. 43.

31 Lewis Mudge asks, "How far along this path is it legitimate to go?," *The Sense of a People: Toward a Church for the Human Future* (Philadelphia, PA: Trinity Press, 1992), 88.

32 James E. Cone, *Speaking the Truth: Ecumenism, Liberation and Black Theology* (Grand Rapids, MI: Eerdmans, 1986), 118.

33 Rigali, "The Future of Christian Morality," 287.

34 Robert Schreiter, *The New Catholicity: Theology between the Global and the Local* (New York: Orbis Books, 1997), chapter 1.

35 Don Browning, *Marriage and Modernization. How Globalization Threatens Marriage and What To Do about It* (Grand Rapids, MI: Eerdmans, 2003), 230. See also: Vincent Miller, *Consuming Religion: Christian Faith and Practice in a Consumer Culture* (New York: Continuum, 2004).

36 Schreiter, *The New Catholicity*, 46–61.

37 Michael J. Schuck, *That They Be One: The Social Teaching of the Papal Encyclicals, 1740–1989* (Washington, D.C.: Georgetown University, 1991), 180. We say this noting also this body of teaching has weaknesses in its treatment of women. See: Christine E. Gudorf, *Catholic Social Teaching on Liberation Themes* (Washington, D.C.: University Press of America, 1981), 249–328.

38 Ruth Chadwick, "Professional Ethics," in a *Matter of Breath: Foundations for Professional Ethics*, ed. Guillaume de Stexhe and Johan Verstraeten (Louvain: Peeters, 2000), 47–49.

39 David Carr, "Professional Education and Professional Ethics," in *Matter of Breath*, op. cit., 15–20.

40 Gallagher, *Clashing Symbols*, 31.

41 Bellah, *Habits of the Heart*, 149.

42 Studs Terkel, *Working* (New York: Pantheon Books, 1976).

43 Bellah, *Habits of the Heart*, 298.

44 See: Joerg Rieger, *No Rising Tide: Theology, Economics, and the Future* (Minneapolis, MN: Fortress Press, 2009).

45 Richard Sennett, *The Culture of the New Capitalism* (New Haven: Yale University Press, 2007). See also: Michael Maccoby, *The Gamesman* (New York: Simon and Schuster, 1976) for an early account of the influence of the business climate on types of managers.

46 Stephen Carter, *Civility: Manners, Morals and the Etiquette of Democracy* (New York: Basic Books, 1998).

47 John A. Coleman, S.J., "Retrieving or Re-inventing Social Catholicism: A Transatlantic Response," in *Catholic Social Thought: Twilight or Renaissance?*, ed. J.S. Boswell, F.P. McHugh and J. Verstraeten (Leuven: Peeters, 2000), 289–92.

48 Lisa Sowle Cahill, "Toward Global Ethics," in *Theological Studies*, 63, no. 2 (June 2002), 333–44.

49 James Gustafson, as quoted by David Hollenbach. See: "Tradition, Historicity and Truth in Theological Ethics," in *Christian Ethics: Problems and Prospects*, ed. Lisa Sowle Cahill and James F. Childress (Cleveland, OH: The Pilgrim Press, 1996), 61.

50 Donal Dorr, "Option for the Poor Re-Visited," in *Catholic Social Thought*, op. cit., 254.

51 Stefano Zamagni, "Humanising the Economy: On the Relationship between Catholic Social Thinking and Economic Discourse," in *Catholic Social Thought*, op. cit., 151.

52 This also calls for moral competence in the professions. See: Tomas Brytting, "The Preconditions for Moral Competence: Contemporary Rationalization and the Creation of Moral Space," in *Business Ethics: Broadening the Perspectives*, ed. Johan Verstraeten (Leuven: Peeters, 2000), 81–88. Johan Verstraeten, "Business Ethics and Personal Moral Responsibility," *Business Ethics*, op. cit., 97–112.

53 Helen Rose Ebaugh, Paula F. Pipes, Janet Saltman Chaftetz and Martha Daniels, "Where's the Religion? Distinguishing Faith-Based from Secular Social Service Agencies," *Journal for the Scientific Study of Religion*, 42, no. 3 (September 2003), 411–26.

Chapter 7

POSTMODERN DISCIPLESHIP: AUTONOMY, INITIATIVE, AND MYSTICISM

It is not hard to recognize the situation of postmodern life in what Mary Douglas describes as low-group and low-grid situations. Role definition is at a minimum. While Context B life (discussed in Chapter Six) engages one in a community of competition, Context C life involves isolation and lack of communication between people since neither group nor grid controls or influences. In Context C one finds a more extreme lack of structures and supports. Relationships are optional and mobile. The lack of structure contributes to the sense that everything is floating. Douglas claims that modern industrial society affords people more opportunities than ever to live as an isolate.

Douglas cites the example of a girl working at a cash checkpoint in a super-market as an example of this culture of minimum grid and minimum group pressure. Within the patterns of such a job there is practically no opportunity to relate to people or to have any sense of belonging. Her analysis focuses less on the external situation of this type of work in a modern city, and more on the changing place of the self within the social organization.[1] The cashier simply punches her time clock, does her job and collects her paycheck, without much sense of professionalism, upward mobility (Context B) or having a distinct role in a wider system of meaning (Context A).

Context C and Church

In comparison with Church–community links in Contexts A and B, the Context C situation offers few supports or symbols to reinforce the religious dimension of life. One is in a totally secularist atmosphere. In the Context C climate, the Church does not enter into everyday life, unless one goes to church. This society is likely the most common for many First World Catholics.[2]

In Gallagher's words:

If the main form of unbelief in "A" is an opting out of the structures of belonging (for instance from church practice), and if in "B" the tendency is to reject God as irrelevant to my life, in "C" the very question of some ultimate meaning and spiritual horizon fades into silence or unreality.[3]

In Context C the question is posed whether the Church has any purpose at all, or has the potential to represent an ultimate horizon of life. The question of Church also can be mute, as life goes on in a culture where one's interactions are devoid of religious symbolism or interpretation. In postmodern society, in the experience that one shares with others a Christian frame of reference can be absent. In Context B there can be a tension between faith and culture. In Context C this may be a non-issue. Typically, when people face key life experiences, those of fullness and emptiness, it cannot be assumed that they will be interpreted within a Christian frame of reference.[4] For Christians these may be moments "when God was silent." For others, there is simply silence with no God or sense of transcendence present.

The Context C situation, where people are detached from one another and from the master narratives which give life meaning, can give rise to two responses, according to Douglas. For some, the situation is so lacking in structures that members become free to build "intentional communities" creatively from below. The very absence of control from group or grid becomes a cultural blessing for new forms of social and religious response. People can seek a personal identity, self-worth, and potential for change in this new situation through freely attending to the Christian narrative. They act in spite of the vast pluralism of the culture, and those who will not search. In this sense a secularist climate provides a fertile ground for individuation and for counter-cultural community in the Church and society. The social order, however, does not demand it. It arises from the desire for it, a desire which the Christian narrative testifies rests on the nature and call of God, and the suffering of the Other.[5]

Some respond to the Context C situation through a type of cultural desolation, where drifting dominates. Lack of support leaves people without any scaffolding for an encounter with religious revelation, a requirement for ongoing conversion, or community involvement. Lack of protection of a church community can lead to manipulation of the soul isolated from the markers of a tradition. The absence of pressures may provoke creative freedom and rediscovery of the gospel for some, but for others it will promote a type of self-created religion without any contact with the traditional wisdom of the churches. Without some belonging to a "group" or some links with the "grid" of other people, people can easily become secularized, un-churched, narcissistic, and lonely.

New Age

New Age religion has been criticized as sharing in the weaknesses of Context C life. New Age religion can be defined as an eclectic set of beliefs, practices, and worldviews which form no set dogma or creed. New Age beliefs are wide ranging, as they have no central organization or membership list, no formal clergy, and no one geographic center. New age practices are often a blend of ancient practices such as meditation, spiritual reading, pilgrimages, and ritual practices. Yet the way the practices are integrated lacks coherence and the ability to promote the conversion the full religious way promotes. One can be a Buddhist and a Christian, without ever submitting to the internal dynamics of either religion in all its dimensions. The New Age movement is not new in the history of spirituality. It arises in an historical period which is believed to be a harbinger of the future, bearing alternative values, and the type of changed consciousness which is necessary for the survival of the planet at the time.[6]

Context C religious practice is compatible with New Age spirituality, as its origins are a movement away from both grid and group forces of social control. However, New Age spirituality is not monolithic. Aspects of it emerge in traditional religions as they seek to adapt to modern culture. In this instance, New Age practices blend with major symbols and beliefs and augment rather than replace central structure of religious practice. In other cases, there is not this relationship. The free-floating nature of New Age spirituality simply joins the amorphous cultural context of Context C life. When this occurs, an anchorless form of spiritual searching of the New Age variety can leave people without filters to sort through a growing barrage of religious nonsense.[7] Criticisms of New Age religion focus on its superficiality, its narcissistic focus, its overstatement of the possibility of personal transformation, and its propensity toward Gnosticism, or a claim to specialized knowledge not available to all.

The rise of New Age religion can also indicate to the Church that a non-transformed Context A life will not meet the needs of those living in the postmodern situation of Context C life. A foreword to a recent Vatican study of New Age religion notes that the research invites the readers to take account of the way that New Age religiosity addresses the spiritual hunger of contemporary men and women. It reminds readers that the attraction that New Age religion holds for some Christians may be due in part to the lack of serious attention in their own communities to important themes of spirituality which are actually part of the Catholic synthesis. Among these are the importance of the spiritual dimension of human life and its integration with the whole of life; the link between human beings and the rest of creation; the desire for personal and social transformation, and the rejection of a rationalistic and materialistic view of humanity.[8]

Rahner, Myticism and the New Church

Karl Rahner has a different approach to a spirituality which fits Context C life in this new time in the Church. His essay, "The Spirituality of the Church of the Future," states that the spirituality of the future must be suited to the new conditions of belief in modern society. "The spirituality of the future will not be supported or at any rate will be much less supported by a sociologically Christian homogeneity of its situation; it will have to live much more clearly than hitherto out of a solitary, immediate experience of God and his Spirit."[9] All spirituality is characterized by an act of freedom whereby a person moves freely in love toward God and others, rather than into themselves in egotism. In the past, however, the movement toward God was done within a more Christian homogeneous milieu. Context A and Context B existences suggest a taken-for-granted Christian life, even though admitting variations of it. Today Christian faith and spirituality must be freshly realized in a secularized world. It must answer the claims of atheism and the trend to locate technical knowledge as the broker of truth, claiming anything which cannot be proved in terms of this thinking is meaningless. For Rahner, this climate of belief and unbelief gives rise to another form of Christian response to God: mysticism. "In such a situation the lonely responsibility of the individual in his decision of faith is necessary and required in a way much more radical than it was in former times."[10] The Christian must make a decision of faith, contrary to public opinion. Not even the public opinion of the Church sustains such a solitary decision; rather the Church itself is sustained by individual decisions of faith, lived out of a wholly personal experience of God and God's Spirit. Context C life fosters such spirituality.

Modern day mysticism is not the mysticism reserved for the saints and those with privileged spiritual experience. Rather it is a genuine experience of God arising from the heart of existence, and open to all people of faith. Mysticism in this sense is moved from the margins of Christian life and made a feature of people's everyday existence as they live the Christian life.[11] Rahner cautions that God is not one mystery among others, but *the* Mystery which undergirds all life, who can never be fully known or grasped: ". . . the concept of God is not a grasp of God by which a person masters the mystery, but it is letting oneself be grasped by the mystery which is present and yet always withdrawing itself."[12] Rahner sees this reality of mystery as the grounding and necessity of catechesis, study of Scripture and focus on Church teaching. These resources are for a purpose; through them a person is able to interpret his or her experience of God, and meet God in Jesus Christ and know the Christian way.

The Christian mystical tradition speaks of both positive and negative "ways" to the mystery of God. There is a positive sense that God is encountered in experiences, for instance of goodness and beauty. Yet there also can be encounter with

God's mystery in a situation of seeming negativity, as when we forgive without acknowledgment, bear pain patiently or take up the burden of responsibility.[13]

Rahner speaks of the diverse life experiences which can be encountered with God:

> . . . the solitary Christian makes the experience of God and his liberating grace in silent prayer, in the final decision of conscience, unrewarded by anyone, in the unlimited hope which can no longer cling to any calculable assurance, in the radical disappointment of life and in the powerlessness of death — if these things are only voluntarily borne and accepted in hope, in the night of the sense and the spirit . . .[14]

These experiences prove to be the real crucible of faithfulness for the adult Christian. In them, the human consent to God's grace at the heart of faithfulness can deepen existentially, or can be refused, as the gospel story of the rich young man who "went away sad" testifies (Mt. 19.16-26).

Consumerism: The Hidden Culture

Forms of social control can be hidden in Context C life, not consciously observed as in Context A and B situations. Douglas claims that the individual in Context C life does not encounter fellow human beings as the principle determinants of social life.[15] In a Context C situation, she argues, people feel dominated by objects, rather than by people. A sense of futility and lack of freedom emerges because of the impossibility of bringing moral pressures to bear upon that which controls. For instance, the social control in a Context C situation can be a sense of being caught in a system, or having no alternatives. Some people today, for example, feel their personal future is positive but have no basis to envision a better future for the human race.[16]

Vincent Miller elaborates this posture in his study of consumer culture. If an antidote to a mystical posture is simply to run away, certainly the consumer culture is a fitting hiding place. Miller is concerned that our current culture weakens religion by treating religious symbols as "consumable decoration" for pre-existing structures of everyday life.[17] Miller sees culture as an internal and intentional horizon of human consciousness that flows from the social organization and behavior of participating in a consumer culture. His concern is that the degree the cultural symbols of capitalism provide a deeper organization of life than the religious symbols of Catholicism itself. Consumerism can be an escape in modern culture. Its maxims, by analogy, can be considered an elaborated code of modern living. However, Miller's study raises the question of whether consumerism has become the condensed code of Western society, in the absence of significant intervention by other forces.

Faithfulness, Mysticism and Context C Activity

The individual in a Context C situation struggles to be faithful without the supports of group or grid. Feeling marginal arises from the structure of the disconnected modern life. For some, it can result from the difficulty of finding a life structure in which to "fit," since the model of role (Context A) and particular identity (Context B) play less a part in self-understanding.[18]

Faithfulness requires a two-fold effort in a Context C context. First, there has to be familiarity with the operating principles of the many facets of modern living. There is no buffer zone for the Context C dweller, where knowledge of the world is irrelevant. Second, one needs a reason for loving and caring at all, beyond one's self-interest. No group demands altruism of the individual, nor do the interpersonal relationships of grid force it.

How does one maintain a sense of the transcendent in its moral form of attending to the truth, sacrifice for the neighbor, and responsibility? How are these markers of faithfulness kept without the cultural supports to reinforce them? John Paul II claims that the world is in peril without them. Only a belief in the transcendent nature of human life, for instance, grounds openness in public administration, the rejection of illicit means in order to gain or increase power, and respect for the rights of political adversaries and others.[19]

Rahner speculated that the future Church, which could no longer rely on the cultural supports Western society once provided, would be in fact one where the mystical experience of faith would be predominant for this very reason.[20] The Christian of the future will be a mystic or he or she will not exist at all. Mystic here means that the source of one's faith is not external as through indoctrination from the outside; rather it is a genuine experience of God emerging from the heart of one's existence. In Rahner's words:

> For, according to Scripture and the Church's teaching, rightly understood, the ultimate conviction and decision of faith comes in the last resort, not from a pedagogic indoctrination from the outside, supported by public opinion in secular society or in the Church. Nor from a merely rational argumentation of fundamental theology, but from the experience of God, of his Spirit, of his freedom, bursting out of the very heart of human existence and able to be experienced there, even though this experience cannot be wholly a matter for reflection or be verbally objectified.[21]

Encounter with God is begun by God, not self-initiated. Yet, it demands the supports of religion, Rahner cautions. The future of the Church will have a continuity with the spirituality of the past: as centered on revelation (not mere humanism); focused on the paschal mystery (not modern theories of progress); and ecclesial (although it might shape a new Church). It will be sacramental; related to the world (political dimension); involving the evangelical counsels and the Sermon on the Mount; focused on hope; and always leaning toward community and a communal discernment of the Spirit alive in our day. The ecclesial dimension of spirituality goes beyond membership. It is an attachment to the Church, a patience with the Church and a respect for it, knowing that without it, ". . . we shall eventually get no further than our own arbitrary opinions and the uncertainties of our own life selfishly caught up in itself."[22]

Context C life contains an essential paradox. It evokes a spirituality which must be mystical and individual; that is, centered in an experience of God, and a free response in return. Yet, this mysticism must be open to the communal in new ways.[23] The first experience of the Spirit was given at Pentecost, at a time of fear and solidarity, and the Church was born. Likewise, the spirituality of Context C life is to embrace a new blend of individuality and solidarity in the ambiguity of our times. This new spirit is implied when we speak of the reality of the Church in terms of Context C life. The faithfulness required for a life of faith amid Context C realities will enliven the Church, in its mediative, sacramental and communal dimensions, in a new and authentic manner.[24]

Context C Life: The Mystical and the Sacramental

"The Church since the Council has to a large extent put off her mystical characteristics," wrote Hans Urs von Balthasar, "she has become a Church of permanent conversations, organizations, advisory commissions, congresses, synods, commissions, academies, parties, pressure groups, functions, structures and restructurings, sociological experiments, statistics . . ."[25] The Swiss theologian von Balthasar offers this criticism of Church life in post-Vatican II times, and raises how the Church's mystical tradition illumines the meaning of faithfulness in the Context C situation. A tendency of modern life is to get caught up in the practice of life, without reinforcing the grounding of one's operations.[26] In Douglas's terms, people create an elaborated code which is not in reference to any restrictive one. The result is the absence of a language to explain why we do things, which can lead to alienation. The Christian life today can be faced with this dilemma.

Context C life is a secular world unmediated by groups or grid relationships. It reflects the Enlightenment project to locate moral life in rational or utilitarian terms. Yet is this enough? No matter how fruitful our conversations may be, they often do not resolve the conflicts we encounter. While we debate technical solutions to our problems, we often lack a language to ground for what and for whom we are responsible.[27] "Reason" can be the code term for my language, my vocabulary and my network of convictions. It is assumed that reason is "universal" when it simply expresses the mentality of the most powerful person in the room. We lack a vision of what is true and good beyond our personal appraisal of it. Postmodern criticism questions this state of affairs. Such lack of a foundational vision leaves little place for Christian conversion in a vision of faithfulness.

The person in a Context C life situation can be caught in this postmodern dilemma. On the one hand, the person is freed from a false sense of reality which is fostered by the narrowness and limitations of grid and group sensibilities. On the other, there is a loss of embeddedness which leaves the individual to take responsibility for his or her life, but also to define the goals, practices, and rules of modern living. Since God is unnecessary in this world, the other-worldly horizon which ultimately gives the actions of a Christian ultimate weight and meaning is left unsaid. Even if God is acknowledged, globalization confronts us with the reality that Christian faith is not the only religious option open to us, and that Christians constitute only a minority of the world's population. Hence a Christian response can be depicted as good as any other, leaving its distinctiveness and importance unexpressed. Caught in this postmodern paradox, the wisdom of "getting by" can take over, with its content loosely defined, detached from group and grid relationships. Is there a way out of this situation, without denying the realities of modern living?

We hold that the Church is a sacrament. At the heart of the Christian life is the life and death of Jesus Christ, which gives the Christian a new life in Christ. This event is sacramentally mediated, and communally embedded. It calls Christians to a way which can give them a degree of critical distance, autonomy and ethical discernment which the postmodern mentality rightly suggests. Yet, it offers them a vision of a center of life and reality which is not only a mooring, but a relationship, not only with God, but with each other in the community of the Church. Without this, work to improve the social condition of society fails for lack of a living community of witnesses to the event which gives their lives meaning. At its core, this is the meaning of Church as sacrament. While the level of society work is always done at the level of what promotes human flourishing, for Christians, we ground what we know to be fully human by looking in the mirror of Jesus Christ. It is our life in Christ which illumines our contribution to the meaningful moral language held by all which speaks of the objective conditions required for human flourishing. Being a disciple of Jesus Christ embraces this task.

Laws in society are necessary but not enough to build a common life among people. Values in society which laws try to uphold cannot simply appeal to self-evident values in some circular manner, because it is not self-evident in modern society why one would want to sacrifice for another, rather than use them for profit. Virtues depend on a vision of personal responsibility and a meaningful life which religion upholds. Stephen Carter comments:

> Nothing in contemporary secular conversation calls us to give up anything truly valuable for anybody else. No politician would dare run for office asking us to sacrifice for others. Only religion offers a sacred language of sacrifice-selflessness-awe that enables believers to treat their fellow citizens as . . . fellow passengers.[28]

For the Christian, all such efforts reflect a vision of life's meaning and purpose as life in Christ. It is this vision which is at the heart of Christian discipleship.

Context C Life: Mystical and the Political

We find that people in a Context C situation can also be invested in the Church, especially in its mystical tradition and its significance for prophetic and political action. Mystics can see the ethical good in society in a way not available to those who live their lives without this deep prayer life. Their prayer gives them "sight" which is socially significant[29] Authentic mystical prayer can cut through the illusion of culture and self-deception to go beyond the weakness of will to do what is good, characteristic of the human condition. Mystics find a freedom in love of God that focuses them on the pursuit of good with a perseverance that transcends their own attachments, and the moral stagnation they can promote. Mysticism, healthfully understood, is done within the Church, not instead of it or apart from it.[30]

A corollary to the mystical life is the call to solidarity, which is also the trajectory of conversion of Context C life and a mark of discipleship. This call is for the regeneration of community life in the Church and creation of new communities.[31] Members today are making a new option for the Church, to offset the deadening forces of a consumer and irreligious culture. The pastoral needs of those in Context C life are also met in new ways by the spiritual direction and retreat movement which maintains an important bridge between socially involved Catholics and the Church. It meets spiritual needs which are not fulfilled in a traditional Context A environment as one's sole Church context. Today's globalized capitalist society generates ecological, societal, and spiritual breakdown as well as a polarization of politics.[32] Joe Holland sees a positive potential of the Context C context to respond to this situation. People can get involved in the local networks made possible by an electronic era to engage in strategies of holistic regeneration, to defend and renew creative communion of life across its ecological, societal, and spiritual dimensions.[33] Attention to the webs and cycles of natural and social ecology also informs investment in this renewal.[34] The lack of social controls of Context C life, its freedom from group and grid restrictions, can be a freedom to engage in these new networks, and through this involvement enrich the Church's response to these issues. Channels of sacramentality, mediation, and communion which speak to Catholic life in a Context C situation link a hunger for a more individuated spiritual life to these important movements of the day.

Autonomy Transformed

Douglas claims that in a low-grid situation like Context C, big rewards go to the innovating individual. In a commercial enterprise, there is no system of controls except those mutually agreed upon to protect respective practices of risk-taking individuals. These mutually provide useful services for successful colleagues, and reject those who can do nothing to increase their range of activities. The main way to measure success in this environment, however, is by the size of following. What begins as an individual transacting with others ends with the individual strongly insulated from others, since there is no formation of an explicit pattern as to how roles are related to one another. The rights of the individual to transcend boundaries of all kinds of social conventions (Context B life) move toward a situation where it is difficult to articulate one's experience in an intelligible way.[35] Douglas notes that the most adaptive response will be a great passivity since there are no rewards, except for "big" responses, and no escapes. In our terms, one just tries to "get by," sometimes with a vague hope that a type of moral progress without conversion might be brought about by alternations in political, social, or economic structures.

Christopher Steck, S.J., in his study *The Ethical Thought of Hans Urs von Balthasar*, indicates some directions required to ground a sense of moral initiative beyond the cultural model of a self-initiated moral style of Context C life, which has no grounding except in the individual's autonomy, or sense of self-direction. We will explore three aspects of the problem in order to see the possibilities of a new sense of direction. First, we will note the difference between a cultural model of autonomy and one upheld by Christian ethics. Second, we will inquire how we can affirm the moral project of all in a universal way, while at the same time giving attention to the unique experiences of Christian initiative and autonomy. Third, we will ask what difference a Christian view of autonomy and initiative makes in a view of Christian ethics.

The first matter to be clarified is how attention to the personal context of a person's life in Context C situation is a different approach to the moral person than a more traditional one in moral theology. Steck argues that Aquinas focused on the one, universal goal of all human persons, and not on the unique "I" that was in journey to that goal.[36] The highest goal was that our minds be attached to God. The person was but one member of the human species. As a rational animal they shared with all human beings common faculties and the same ultimate goal. Concern about how the unique individual, the unrepeatable and irreducible core which theology refers to as person, was to be realized in the moral life was not something Aquinas addressed.

Aquinas did hold that human actions always had a purpose, included in which was the fulfillment of the person themselves. However, he saw fulfillment as a type of linear development of human capacities that all people shared, or our progress in virtue. Von Balthasar, however, sees purpose more as a narrative, in that our actions seek to add up to a meaning which is personal, our life story. The contingencies and concrete events of one's life in other words, tell a story. The actions of an individual are given purpose by being united by and interpreted within a story that says something true about the person, an inner truth so important that it is constitutive of the person themselves. We might refer to a person's "truth" as something which gives unity to their lives.

When a person reflects on their life, perhaps looking back and thinking of wasted years spent in rebellion; opportunities missed through fear; a failure which opened a door to another opportunity, they try to make sense of their life through the type of insight which von Balthasar suggests. They put life's isolated situations in a wider context of meaning in order to explain themselves to themselves.[37] The image of life as a river, flowing along, never to be retrieved, is a popular image of thinking of one's life as a whole.

Steck claims that Aquinas termed these broader situations of life, like aging, betrayal, leaving home, and forming significant relationships, as the *circumstances* of the act. Von Balthasar, however, argues that we do not identify ourselves with the isolated acts or the facts of our lives but with the meaning they come to represent in being part of our story.[38] We judge past and future actions in light of how they "fit" into a life course, or story, which we have begun. We can either enrich this story, or deplete it through neglect or rebellion.

Is von Balthasar's sense of a unique life course different from the personal struggle of the individual in Context C who deals with a loss of embeddedness? In Context C they are left not only to take responsibility for their life, but also to define the goals, practices, and rules of modern living. Is "one's story" simply another self-construction? For von Balthasar, the narrative identity is not self-constructed alone, it is given by God. In addition, von Balthasar visions a gap between one's true identity and how one understands one's story. Even though the person has to interpret this story, the narrative "I," how it is understood by the person, and their true inner identity, the subject "I," are never the same. In other words, the human person cannot give to themselves the ultimate validity which can only come from God. Rather their true identity in God is revealed to them over time in continued encounters with God. Steck summarizes, "Thus, while for Thomas the highest act (the one that represented the fulfillment of the person) was the knowing, willing and loving the absolute, for von Balthasar, it is becoming a 'self' in relation to the Absolute, to relate the unique 'I' that is one's identity to the absolute."[39] While a role in life gives one a sense of this bigger picture — I am a mother, I am an advocate of justice — it is not enough. The inner "I" might remain alienated in this public role. However, if a person embraces this alienation and looks to the divine, one can separate themselves from their stance in this life and anchor their identity in the divine. The paradox is such that a stand in eternity grounds one fully to engage in the finite.

Mentally this construction makes sense, however, some might say, it is simply a mental construction. A better understanding is given when we imagine this dynamic in the form of a relationship. One understands self not simply by using a mental construct; rather one enters into a relationship. For von Balthasar, the achievement of personal freedom (the person's free choice of this identity) occurs when one is able to grasp one's deepest identity and not just know it but to express it to the other. At a spiritual level, this occurs by invitation only, and is freely given. God's way is to awaken through love a free response that embraces God's freedom and with it God's vision of the identity of each person. One possesses oneself through relating to the other, and by responding to the other, one expresses and forms self. Key to our concern is that the two movements require a type of suspension of one's own agency alone, as in the cultural model, in order to also receive what is the other. We interpret our lives in terms of the absolute and we listen actively to the personal address of the other. For Christians this is done in relationship to Christ.

Are There Christian Ethics?

How then does one affirm the universal sense of ethics which we discussed earlier in terms of the call to the natural law, and the Christo-centric understanding of autonomy given above? Norbert Rigali describes ethics, that is, where rightness and wrongness of conduct is concerned, as having four levels.[40] These distinctions are helpful to understand the relationship between the universal call of all people and a sense of Christian faithfulness, which is the concern of this book. First there are essential ethics. These include norms that are regarded as applicable to all persons, where one's behavior is an instance of a general, essential moral norm. Rightness and wrongness of acts of killing, promise keeping, not stealing, are included as well as all actions which are rooted in the dignity of persons as human beings.

Second, there is an existential ethic. This refers to the awareness that "this ought to be done by me." This is a choice of a good that the individual as an individual should realize, a sense of "ought," as an absolute ethical demand, which is addressed to an individual. I ought to go to that funeral. I ought to use my talents for accounting and help that non-profit organization.

A third is essential Christian ethics. These are ethical decisions a Christian must make because he or she belongs to a community to which the non-Christian does not belong. These are moral demands placed on a Christian as a Christian. To belong to a worshipping community, to educate one's children in the faith, to attend to the teachings of the Church would be included.

The fourth is an existential Christian ethic. These are decisions that the Christian as an individual must make. For example, this could be a call to follow a religious vocation, to accept a responsibility in the community, to be a missionary. In light of what Rahner called everyday mysticism, Christian existential ethics would embrace many facets of a faithful life and carry with it a fuller sense of conversion which logically might be missing from the other types. What marks a Christian ethic is not just a difference in motivation on the part of the Christian, i.e. what I do, I do in union with Christ. In some instances, it could evoke a different response in content, as we will see. Here again von Balthasar can be instructive.

He claims that the Christian's response to Christ in love is not simply one-directional, i.e. we love Christ. Rather it is found in a two-fold movement whereby we receive Christ's love and then we act.[41] He draws on St. Ignatius of Loyola, who states that we are created first to praise, reverence and serve God, and all things are to be ordered to this first calling.[42] To accept this vision of life, we surrender to God, and then make choices. This is quite different than the self-realization of the autonomous person. Instead there is a giving of self to God and a reception of self from God. The person asks, how does this decision look in God's eyes, not simply the God of the commandments, but God who loves me and calls me to my true identity? This is the two-fold movement of interpersonal love. Christ moves toward me, a creature, in self-emptying, and the human being reaches toward God. Here the person allows himself or herself to be changed by this encounter, and to allow emotions, ideas, plans, and strategies to be altered by what one learns in this personal exchange. If Rahner and von Balthasar are right, this is not an encounter for spiritual specialists alone. It is the model for the daily life of Christians in postmodern society. George Aschenbrenner comments on the paschal mystery at the heart of the Christian life:

> The drama whereby Jesus entrusts himself in dying and the Trinity miracu-lously raises him to life presents an example for the daily life of us all. The challenge facing us Christians is surely not to raise ourselves. However much

we may desire such fulfillment, no Herculean efforts can possibly achieve it. Rather, our challenge is to learn, in everyday situations . . . a life not centered on ourselves but heartily engaged in a personal, real relationship with our consoling Companion whose faithfulness is beyond doubt.[43]

Initiative Transformed

Human fulfillment, according to von Balthasar, has two dimensions: the desire to overcome the meaninglessness associated with contingency, to achieve a personal identity grounded in the absolute; and the desire to gain self-possession through interpersonal love.[44] Obviously, the achievement of both goals demands a going out of self and embracing what is other. A type of distancing is necessary. In fact, indifference to the world has been a hallmark of Christian spirituality. Traditional teaching on indifference is the belief that in order to attend to things of an absolute nature, one must distance oneself from things of this world. Von Balthasar, following Ignatius, suggests a different kind of indifference, one that grows out of a dynamic relationship with God. There is a certain amount of indifference required to move toward God, in response to God's movement toward us. Over-immersion in daily life will make reflection on the deeper meaning of things impossible or simply drown out the desire. This leads to the "floating" and overwhelmed sense of Context C living without grid or group moorings. In order to make oneself attentive to divine movements therefore, an appropriate level of indifference is necessary, a type of freedom *from*.[45]

However, encounter with God also leads to a freedom *to*. Steck remarks:

> . . . Ignatian indifference is not so much a permanent stance vis-à-vis creaturely things, but rather one moment in a dynamic posture toward them. Indifference moves back and forth, from an initial detachment in regard to earthly goods . . . and toward a reengagement of those goods, now with desires and love attuned to those of God.[46]

Since the individual cannot predict or anticipate all of the free expressions of God, there can be a "break" or "discontinuity" with what has been anticipated. Human initiative therefore may express an action which is not a typical response to a situation, or something which is a new posture on the part of an individual.[47]

Political theologians also speak of this "break" or "discontinuity," which marks an ethical response that flows from relationship to Christ. It is not just any doing or activity that leads to true freedom. It is action that imitates the love of Jesus in the concrete realities of one's social situation. Jesus Christ is the one who frees us to know ourselves, to experience our freedom in a way we could not by ourselves.[48] Christianity in this sense contains an inherent paradox. Autonomy and initiative understood through the Christian mysteries lead to an increasing dependence on God. Dependence on God fosters a deeper and more radical autonomy and initiative. However, knowing God as one's supreme good is not the same as knowing what to do in a concrete situation. In this sense, Context C life requires its own rules of discernment suited to its absence of grid and group situations and the moral direction they can provide.

The Mystical-Political Discipleship

Context C life draws the Christian into a basic tension. Instead of intuiting a great order to things, life appears to dictate on a daily basis that the only order which exists is the one we make for ourselves. Faith puts the Christian in touch with ultimate reality and locates us and our situation within it. However, we only know what is ultimate by some partial realization of it in a situation. We know love through loving situations. We know justice by seeing it in action. Therefore what we create and what we do are not asides to the more primary task of contemplation of God.

In modern times the following of Christ is a search in the darkness. It is an affirmation of values of human worth and dignity before obstacles, frustrations and setbacks. While on the one hand, we only know what we have experienced, some things we experience only in a contrast experience. We say no to the world as we find it, and implicit in this no is a yes to something better, which we may only perceive vaguely. Political theologians remind us that we only follow Christ as disciples in an obscure and searching freedom in which we come to know not only Jesus, but our true selves. This is discipleship in a Context C situation.

Because of the great suffering in modern society, the following of Jesus can only be done in hope, in the midst of the concrete realities of the present day. It is not done simply within oneself, through personal reflection, but in a co-world with others, where the freedom of the "other" affects the possibility of concretely living out one's own ultimate freedom.[49] Political theology does not deny the individual's relationship with God, such as von Balthasar stresses. However, it affirms that the promises of the Reign of God that the New Testament guarantees, freedom, justice, peace, and reconciliation are not just private realities but public ones as well. The longing one feels for these in personal religious experience does not exhaust their meaning. These promises make the individual free in that they commit them to critique their absence in society and work toward their creation. The following of Christ therefore is done in community and society, albeit from the solitary stance of the Context C Christian. Political theology does not seek to return the world to a less secularized society, but rather to create within secularized society the realities of the Kingdom of God.[50] Politics is the deliberation about how we organize our life together to make human goods possible. Because such decisions are made in a limited world, mysticism also gives way to a practical realism in action.

Context C life provides an opportunity to think about society's influence on people's thinking, or how human reason enters into decisions which we take for granted. People can consider themselves "radical" or "progressive" thinkers, especially when they live apart from group and grid influences. Yet these people can share in the human condition of being conditioned by the "common sense" of their society. It is very difficult for people to break through to a new vision of things which addresses the concerns of those not established or valued in the society.[51] When we think of the future, we too often think of the fulfillment of our plans, not the needs of others. However, here is where von Balthasar and Metz blend. God's kingdom is known to "break through."[52] To shape the future critical reason is needed, one that accepts the future promised by God cannot in any way be adequately conceived under the conditions of the present.[53]

Context C Life and Moral Discernment

The social organization that seems natural in different cultures constitutes a particular "path" of decision making for the members of that culture, according to Douglas.[54] A central argument of cultural theory is that culture itself is constrained by its own different logical base. This helps to explain how any type of collective can resist pressures to transform. Some see Context C life, detached from group and grid social forces, as a reflection of the state of ethics in modern society. Alasdair MacIntyre in *After Virtue* claims that once morality becomes detached from customs, tradition and from religion it is given a type of pseudo-rational foundation which emancipates the individual from any obligation vis-à-vis the authorities which these institutions represent. At the same time, both virtuous living and theorizing about the moral life are impossible unless those who engage in them have been educated in the stories and ways of acting and thinking of a particular historical tradition.[55] Miller and Bellah argue that this detachment does not leave the individual in a vacuum; rather market forces and the state absorb the moral imagination and appear as "common sense."

In a later work MacIntyre describes a tradition as a tradition of inquiry.[56] The fact that there is pluralism in a grounding tradition does not necessarily lead to relativism. A mature tradition acts upon its past and reintegrates what is useful. It is also able to assimilate ideas originally discovered elsewhere. These ideas do not automatically replace the ideas in place. Rather they are placed alongside them and over time, through a process of what we would call discernment, some are absorbed, some are rejected, and others penetrate the culture and become a new "common sense."[57]

A working tradition therefore is dynamic, self-critical, and open to knowledge gained from the outside. Inquiry into the tradition begins with the stories, images, and traditions of the past as "received." However, the tradition itself has to adjudicate the plurality of experiences which arise from its members, some of which have not been addressed in a previous synthesis. These experiences give rise to various and at times conflicting interpretations, and judgment has to be passed on them. Also, the tradition encounters new questions raised in the broader environment, as well as alternative traditions which confront it with different accounts of how things are or ought to be. These insights certainly provide for those in a Context C situation to consider how the Church as a living tradition enhances their lives and sense of faithfulness.

If members of the Church in Context C situations can overcome the implicit indifference to religion contained in their way of life, they can find ways through autonomy and initiative to bring the questions of secular society into the more traditional circles of Context A church life. Instead of adopting the anchorless religion of the New Age variety, they can opt to retrieve from the tradition those things which serve the present and be pro-active in seeing that their families and communities, as well as the world at large, have the opportunity to engage with the tradition of the Church. If Rahner is right about everyday mysticism as the faith stance of the postmodern person, and von Balthasar is accurate about encounter with God as key to a renewed sense of autonomy and initiative in the moral life, then MacIntrye offers a framework for understanding the process by which we understand the good to which we are called in the concrete without leaving faith out of the process.

What God demands for us is not given once and for all, but must be discerned in a process of discovery. God is involved in history, in the signs of the times. While society would say decisions in society are based on rationalistic claims alone, the faith community holds that both the head and the heart are engaged. The obedience of faith is a surrender in which a person entrusts herself or himself freely to God. Faith is made possible through a gift of the Holy Spirit. This surrender involves not just the head or the heart, but the entire personality.[58] In this encounter, one meets God, not just knowledge about God.[59] In the revelation of this encounter in faith the truth of God and the truth of being a human being are revealed together. *Gaudium et Spes* 22 says that Christ reveals the truth of every person to themselves. Faithfulness in modern society involves drawing on both faith and reason in their mutual interaction in order to know what is right.

Away from the influences of group and grid, the person in a Context C situation can slip into two patterns in making moral decisions. One is to follow a cultural ethic alone. This implies living in a culture of conflicting standards, none of which has any ultimate claim or method for grounding except that they are the personal convictions of an individual or group. This practice is grounded in the widely held view since the eighteenth century that moral beliefs are different than factual beliefs. The separation of facts and values implies that moral beliefs are simply the expressions of our approvals or disapprovals, and cannot be proved true or false. Such thinking has trickled down to the population at large, so that today it is a basic assumption. Without group or grid influence, Context C life is most susceptible to the ambiguity such a belief suggests. The person is left steeped in "emotivism," the belief that moral opinions are simply that. Others may follow a more socially oriented view that we are simply indoctrinated into a cultural system, however the end result is similar. Both views hold that right and wrong can never be grounded.[60] One is left with the need to be tolerant, to accept people have different values, and it makes little difference whether we try to resolve these differences among ourselves. The isolated life of Context C existence may lead to an acceptance that this is all that is possible.

A second option is to embrace Context C life yet with a commitment to move toward community in new ways and to retrieve from the faith tradition the perspective and convictions to deal with new issues; articulate experiences from the margins; and offer to the world new solutions to its problems. John Paul II captures the moral challenge to the situation of Context C in his focus on how Christ's redemptive mystery adds impetus to overcoming social evils as an integral part of the Christian life. John Paul II's redemptive theology is not indifferent to these concrete forms of evil in this world, nor does it advocate a flight from the world, taking up a "nothing can be done" mentality. Rather he sees confronting evil in the Christian life in a manner which goes beyond an anti-world view as fallen creation alone. His theology is more positive, based on the redemptive mode of God relating to the world. Grace rather than sin predominates.

This mode "sees the nature of the international order in the persistent struggle to bring the human oneness established in Christ to transforming historical concreteness in the relationships that actually exist among human beings and their groups."[61] Obstacles to development have to be noted, but prophetic denunciation is not enough. John Paul II claims, "the Church must strongly affirm the possibility of overcoming the obstacles which . . . stand in the way of development." And she must affirm her confidence in a true liberation "based on the Church's awareness of the divine promise, guaranteeing that our present history does not remain closed in upon itself but is open to the Kingdom of God" (SRS 47).

Context C life brings to this effort the freedom of individuals to work in their various sectors as individuals of conscience, yet to come together in new movements to sustain each other in a faith commitment and in common action for change. The language we use to talk about this effort religiously is "we listen to the Spirit." Yet such an experience is often something difficult to articulate and easy to overlook. Karl Rahner captures our normal ambivalence toward it: "It is an experience which exists, even though in the routine of ordinary life we mostly overlook it, perhaps suppress it, and do not want to admit it."[62] Yet the work of the Holy Spirit in our lives is often the core experience which sustains us in the ambiguities and darkness of living in a time of transition. We are embraced by the Spirit of God especially in those times when only this connection explains our faithfulness. Rahner depicts a few of these experiences as icons of the rest. We experience the Spirit in our failures, when we still have hope; when we take up responsibility, even though no evidence of success or advantage can be produced; when we accept death in the hope of new life; when we feel a confirmation of a life of ups and downs; when we know the judgment could be just as well stated in reverse; when we experience in a fleeting manner love, beauty, and joy, and we see these not cynically as confirmations that "the glass is half full" but as promises of the true life which underpins all else; when we experience life as bitter and disappointing, yet experience an inner strength we cannot explain or bring under control.[63] Then God is present with his liberating grace. Here we experience the Spirit as more than a part of this temporal world. We experience our meaning as human beings as deeper than the success models of postmodern society. We experience the secret passion of the saints in the mysticism of ordinary life.

From this inner life the Context C Christian uses their secular everyday abilities as well as their gifts of character and grace for the community. Rahner concludes: "We can safely say that all powers and possibilities of Christian action, as authorized, sustained and animated in the last resort by the Holy Spirit of God, are charisms, gifts of the Spirit."[64] Each person, in the routines or his or her life, experiences the call of a charism. They are often possibilities which are more than an individual with his or her limited powers and time can actually realize. Life demands that the person must makes choices; they must distinguish between options and choose one over another. However, if chosen honestly, seeking the Spirit in them, one can experience being in harmony with God's will, a desire of a disciple of Jesus. These choices are beyond the rational, but include it. Discerning them includes an awareness of whether they lead to or obstruct an experience of this harmony with the Spirit and an everyday duty. This is a harmony with the Spirit which we never appropriate, we simply seek. We can never really say we have it, nor is it ever that far from our desire. When we reflect on our desire to be faithful, is it not something of this journey, where from time to time we are given the experience of arriving at where we are heading? The Christian in a Context C situation has this opportunity for a different type of confirmation, one that is unique to the solitary dimension of Context C life, but which is also dependent on Context A life and Context B life.

The Christian community acts on values like the right to work, to participation, the inherent equality of all men and women, the right to food, clothing, and shelter, and education and health care as outgrowths of the Church's belief in the dignity of the human person. The more formal teachings of Context A life support the faith of the Context C Christian. The belief that love is worth our effort; that sacrifice is indigenous to life; that creation is for the good of all; and the belief in solidarity are values and visions held by the Church and celebrated in her liturgical life.

Church membership is linked to a value stance toward life, and is not extraneous to the Context C Christian. Without group and grid experience, Context C life lacks the clarity of Context A living, yet the personal faith of the Context C Christian sustains the local experience of Church. The Church affirms that being the disciple of Jesus Christ constantly impinges on our realm of values.[65] Christian action in the world of Context C, however, arises from a tradition of faith which provides a "way" of being in society and the world. What is revealed in the process is more than a plan of action. It transcends the life of any particular group, class, gender, or race (Context B life). Rather, it is a way of faith to God, and connected to the deepest mystery of the Church.

The search for faithfulness is never resolved. It always relies on surrender to the truth and call of God, reliance on God's mercy and care, and an investment in service of others. It requires community, commitment, and the conviction that love is worth the effort. However, as Christians, this is a way which is not new, but is the path of the disciple. The search for faithfulness is the tradition of faith. As the tradition it rests in the surety of the presence and accompaniment of the Risen Christ and His promise of its ultimate fulfillment.

Notes

1 Michael Paul Gallagher, *Clashing Symbols: An Introduction to Faith and Culture* (New York: Paulist Press, 2003), 31–33.
2 See: Cardinal Paul Poupard, "Le defi de la non-croyance et de l'indifference religieuse," *La Documentation Catholique* (May 2, 2004), 419–22.
3 Gallagher, *Clashing Symbols*, 32.
4 Lieven Boeve, *Interrupting Tradition: An Essay on Christian Faith in a Postmodern Context* (Louvain: Peeters, 2003), 148.
5 See: Edith Wyschogrod, *Saints and Postmodernism* (Chicago: The University of Chicago Press, 1990), 255.
6 Valerie Lesniak, "New Age," in *The New SCM Dictionary of Christian Spirituality*, ed. Philip Sheldrake (London: SCM Press, 2005), 460–62.
7 Gallagher, *Clashing Symbols*, 32.
8 *Jesus Christ the Bearer of the Water of Life: A Christian Reflection on the "New Age"* (2003), as quoted in Jos Moons, "The Search for an Attractive Form of Faith," *The Way*, 46, no. 4 (October 2007), 17.
9 Karl Rahner, "The Spirituality of the Church of the Future," in *Theological Investigations*, 20 (London: Darton, Longman and Todd, 1981), 148.

10 Ibid., 149.

11 See: Declan Marmion, *A Spirituality of Everyday Faith: A Theological Investigation of the Notion of Spirituality in Karl Rahner* (Westminster, MD: Christian Classics, Inc., 1985).

12 Karl Rahner, *Foundations of Christian Faith* (New York: Seabury, 1978), 54.

13 See: Patricia Carroll, "Moving Mysticism to the Center," *The Way*, 43, no. 4 (October 2004), 41–52.

14 Rahner, "The Spirituality of the Church of the Future," 150.

15 Douglas, *Natural Symbols*, 92.

16 June O'Connor, "Making a Case for the Common Good," *Journal of Religious Ethics* 30 (Spring 2002).

17 Vincent J. Miller, *Consuming Religion: Christian Faith and Practice in a Consumer Culture* (New York: Continuum, 2004).

18 James W. Fowler, *Becoming Adult, Becoming Christian: Adult Development and Christian Faith* (San Francisco: Jossey-Bass, 2000), 1–13.

19 John Paul II, *Veritatis Splendor* (Vatican City: Libreria Editrice Vaticana, 1993), no. 4.8.

20 Karl Rahner, *The Shape of the Church to Come*, trans. Edward Quinn (New York: Seabury Press, 1974).

21 Rahner, "The Spirituality of the Church of the Future," 149.

22 Ibid., 153.

23 This is another instance of the need for a new blending of an elaborated and restrictive code.

24 One wonders whether this is an aspect of the spirituality which many religious orders are living in post-Vatican times.

25 Hans Urs von Balthasar, *Elucidations*, trans. John Riches (San Francisco, Ignatius Press, 1998), 109–10.

26 See: Peter Bisson, "The Postconciliar Jesuit Congregations: Social Commitment Constructing a New World of Religious Meaning,' *Lonergan Workshop*, 19 (2007), 1–35. Bisson observes in his study of changes in the awareness at the Jesuit Congregations. It is not simply a matter of the Society's "reflecting on the quality of its engagement with the world, but on the quality of its engagement with Christ actively engaged in the world" (32).

27 J. Brian Hehir, "Personal Faith, the Public Church, and the Role of Theology," *Harvard Divinity Bulletin*, 26, no. 1, 1996.

28 Stephen Carter, *Civility: Manners, Morals, and the Etiquette of Democracy* (New York: Harper Collins, 1998), 75.

29 Cynthia Moe-Lobeda, "The Mystical Roots of Morality: Christian Ethics and the Dangerous Art of Seeing," unpublished paper given at the Society of Christian Ethics. Pittsburgh, PA (January 10, 2003).

30 Janet Ruffing, *Mysticism and Social Transformation* (Syracuse, NY: Syracuse University Press, 2001).

31 Judith A. Merkle, *From the Heart of the Church*, (Collegeville, MN, 2004), 241–44.

32 Joe Holland, "From Industrial Revolution to Electronic Revolution: The Postmodern Challenge of Catholic Social Thought in the Catholic University," 7. Available online at http://www.stthomas.edu/cathstudies/cts filetype:pdf.

33 Douglas claims, "In a complex society, networks are the minimum level at which social relations can be investigated. They are the sustaining base line of social ties from which corporate institutions rise." *Natural Symbols*, 89.

34 Joe Holland, "From the Industrial Revolution to the Electronic Revolution," 14.

35 Mary Douglas, *In the Active Voice* (London: Routledge and Kegan Paul, 1982), 209–11.

36 Christopher Steck, *The Ethical Thought of Hans Urs Von Balthasar* (New York: Crossroad, 2001), 73.

37 An Ignatian prayer process for doing this is called "graced history." See: John J. English, S.J., *Spiritual Freedom* (Chicago: Loyola University Press, 1995), 261–73.

38 Steck, *The Ethical Thought of Hans Urs Von Balthasar*, 74.

39 Ibid., 76.

40 Robert Rigali, S.J., "On Christian Ethics," *Chicago Studies* 10 (1971), 227–47.

41 Steck, *The Ethical Thought of Hans Urs Von Balthasar*, 77–79.

42 See: Tim Muldoon, "Postmodern Spirituality and the Ignatian *Fundamentum*," *The Way*, 44, no. 1 (January 2005), 88–100.

43 George Aschenbrenner, "A Consoling Companion, Faithful beyond Any Doubt," *The Way*, 46, no. 3 (July 2007), 67–83.

44 Steck, *The Ethical Thought of Hans Urs Von Balthasar*, 72.

45 See: Johann Baptist Metz, "Freedom as a Threshold Problem between Philosophy and Theology," *Philosophy Today*, 10 (Winter 1966), 271.

46 Steck, *The Ethical Thought of Hans Urs Von Balthasar*, 79.

47 The nuance in Von Balthasar's ethics is how he straddles a full divine-command ethics like Barth, and one which also takes human initiative seriously. For his distinctive stance vis-à-vis Barth, see Steck: 81–83.

48 Johann Baptist Metz, *Faith in History and Society* (New York: Seabury Press, 1980), 54.

49 Johann Baptist Metz, *Followers of Christ* (New York: Paulist Press, 1977), 40. See also his *Faith in History of Society*, 51–54.

50 Merkle, *From the Heart of the Church*, 134–46.

51 We think here of the difficulty in moral reflection to deal with something like the systemic oppression involved in institutionalized racism in the United States and its impact on public decision making. See: *Interrupting White Privilege: Catholic Theologians Break the Silence*, ed. Laurie M. Cassidy and Alex Mikulich (New York: Orbis Books, 2007).

52 After a healing, Jesus would say, "Know the Kingdom of God is upon you."

53 Johann Baptist Metz, "Political Theology," in *Encyclopedia of Theology: The Concise Sacramentum Mundi*, ed. Karl Rahner (New York: Seabury Press, 1975), 1240.

54 Gallagher, *Clashing Symbols*, 34.

55 Aladair MacIntyre, *After Virtue* (Notre Dame, IN: University of Notre Dame Press, 1981).

56 Alasdair MacIntyre, *Whose Justice? Whose Rationality?* (Notre Dame, IN: University of Notre Dame Press, 1988). Here he means tradition can change and develop.

57 See: David Hollenbach, S.J., "Tradition, Historicity, and Truth in Theological Ethics," in *Christian Ethics: Problems and Prospects*, ed. Lisa Sowle Cahill and James F. Childress (Cleveland, OH: The Pilgrim Press, 1996), 68–69.

58 Merkle, *From the Heart of the Church*, chapter 2.

59 Dulles remarks, "Without denying the historical mediation of faith, we may continue to insist that God succeeds in making himself immediately present to the human spirit, as the transcendental theologians have so lucidly shown. If this immediacy of God were allowed to be obscured . . . faith might seem to be a reaction to the historical situation rather than a response to a personal call from God."

Avery Dulles, S.J., "The Meaning of Faith Considered in Relationship to Justice," in *The Faith that Does Justice*, ed. John C. Haughey (New York: Paulist Press, 1977), 39.

60 Brian Hebblethwaite, *Ethics and Religion in a Pluralistic Age* (Edinburgh: T&T Clark, 1997), 25.

61 Johann Verstraeten, "Catholic Social Thinking as Living Tradition that Gives Meaning to Globalization as a Process of Humanization," in *Globalization and Catholic Social Thought*, ed. John A. Coleman and William F. Ryan (New York: Orbis, 2005), 42.

62 Karl Rahner, S.J., "Experience of the Holy Spirit," *Theological Investigations*, 18 (London: Darton, Longman and Todd, 1983), 195.

63 Ibid., 202–3.

64 Ibid., 208.

65 We are suggesting that the tradition of the Church to seek to be faithful to God in response to the gift of salvation encompasses its official teaching. However, through the witness of its people in ordinary life, its martyrs, its social action, community life, and sacramental life the Church also concretizes its faith in action.

Chapter 8

TAKING A POSITION: IDENTITY, ADVOCACY, AND PLURALISM

Life is full of choices. Choice as to how we connect with others is one of them. It is clear that the Church sees group life as a choice, not an inevitability.[1] The quality of this choice, not simply that it exists, has connotations for our moral lives, and a sense of faithfulness.

Revisiting a Grid-Group Analysis

Mary Douglas reminds us that individual choices have bearing on the social situation. Grid-group analysis does not suppose that the choices are predetermined, though it may be costly to act against the parameters of a particular context. In her words:

> The method allows for the cumulative effort of individual choices on the social situation itself: both can interact, the individual and the environment, and either can move, because the environment is defined to consist of all the other interacting individuals and their choices.[2]

A group is not understood to be formed or existing independently of the choice of its members. Their investment of time and energy sustains the group and marks its boundaries. If members withdraw commitment to the group, it dissolves away in time. When members act to sustain the group, its very existence serves as a powerful justification for controlling individuals.

In the case of groups marked by high-grid relationships, the one single cultural value that drives the movement toward low grid is the unique value of the individual. Since the individual is of such high value, each person is justified in reacting against constraints on his or her freedom. Conflicts therefore are solved through negotiation. Each basic starting point, the value of the group, or the value of the individual, justifies action which is to generate new life. When one wins against the other, there is a slide toward strong group or toward low grid. When each pulls against the other, the dialogue which results in society is fed by the presuppositions regarding which form of life serves best. An individual can move from one context to another; in fact, it is likely the modern person moves in and out of the logic of these contexts through a stance of "multiple belonging." Grid-group analysis then is a method of identifying cultural bias, or finding an array of beliefs locked together into relational patterns. It is fair to say that when one steps into such a pattern and acts in terms of its logic the wind is at your back. When one acts against it, the wind is in your face. The contexts in themselves appear to have no moral weight, as one being better than the other. Their moral value appears to be in what they enable, and what they constrain.

Douglas claims that individual decisions develop a collective moral conscious-ness, which actually reflects a vision of the human and his or her place in the universe. In her words:

> The action of social context, is placed on a two-dimensional map with moral judgments, excuses, complaints and shifts of interests reckoned as the spoken justifications by individuals of the action they feel required to take. As their subjective perception of the scene and its moral implications emanates from each of them individually, it constitutes a collective moral consciousness about man and his place in the universe. The interaction of individual subjects produces a public cosmology capable of being internal-ized in the consciousness of individuals.[3]

Douglas does not assume that people must act in terms of their context and its inherent logic or bias. Experiences of social change would contradict a pure sociological determination of thought. Disagreement, dissent, rebellion, organizing to change the whole context, or simply moving to a more congenial location are all possible. The goal of the group-grid method of analysis is to offer not an explanation for individual choice, but rather the "range of cosmological possibilities in which they can possibly land themselves by choosing to deal with their social problems in one way or another."

Douglas does not assume that all members, say of Context A, have all the defining features of its characteristics, but rather most of them, and in different intensities. In addition, while one can have a predominant leaning toward one classification, there can be behaviors which hold together with a dominant pat-tern, but are not characteristic of it. Finally, while we spoke of Context A as a church model, Douglas would see the Catholic Church itself as too big to exert pressure of control on an individual. Rather her focus would be on the face to face relationships which exert pressure one to another, draw the same boundaries, and accept the alignment of insiders and outsiders.

For example, the parish is the primary experience of the Church for most people, extending perhaps to a diocesan consciousness. "The strongest effects of group are to be found where it incorporates a person with the rest by implicating them together in common residence, shared work, shared resources and recreation, and by exerting control over marriage and kinship."[4] In an age of technology and mobility with fluid boundaries and communication across distances, along with the fact that the modern person might belong to multiple groups at the same time, Douglas's alternative criterion is useful. She asks, at what level do people have to explain to one another why they behave as they do? By extension, it seems fair to conclude, that the same can be said for professional boundaries, women's consciousness groups in Context B, as well as networks of reciprocity in Context C.

In contrast, an individualist environment can be measured by changes in the direction of increasing autonomy given to the individual. A high-grid situation will afford a person a substantial degree of autonomy; that is, freedom in terms of how a person disposes of time, goods, selects companions or collaborators, chooses clothes and food. Autonomy joins with control and competition in this analysis, as a different social experience comes from having personal autonomy along with control over the autonomy of another. Added together one has a "universe of independent autocrats each controlling a servile population . . ."[5] This can be done because a low-grid situation is subject to fewer society-wide rules. The individualists must negotiate their relationships with people of somewhat equal power. In a competitive individualist environment, all rules will be negotiable, or people simply break negotiated rules when it is advantageous to do so.

Douglas concludes that if you belong to no group, you are controlled from someplace else. Control comes from groups from which you are excluded or from the blind forces generated by competition in a low-grid situation.

Context D Life

Context D represents a radically different response to the complexity of today: a community formed on withdrawal from others. People respond to the chaos of our times through a search for identity in a group. This is a weak-grid/strong-group community culture, or an enclave. The social experience of the individual is constrained by the external boundary maintained by the group against outsiders. Members gain their whole life support from the group as such. The grid is weak because the members only relate to each other, not to people outside the group. In fact, the more a member relates to people outside the group, the weaker are the controls the group exerts. Individual behavior is subject to controls exercised in the name of the group.

The desire to insulate the tight group from the surrounding world renders a low priority given to horizontal relationships between people, or the grid. Allegiance is really to an authority. Scope for individual initiative is narrow.[6] Even though this kind of group might present itself to itself as egalitarian, group membership is accompanied by "rules" about non-conformity of any kind. There is a danger of authoritarianism that discourages individual creativity or freedom. The absence of scope for individual initiative and its certain suspicion toward non-members characterize this group.

Context D life is different than Context A because the content of the authority structure is not a system of belief itself, upheld more objectively by a hierarchy of people, who are also subject to its laws. In a Context D situation there is a lack of coherence of an objective system; rather laws can be formed by strong personalities in it or by the needs of the group for boundaries of identity. While this is not Douglas's insight, it seems this identity could also be stipulated by a "cause," but attention to a cause under specific conditions which will be discussed below. It is difficult to resolve differences in Context D groups, and they tend to simply go underground: ". . . only the sanction of withdrawal of privileges of membership and resulting expulsion from or fission of the group can be effectively applied."[7] People simply leave the group and begin another one more to their liking. Context D social control is equivalent, according to Douglas, to the infant in the world of parents. It is not the objective rules, but the subjective demands of parental interpretations that shape the rules. It is for this reason that this group seems to be given less attention in Douglas's work, as it is a default group, one that cannot be sustained over a long period of time. In a child's life further socialization mitigates rules and the child develops a center of self as they are socialized. In the life of the group, what might begin as a Context D relationship could mature into another form. As it stands, the future of a Context D situation is not positive: ". . . the group will tend to be small and hopes for its long persistence disappointed; it will be subject to fission."[8] Douglas's description of Context D life raises the question. Why? Why would someone want to be part of such a group? If we search our experience of groups, we see they can be healthy and unhealthy, non-dialogical and open to others, peaceful and violent, destructive and agents of change. Let us explore some of these variations in order to grasp the challenges Context D life presents, and its own trajectory of conversion.

Fundamentalist Groups

Fundamentalist groups are one variation of Context D life. George De Schrijver sees fundamentalist groups as reactions to the pressures of modernity. De Schrijver draws on the work of Hans Urs von Balthasar to comment on "new religious movements" of a certain type. These hold on to a traditionalist concept of tradition, as well as strive for occupying power positions in the Church and in society at large.[9]

In contrast to groups who engage in commitments of solidarity to create a more humane world, these groups try to move the world forward by holding on to a few abstract, fixed principles. The former try from within to experience how the various dimensions of historical reality are interconnected and how they influence each other. The latter try to mold the world through strictly applying principles of revelation, principles as such which cannot be found in the secular world. The former tend to bring the natural and supernatural closer together, seeing in the people of good will, even those outside the Church, who seek to make ethical decisions, an image of God's love. The latter tend to be fearful and constrained, and find a closed domain of the supernatural pitted against a closed domain of the secular.

Marks which distinguish these groups from others in the Church include their self-righteousness. This is expressed in a lust for power, clinging on to tradition, and rigid system building.[10] Another mark is that they tend to place themselves in the center of the Church as a more pure elite, or against the movement of the whole, like in a rejection of Vatican II. The characteristic of Context D life, of moving against others, is shown in these groups as they adapt an inflexible attitude toward others, seeing themselves as the true custodians of the faith. Others are viewed as backward, who through a simple faith try to respond to the changed conditions around them.

Von Balthasar states that whenever there have been changes in the Church, groups emerge which are uneasy with the direction taken by the Council, and want to return to what was done before. Money is usually given to these groups by the wealthy because these groups serve their interests: maintenance of old privileges and lifestyles.[11] What was so attractive about previous ways of living? Modern society makes it difficult to opt for one single encompassing worldview or belief system, as it appeared in pre-modern times. This results in groups being formed which try to take one insight into reality, and fit everything in life into it. The one ideological perspective becomes the integrating point of the whole. Everything is viewed through the single lens. These groups are not just formed on pre-modern ideals; they can be created around a "modern" concept, like ecology or equal rights. To the degree that this one all-encompassing idea is used to explain all of life they might sound modern, but they remain pre-modern. On the other hand, a more conservative position may make a selection of points in traditional doctrine and make them the litmus test of orthodoxy. Both responses absolve an individual from facing pluralism and finding their place before it. The strain of having to adapt to new situations, make new choices and decide appropriate responses is removed. The energy it takes to engage in continuous discernment, trial and error and openness to others and new situations seems not worth the effort. Better is to cling to a practice of the Christian life as they have always understood it. From our perspective, what might look like an effort to be faithful can be a flight from its responsibilities. We need to note that Context D groups also differ from Context B groups, in that the latter are based on similarity in race, ethnic background, gender, or profession — grid relationships which convey expectations of how to be in this world. While Context B groups might also engage in advocacy in society, they will do so from the common element which unites them.

The mark of refusal to dialogue, however, marks the fundamentalist type of Context D group. Instead of facing the new circumstances in which to live their Christianity, which will require some negotiation and cooperation with modern values, these groups will rest on a fixed point from the past or try to reduce a complex reality to a limited set of clear positions. Modern values such as human autonomy, accountability, assuming responsibility, respect for human rights, and dealing with oppression challenge the identity of these groups of Christians, who have located their identity in a self-construct of nostalgia or selected values. The modern challenge for Christians is to live their faith in the face of the challenges of the times and to witness to others of its relevance and meaning. This call to inculturate faith is interpreted differently by these groups. Fundamentalists live in a construct which is their own. Some will even reject teaching of the Pope, and return to teachings of previous popes who reflect their own foundations of certainty.[12] In terms of our description of Context D life, the personalized dimension of constructing a vision of the Christian life is not there. Rather, individuals will take on an interpretation of the group, either generated by a strong leader, or a cluster of factors in response to the need to insulate themselves from others. The use of hermeneutics, principles of interpretation which might help translate values from the past to situations of the present, is absent. Tradition needs to be interpreted in new times if it is to be a living tradition. Instead of "seeing God in all things" or "reading the signs of the times," fundamentalists prefer top-down thinking of a hierarchical kind which focuses on essentials of the faith without relating them to the conditions of modern times. They are closed to others, who they view as evil. Simultaneously they credit some in their circle with a direct relationship to God. Through this relationship, the voice of God comes through them, a voice they uncritically accept.

Modern life requires a balancing of the tradition and the communication of its relevance. The Church can try to be so relevant that it loses its identity, or it can so affirm its tradition (without relating it to the times) that it becomes irrelevant. However, these conservative-progressive leanings do not concern fundamentalists. Their need is to promote their own identity and that of their movement. They do not engage in dialogue because they perceive that they have the truth. They engage in a monologue with the world. Fundamentally, they do not trust the world, nor trust themselves to find their way in it.[13] A faithful Christian will be able to find good also in those who stand outside his or her circle.

The Enclave Culture

The dynamics of Context D life enter into what sociological research calls the enclave culture. Emmanuel Sivan claims that leadership emerges in traditional religious organizations through the impulse to protect the organization from losing many members. If the world outside the enclave is attractive, it provides material and social temptations of a wider community which enjoys a type of prestige, material security; the need for boundaries is heightened. If the outer world offers all these attractive rewards, the enclave must offer something in comparison. Since it cannot compete on a material level with the outside world, it offers moral rewards.[14] The enclave stresses the voluntary character of its membership, by asserting that people are members because they have a higher calling. Their membership is based on being set apart for a holy cause. This means that the people outside the enclave are perceived in sharp contrast to those within it. While of the same tradition, the others are inferior members of it. The enclave sees itself as the rightful representative of the tradition, while the others occupy a place from "weaker" to "apostates," depending on the group. The outside is polluted, contagious, and dangerous.[15] It is best for members to stay away from those outside, or to engage them and bring them into the true fold; the latter even to the point of violence. Members in the group are valued, but distinctions or uniqueness among them is downplayed.

Sometimes modernity itself is seen as the enemy to the enclave. In American fundamentalism there are attacks on the social-service, self-help "me-generation," and the ideas of secular humanists who advocate reliance on human judgment and cultural pluralism. Those who hold beliefs which are counter to the enclave's proposed boundaries and identity are thought to be the enemy. A viable enclave wields efficient group constraints capable of having its members conform to the same public norms. This gives them a unique social space.[16]

The group can impose heavy constraints on the time, space, and behavior of its members. These come not from grid expectations but from authority either in the form of ideas gleaned from a perceived Golden Age of the tradition or from charismatic leaders. Authority is usually vested in a small number of individuals, or one per community. These leaders are established through charisma; formal training may or may not enter into the dynamic. Perception of virtue, decision-making ability and mastery of the tradition sets one person apart from the rest. Usually such authority is unquestioned. Yet the members of the group are perceived as equals, as their membership is always purely voluntary.

One might ask, why would someone want to join an enclave? Sivan suggests that people who find themselves in a social context that requires subordination are the most likely to be attracted to what we are calling a Context D situation. Individuals living in such a context in modern society are constrained, in an inegalitarian manner. They are told how to behave according to their rank, a place in a business or social class, yet they do not enjoy the protection and privileges of group membership. Sivan remarks: "They are manipulated, are peripheral to all decisions that may determine their destiny, and have a limited scope for forming alliances."[17] Passive, isolated, and conformist, they feel alienated. American commuters living in suburbs can feel stuck in a midlevel job in a large corporation. Migrants to large urban areas can feel displaced because their old reference groups have been disrupted. College students in large universities can feel anonymous in congested and understaffed universities where they feel "like a number." Anxious about the future, whether the job market will give them a place after a considerable investment in an expensive education, college students are prime candidates for an enclave experience. The group conveys to them an identity they cannot get in their daily lives.

The Lifestyle Enclave

Identity in a community is based on its ability to be a place of manifold engagement.[18] True community is an inclusive whole where people live interdependently with one another, sharing both a private and a public life. In community, one generation initiates the next into a way of life. As a center of manifold engagement, community gives each member a significant place in day by day participation. Manifold engagement creates important bonds that tie the members together and gives them a sense of identity in the group. In the terms of this book, such community would be closer to a Context A environment.

Robert Bellah describes a form of Context D life which emerges from consumer culture: the lifestyle enclave.[19] It is often mistaken for community today. In contrast to a community, which involves both private and public life, a lifestyle is segmental and based on similarity. A lifestyle enclave shares the "separate" over against quality of Context D life. First, it deals only with a segment of the individual's life, leisure and consumption. Second, it includes only those who share this level of lifestyle. "The different, those with other lifestyles, are not necessarily despised. They may be willingly tolerated. But they are irrelevant or even invisible in terms of one's own lifestyle enclave."[20] The changing nature of work in American society has led people to seek a place more in a profession than as a leading citizen, for example, in a community. Social status and class come to depend less on local communities and more on the national occupational system.

In contrast to ethnic communities that tried to reproduce a total institutional complex which provided for most areas of life for its local members, professional lifestyles make people less dependent on local communities. People can withdraw and create association with others according to selected similarities and preferences. "Youth culture" itself is based on patterns of recreation, dress, music, and internet networks, and are shared by young people across class boundaries.

A lifestyle enclave can be understood as a form of collective support in an otherwise individualistic culture. Selfhood or identity is affirmed there, based on the perceived standards of success, with others who share these standards. However, in a society where the self is entirely self-constructed, the self as well as the enclave appears to have a shallow foundation. In Bellah's words:

> What appears to be a self is merely a series of social masks that change with each successive situation. An absolute autonomous self and a self determined completely by the social situation do not, then turn out to be opposites.[21]

In the traditional enclave of the fundamentalist nature, and the consumer-oriented enclave of the lifestyle enclave, there is an eclipse of self where definitions from the group provide an identity over against either a hostile world, or one of "others" who do not reinforce one's identity based on an escalating scale of consumer standards.

Groups of Advocacy and Solidarity

Context D groups, however, can move from the strict boundaries of an enclave to a more outward-looking perspective. If they are open to needs beyond themselves, they can become groups of advocacy. In fact, in the presence of strong religious beliefs which are reinforced in an intense way, these groups are often drawn into politics. First let us examine a positive way this can happen, then look at the pitfalls of such an endeavor.

Authors of the Fundamentalism Project originating in the University of Chicago detected four patterns of fundamentalist interaction with the world. They are the world conqueror; the world transformer; the world creator; and the world renouncer.[22] The authors hold that intense focus on enclave existence need not remain static. Rather a group can move outward. The reasons an enclave was formed in the first place can be transcended, and instead of a stance of over and against others, the group can work to translate its religious values into the humanitarian needs of the society.

One moment is this movement is *withdrawal in order to connect*. We hear echoes of a call to Christians to be a world transformer and world creator in

John Paul II's call to solidarity. Solidarity, the readiness to accept one's share in the community, and opposition, the capacity to work toward a better realization of the common good in community, are both virtues which build up community. Both require dialogue which is a process of discernment and judgment wherein the community seeks the truth and acts together with others in realizing it.[23] This call to dialogue challenges a static Context D life which embraces no dialogue with others as a signature of its identity and a way to reinforce its boundaries.

Withdrawal to Connection

Withdrawal from society is not foreign to the Christian life, as for centuries people have sought the desert as an alternative context in which to know and worship God. "You shall love the Lord, your God, with all your heart, with all your being, with all your strength, and with all your mind" (Lk. 10.27). However, withdrawal in Context D life can mimic both the unhealthy and healthy forms it has taken in the history of Christian spirituality. In the early Church, people fled to the desert for many reasons, among them the judgment that Roman society was so corrupt that it was not a place where one could live the Christian life. Going to the desert today, religiously, not geographically, withdrawing from whatever is perceived as distracting one from the Christian life, can be expressed in Context D life, for some. One can take on the group identity as an expression of this withdrawal and a new seriousness in concrete form. However, traditionally withdrawal is spiritually healthful, usually as a place or time of transition. When the struggle of the withdrawal is over, the desert is transformed, and no longer exists. "The desert and the parched land will exult; the steppe will rejoice and bloom. They will bloom with abundant flowers, and rejoice with joyful song" (Isa. 35.1-2).

It is possible, through the focus of a Context D group, that a Christian can express a need to pull back from society and gain some *critical distance* to live the Christian life more fully. The group itself can stimulate or express this desire. However, when the withdrawal becomes an end in itself, the Christian mimics people who have gone before who have hid in situations of withdrawal from the commitments necessary to be faithful in their respective societies. No group can express our personal response to God and our acceptance of God's salvation. Such groups become the same empty shells as lifestyle enclaves, where an absolute, autonomous self hides in a group instead of becoming a deeper self in Christ. Instead they seek to be a self-determined completely by the social situation. The personal identity needed for true faithfulness is escaped in the false identity of being defined in terms of whom one is over and against. Only extreme situations would merit an over-against behavior toward society as an expression of Christian faithfulness. Healthy withdrawal, modeled on Jesus' withdrawal to pray, always contains Jesus' own mission, for which it is a preparation. This model of Christian discipleship is exemplified in the season of Lent as a preparation for baptism and a full life in Christ in mission.

John Paul II reflects this model of spirituality in his caution that Catholic Social action not only has the task to condemn actual injustices in the light of an adequately understood concept of human dignity, but must also proclaim a meaningful new future (SRS 42). This new future includes coming up with constructive proposals to remedy situations and to work toward them with others. He offers a rule of discernment to be used in making choices between concrete options in society.[24]

Hence a transformed understanding of Context D life is to facilitate the moral posture of standing against culture as a moment to stand for a value. This has traditionally been the motive for withdrawal from society in the Christian life, and can be retrieved in modern society through the support of groups of identity as Context D life prescribes.

From Purity to Mediations

"Withdrawal" characteristics of Context D life can also be expressed in the theological method of the group. When addressing concerns which are a matter of public policy, there can be a move from Scripture to policy, without passing through the public discourse and culturally mediated understandings of the problem which are open to public debate. When the democratic process is avoided and the possibility of arriving at socially shared visions of alternatives is not valued, the shadow side of Context D life is in evidence. It is one thing not to find common ground in the public arena; it is another thing never to intend to look for it. If the identity of the group is based on a perception of others as "lost," then openness to anything they might have to offer to a situation will not be present. When this occurs there can be a refusal to frame one's position in terms that can understood beyond the circle of the initiating group.

There are times when an over-against stance around a public question is needed. Brian Hehir claims that "standing against" as well as "standing with" others is part of a pedagogical prophetic ministry in the spirit of this model.[25] For instance, public policy formation in military, bioethical and sexual areas in the U.S. is requiring that the Church take more counter-cultural stances. Commenting on a growing state in American society where there is a diminishment of the common ground of shared perspectives into which to integrate Catholic principles and positions, Hehir predicts a "Mennonite future" for the Church.

How shall we engage the society and culture? Hehir reminds us that the document on the Church in the modern world, *Gaudium et Spes*, seeks a balance between compliance with society in all cases, and a constant being against society. It rejects the notion that the Church must inevitably be in constant and permanent opposition and conflict with the world. It also rejects the notion that the Church should be dominated or directed by the world. Rather the Church's relationship to the world is dialectical. It involves shared objectives and common ground, yet will always entail some conflict and opposition to the world. The fulfillment of this dialectical relationship is sustained by dialogue with the world.[26] Dialogue assumes the Church learns from the world and also witnesses to it. Context D life can be one vehicle in the Church through which this dialogue takes place. However, to do so requires the group to move beyond its group's tendencies.

Context D groups do not speak for the Church, but can arise from the Church or through collaboration with other movements in society. An example of this would be the Peace Movement, of which Pax Christi is a Catholic expression. Groups in Context A tend to officially represent the Church and operate through its sponsorship. There is a difference in Church groups between people in Context A who adopt a prophetic stance and people in Context D whose identity depends on being over and against. The fingerprint of such identity is its non-dialogical tone. Groups themselves would need to acknowledge that hostility to others actually functions as an element of their identity, and accept the challenge to form their identity on something better. The trajectory of conversion in Context D life is dialogue, inter-group, inter-cultural, and inter-religious. Context A groups could also examine whether they are operating out of Church standards of dialogue, or have slipped into the dynamics of unhealthy Context D.

What then might Hehir mean by the Church adopting a Mennonite future? Here he is not speaking of the Church taking an over-against stance because of needs of its own identity. It is taking such a stance because of current conditions in American culture. Hehir reflects that the Church has functioned in the United States traditionally under the conviction that large sections of its social teaching and social policy could be shared beyond the community of faith. The Church traditionally has adopted a natural law perspective. However, when it brings this perspective to the public realm it seeks a common ground of conviction about human flourishing it can share broadly in the public realm. The Church does not get to its interpretation of the natural law in society by subtraction of faith and revelation. For Catholics, natural law interpretation happens within the Catholic community and is developed in the tradition. Dialogue with others in society arises from a stance of standing in the Church yet seeking a common ground on social, political and economic issues, as well as sharing moral wisdom on bioethical and sexual issues.

When Christians search with others for the common good in society, they have to look both to some objectivity of the good and a concomitant societal consensus about public goods and the institutional relationships necessary for human flourishing.[27] The cultural change today is that on some issues, the distance between the Church and the public agenda has widened and the Church finds itself in a defensive position, claims Hehir: "Not only differences in principle, but also the ability of Catholic health care and social service to function effectively and with institutional integrity are at stake."[28] Hehir goes on to say it is still possible for the Church to enter into socio-political, domestic, and foreign policy debates, but it is important for it to judge this possibility on an issue by issue basis. Such judgment needs to be made before a strategy and policy position is formed. A coherent Catholic strategy can be maintained even while facing the necessity of taking a defensive stance on some issues. Hehir cautions, however, that this is not a defensive stance on all issues, as a Context D identity would dictate. "Coherence lies in using Catholic assumptions but recognizing that 'standing against' as well as 'sharing with' others is part of the pedagogical-prophetic ministry."[29] "Standing against" therefore is a moment in "standing with" in Hehir's analysis. Standing against is not the way Catholicism has usually viewed its relationship with civil society.

Those who enter into a Context D life who have ceased to turn solely within can express this. F. Schussler Fiorenza reminds us: "The interrelation among the notions of equal rights, solidarity, and common welfare is not simply a formal logical or ethical interrelations, but it is an interrelation historically rooted in a religious tradition and history with their vision of the individual's value in relation to a community and to God."[30] This tradition is not just in ideas, but in movements and actions in society which witness to these values. At times a Context D response is a possible avenue to express this when a Context A response is not.

Approaching Pluralism

Context D life, which becomes an expression of fundamentalism, faces the problem of a faithful life by a withdrawal that disengages it from the problems of modern day life. By thinking and acting in categories of absolutes and eternal truths, and through the posture of exclusivity, it fails to mediate those truths to a wider world because it fails to relate them to the common ground of humanity it shares with others. Faithfulness today requires the energies and ingenuities of human beings to work toward a better future in that world that believers share with non-believers, the *saeculum*. There is no disengagement from the problems of history. The fact of our world today is that another world, not the world of the Kingdom, is in place to name our collective future. A world of the homogenization of globalization, the violence of nuclear war and its links to terrorism, the erosion of standards to judge human rights violations, the trafficking of human beings, or the threat of ecological disaster — these are real evils which will rob people of their possibility for human flourishing if not checked. They inculcate the spiritual evil which an unconscious fundamentalism flees in its drive for the absolute. Answers to complex human problems are often not clear, while the drive for the clarity of black and white thinking is characteristic of a fundamentalist posture. Often societal problems are solved in small steps, rather than in once and for all solutions. Having the answer before one meets the reality translates to no need for dialogue to get a deeper understanding of reality and the mystery permeating it. Nor is dialogue needed to become more alert to all the values involved in a situation and their conflicts. The Church stands for deeply held convictions. The issue here is how those convictions penetrate the secular society.

In order to be a group who can be transformative, two extremes have to be avoided. First, the problem being faced cannot be defined through social scientific analysis alone. People of faith do not rely solely on sociological, economic, or political data to name the reality.[31] This data does give information regarding the complex relationships involved in the problem and can alert people to aspects of a situation which might go unnoticed. However, judgments have to be made regarding the correspondence between the data gathered, its interpretation, and Christian values. Judgments have to be made as to what data will be taken seriously. From what perspective is this analysis given; does it explain what is working in a situation or what is not working? For instance, a functionalist analysis explains how the disparate factors actually work together to function as well as possible in a particular situation. Such descriptions often cover up the conflicts and real problems the marginalized, the poor, and the working class have, as a situation might work well for some and be difficult for others. Awareness of the selectivity involved in such analysis has spurred the Church to adopt an "option for the poor" not just in its religious conclusions about a situation, but in its selection of what data to use in framing the problem. The Church asks how the situation appears through the eyes of those who do not profit from it. Here the question of truth enters in. Christians ask, does this analysis reflect the whole truth, or just the truth of the status quo, which confirms that nothing further needs to be done?

Another extreme is to simply reiterate verbatim a stance in Scripture or Church belief in the public domain and to expect its meaning will be both obvious and capable of meeting the concerns of alternate rationalities which are used to frame a public debate. A literal rendering of the text or dogma is deemed sufficient to be faithful, without analyzing what God-human relationship this passage or belief questions or affirms, or what behavior it asks of us now in this situation in the Church or society. Another form of this fundamentalism is to seek a correspondence with a scriptural text; one speaks it purely in terms of a person's private faith understanding, without hermeneutically linking its meaning to the cultural values of the times, which have bearing on one's perception of the situation. One desires unmediated truth in a world where truth is always mediated.[32] This is not the spiritual connection which coming before God in order to receive a sense of what really matters, or is absolute, as von Balthazar described, connotes.

Hehir suggests that in some cases we as the Church are not able in the public arena to find sufficient common ground to enter into fruitful policy formation. In these cases, we seek to share moral wisdom in the debate, in the midst of taking a defensive position to hold the line in a policy direction.[33] However, the inability to speak Catholic principles and positions in a language of the historical realities that all people share will not bring them to the table of public debate.[34]

The theological gaze that a mystical insight contributes is not just subjective. It allows us to view a concrete situation in terms of grace or sin, how its concrete appearance relates to the order of creation and redemption, not just for ourselves, but for others. It challenges us to examine our position before God, who loves us, as well as our neighbor, and opens us to intellectual, affective, moral, and religious conversion. However, this gaze, while always personal, is also mediated to us through openness to the concrete other in our lives.[35] Without dialogue, immersion, option for those who stand outside the circle of inclusion in a situation, it is hard to verify that it is God on whom we look, for God is love.

The Option for Solidarity before Pluralism

We began this chapter with the insight that we choose to join groups. However, we do so in a situation of pluralism, unlike those of the past who practiced Catholicism through special forms of Catholic organizations in society and a monolithic approach to Catholic life and doctrine.[36] After Vatican II, Catholics moved into the mainstream in American society; their identity was no longer formed in the Catholic ghettoes and parallel style of society marked by the 1950s. Catholic identity had to be continually negotiated and re-expressed. What it meant to be a Catholic could no longer just be given; it had to be negotiated with influences beyond the boundaries of the Catholic Church and their subsequent integration into Catholic life and practice.[37] By Vatican II, Catholics in the First World lived in a pluralistic society. Pluralism suggests that a variety of viewpoints, explanations or perspectives are offered as accounting for the same reality.[38] However, pluralism is not an absolute value in life as it can generate relativism, the attitude that one truth is as good as another, and that there is no truth to be pursued. Rather, pluralism has to be held in tension with other values which function in a communal situation to respect the dignity of persons and enable optimal participation.[39] When pluralism gives way to relativism, there are no means to mediate between your truth and my truth. However, in practice, the human community does have to mediate between "truths" and make decisions which affect its common welfare.

The challenge of politics in a pluralistic world is to settle disputes regarding what vision of life, whose needs, and what concerns will be included in a public consensus. No one group in a pluralistic society will have the complete answer to societal problems, including the religious community. Paul VI made this clear for Catholics: there are no Catholic answers to social problems (PP 81–86), the Church needs to unite with all people of good will, government authorities, and people of learning to work toward solutions to world problems. Context D life in its positive form can be a vehicle to pursue the compelling truth, the truth needed for the common good at this time.

It is also a truth that represents a good which calls us out of ourselves. It is not just a good which concerns our perfection.[40] Rather it is a good to be done. Often if it is a public good, a good which deals with the welfare of others, it can be practiced best with others, or through communal or political action.[41] The Church and its members can become better as they interact in society. We remember that in the U.S. the race movement, the peace movement, the feminist movement, did not begin in the Church, but the Church entered into these new movements in dialogue, support, and critique. The Church can both learn from society and contribute to it its moral wisdom.

A fact, however, of a modern individualistic and pluralistic culture is that there is no automatic movement from a life of self-fulfillment, as defined by the culture, to an act of solidarity with others either to witness to the truth or to join them in their efforts to transform their lives. Culture suggests human success is a type of upward mobility where one moves farther and farther away from one's neighbors. Their concerns impinge less and less on one's world.[42] Yet the person is dependent and interdependent, rational and a symbol-using animal, claims Catholic philosopher Alasdair MacIntyre.[43] It is possible that joining a group of advocacy or concern, which is counter-intuitive in the culture, is a symbolic act whereby a person in faith makes a statement counter to this cultural stance.

These groups of advocacy receive their identity directly from the radically social nature of the human, which an individualistic culture passes over.

The action of solidarity with others therefore must be chosen. If it is simply another act to prop up a feeble identity, it will be an act of self-identification over against others, as in an unconverted Context D life. However, if it is an act of self-emptying in order to move toward others, it is done in the imitation of Christ. John Paul II asserts that the specific Christian dimension of such action is a solidarity that overcomes fragmentation caused by sin (SRS 40). Going beyond the secular language of rights and equality, John Paul II uses theological language to point to the ultimate mystery that encompasses such Christian action. One's neighbor is "the living image of God the Father." Being all under God brings a new criterion to interpret the world (SRS 40.3). "Beyond human and natural bonds, already so close and so strong, there is discerned in the light of faith a new model of the unity of the human race, which must ultimately inspire our solidarity" (SRS 40.3). This unity is not only horizontal (in our terms of Context D life), urging a fragmented global world to a new unity, but also is a "reflection of the intimate life of God" and what Christians mean by "communion." Such communion is expressed in those things which move Context D life to a more altruistic identity, gratuity, forgiveness, and reconciliation. When Context D life is inward-looking, violent and unable to dialogue, it lacks the quality of movement toward communion which is its path to conversion.

Such action of Context D life can be interpreted in John Paul II's terms as sacrament: "This specifically Christian communion, jealously preserved, extended and enriched with the Lord's help, is the soul of the Church's vocation to be a "'sacrament,' in the sense already indicated" (SRS 40.3). This sacramental dimension of Christian faithfulness is not simply a luminous symbol of God's love; it is also an efficacious presentation of God's love to others. The efficacy of the sacramental activity of Christians is not such as to make other recognize God's love in action. It is a true human presentation of God's redeeming love, which invites others to recognize and receive that same love.[44] Groups of solidarity witness not only to the miracle in modern society that people can act beyond themselves, but they also witness through the quality of their efficacy in representing their concern in the public realm. These can be dimensions of faithfulness in the Christian life now possible in our times.

The Church depends on the world, and lives in the world. It needs other contexts of life, economy, government, educational system, agriculture, the arts, and more for its material well-being. Robin Lovin remarks: "No context can provide all that it needs to maintain its distinctive goods. It makes claims on other contexts to survive."[45] However, the Church also has a unique contribution to other contexts. It advocates an option for the poor, a priority of care for the basic needs of members of society, rather than allowing the power relations of the group alone to set whose needs are met. It fosters a type of participatory justice, that is, it enables those without voice to have some real chances to have their needs represented in the mix from which political consensus is reached. Context D groups can play a large role here, either through solidarity with those seeking to have their voice heard, or through fostering in these groups themselves ways of enablement. In the realm of these public debates, the Church is a context among others. As one voice in the democratic process it cannot participate in the larger process of claims and counter-claims which makes choices in society and sets direction for the future if it is unwilling to dialogue with those who challenge or even oppose its assumptions. If it does so, it will be marginalized from public debate. Here Context D groups might be early conversation partners in public debate and bring to Context A church presence the experience and wisdom they have learned through their investment. Context D groups can locate the Church close to the ground on social issues, while Context A groups, especially at national and regional levels, often provide more comprehensive study papers and lobbying efforts to shape issues both domestic and global. For instance, documents on globalization have been issued by the bishops of Asia, Canada, Spain, the Philippines, and Brazil; they have also come from interregional conferences of bishops in Africa, the Americas, and Europe.[46]

The Church as a major religious voice has a unique contribution to the public debates which shape concrete life across the globe. Religious voices can hold out to the world the message of the Kingdom: "Another world is possible." They can think of this other world concretely, both in terms of root metaphors and overarching worldviews which have concrete ramifications for the shaping of public policy. Instead of the cultural view of the world order, there is a clash of civilizations; religions of the world can hold out the possibility of dialogue among civilizations.[47] However, negative developments across the globe suggest that social forces aligned to globalization act to ensure that movements to constrain their efforts by structures responsive to the public good are pulled back. Richard Falk imagines a new clash across the world: "This confrontation can also be schematically simplified as an encounter between globalization-from-above (transnational corporations/banks/states) and globalization-from-below (transnational civic initiatives/women/indigenous peoples/human rights/environmental activists."[48]

Falk contends that progressive movements of resistance will not have sufficient political leverage, or will be reduced to either local influence alone or dismissed as "fringe movements" unless they are strengthened by religious commitments and by support from important sectors of the organized religious community. He admits that religion can take a constructive or destructive reaction to the challenges of modernity and the constraints of an economic secular view of the human future. It can be a potent force in human affairs by proclaiming a relevance to the concerns of the public sphere as well as the private sphere. However, it can also disclose a range of regressions which makes its opposition to secularism "a terrifying descent into repression and violence."

Falk contends that the relevance of religion cannot be separated from its persistence in human consciousness and its role throughout history in the social construction of human nature.[49] Among its contributions are its potential to take suffering seriously; civilizational resonance or ability to mobilize masses; an ethos of solidarity; normative horizons; belief in the transformative capacities of ideas, sacrifice and spiritual energy; a sense of limits and human fallibility; a sense of human identity not given solely by the state; and a belief in the possibility of reconciling science, reason, and spirituality.[50]

The Kenosis of Community

The asceticism of belonging to a group is actually counter-intuitive in modern society. If one joins a group, he or she is not "free" to do whatever he or she wants. When freedom is considered an absolute value, giving up any facet of freedom does not make sense in a cultural understanding of life. To act in solidarity with others, one must consciously set aside some legitimate freedoms, the freedom for instance to express an issue in one's own terms, in order to take up the greater truth which the group represents. Advocacy means the needs of the other transcend the pleasure of an individual Christian to certain forms of self-expression, in order to say the one thing necessary, for the sake of political impact. The person may need to "withdraw" from one set of associations, and "connect" with another. A person may need to write letters, march in rallies, participate in various forms of political action, not necessarily because the strategy is to his or her liking, but because of the value of group action. Here a mature person can enter into a group as an expression of Christian discipleship.

Groups which are non-dialogical cannot bear the Christian message to the whole, nor offer their interpretation of it to the process of public debate. Groups whose ultimate identity is simply to be over and against may be caught more in a web of self-righteousness than in a network of care. Context D life can go either way. Groups of resistance during the Second World War were certain that the evil they were confronting demanded a total over-against effort to oppose. Whether this exists in current modern society is a matter of discernment.

The Banality of Good and Evil

The banality of evil is a phrase used by Hannah Arendt during her observations of the Eichmann trials for Holocaust crimes. As an analytic tool, it refers to the ease with which normal people are drawn into doing unbelievable evil. The banality of evil has been construed to mean three things: evil which is normal, prosaic, or matter of fact; evil which is rationalized as good because it is obedient or because it serves a larger purpose; and evil which is trite, hackneyed, or stale. Evil appears as "good" because its immorality is cloaked through rationalization or routine. However, the evil itself is so horrendous it ruptures the very coherence of our language about human beings, relationships, and the meaning of life.[51] Abuse, for example, may not be named for the evil it is, rather it is perceived as moral, prosaic, matter-of-fact, and even rationalized as a greater good.[52] John Perry alerts us to how torture in a post-9/11 society relies on constructs or narratives that allow us to harm the "stranger." The banality of evil is shown by how people become desensitized to their actions, how declaring war or any "special situation" loosens checks and balances, and how bureaucracy can separate us from moral responsibility for actions and the violence we can allow in our own institutions. We diffuse responsibility, we demonize victims, we advance a just cause to explain our violence and we cloak violence in professional mandates.[53]

The banality of evil is fed in part by a false sense of obedience. People have a deep need to be part of a hierarchy and can have a natural penchant to do what they are told. This is stimulated especially if they are relieved of their responsibility by legitimate authority figures. When Bernard Haring wrote his text on moral theology shortly after the Council, the memory of the placid obedience he observed in Germany during the Hitler regime spurred him to focus on a new sense of responsibility in Catholic ethics.

Good, however, can also be banal. Clichés, stock phrases, adherence to convention, and standardized codes of expression and conduct have the socially recognized function of protecting us against the challenge to think, what is really good in this situation?[54] Yet the above also codify a common understanding of the good that has helped society through the centuries. We need to honor the ways the common life of the Church has been woven with the temporal ways in which the good is understood and realized in a genuinely contingent world.[55] It is when these stock ideas and traditional understandings are used in situations where they replace a thoughtful search for the true good that they become banal. Postmodern life and its criticisms of evils which have been perpetrated in the name of the good have moved away from a vision of ethics where the "good" is only a known quality to stress that insight into the good grows with the process of conversion of life. The problem is that the good is difficult to know, especially when it is embedded in new social contexts with complex and competing understandings of the factors which comprise it. Then we are faced with the same problems facing social analysis of a situation. Do we call upon ideas which reinforce an image of the world of order, harmony, and equilibrium or ones which reveal a dialectical tendency toward conflict, tension, and struggle?[56] Metz encourages that a memory of suffering and a sense of the future are essential for understanding the good.[57] Closer scrutiny reveals that many moral ideals are flawed and limited in some way, and the question becomes whether the ones we have available have some capacity to change prevailing practices which are not good to become better.

John Paul II also recognizes this problem of ascertaining the good in concrete situations where cultural ideas regarding human flourishing conflict. He comments on relationships where a cultural reality requires a transcendent or religious perspective to focus it to serve the human good. Similar to his assertion that justice needs mercy and love, he argues that freedom needs truth; human autonomy requires the perspective of community; and political life must incorporate the outlook of transcendence. He cautions that detaching human freedom from its essential and constitutive relationship to truth leads to contemporary relativist thought.[58] Failure to search for the truth of human dignity in its transcendent and permanent nature undermines the vision needed for essential political conditions in our world. Without the transcendent horizons of truth and community, the cultural realities of freedom and autonomy fail to accomplish the humanizing goals to which they aspire. Groups can be blind to the truth, giving a cultural sense of truth or freedom an absolute value. Holy wars and "national security" mentalities are distortions of the truth fed by need for identity and protection of the status quo. A greater truth is only accomplished through dialogue, openness to which is more evidence of the search for transcendence. Contrary to those who hold that religion is extraneous to public debate, John Paul II teaches that it is central. Religion takes seriously that human beings have a transcendent goal. Without attention to the ethical relevance of transcendence, which the relationship of justice, love, and mercy holds out, society is at peril.

This does not happen automatically. In American culture today there is a drive to belittle faith and obscure its importance to our history and culture.[59] Context D life can function to carry these beliefs into the public realm and express them in terms of concrete needs and policies for the good of the neighbor. Rahner notes that there are some institutions which are created for the special purpose of contributing to freedom by counteracting the effects of other institutions.[60] Entering into the mix of public debate, however, requires the kenosis not to circumvent the democratic process, but to enter into it, accept its limits and potential for human flourishing. It requires the model of discipleship that lives in the tension between making a Christian community consistent with its belief, and fostering a sense of peace and justice in this world, to build the *humanum*. Where a group stands in this tension will reflect its capacity to engage in dialogue with those who do not understand its view of life or disagree with it, or withdraw, not as a moment in the process of engagement, but as a stance toward society. The latter is the option of Context D life as Douglas finds it in society, and remains a core temptation for these groups.

Notes

1 Christian anthropology depicts human beings as essentially social, however, one's essential social nature is expressed in choice.
2 Mary Douglas, *In the Active Voice* (London: Routledge and Kegan Paul, 1982), 198.
3 Ibid., 200. The following is drawn from this important essay at 183ff.
4 Ibid., 202.
5 Ibid., 203.
6 Michael Paul Gallagher, *Clashing Symbols: An Introduction to Faith and Culture* (New York: Paulist Press, 2003), 34.

7 Douglas, *In the Active Voice*, 206.

8 Ibid.

9 George De Schrijver, S.J., "Fundamentalism: A Refusal to Recognize a Religious Dimension in "Secular Existence," in *Fundamentalism and Pluralism in the Church*, ed. Dennis T. Gonzalez (Manila: Dakateo, 2004), 1–28. In the following I draw on De Schrijver's analysis.

10 Ibid., 3.

11 Ibid., 10.

12 See: Emmanuel Sivan, "The Enclave Culture," in *Fundamentalisms Comprehended*, ed. Martin E. Marty and R. Scott Appleby (Chicago: The University of Chicago Press, 1995), 37–38.

13 Ibid., 15.

14 Emmanuel Sivan, "The Enclave Culture," 17.

15 Ibid., 19.

16 Ibid., 27. Contrast with Tanner's view of the Christian community as having more fluid boundaries. Kathryn Tanner, *Theories of Culture: A New Agenda for Theology* (Minneapolis, MN: Fortress Press, 1997), 38.

17 Ibid., 57.

18 Larry Rasmussen, *Moral Fragments, Moral Community* (Minneapolis, MN: Fortress Press, 1973), 139.

19 Robert Bellah, *Habits of the Heart: Individualism and Commitment in American Life* (Berkeley, CA: University of California Press, 1985), 71–84.

20 Ibid., 70.

21 Ibid., 80.

22 Gabriel A. Almond, Emmanuel Sivan and R. Scott Appleby, "Explaining Fundamentalism," in *Fundamentalisms Comprehended*, op. cit., 426.

23 Karol Wojtyla, *The Acting Person*, trans. Andrzej Potocki (Dordrecht and Boston: D. Reidel Pub. Co., 1979), 283–88.

24 John Paul II, "Address to the United Nations on the Declaration of Human Rights," AAS 1156, para. 17, as quoted in Donal Dorr, *Option for the Poor: 100 Years of Catholic Social Teaching* (New York: Orbis Books, 1983), 275.

25 J. Bryan Hehir, "Can the Church Convincingly Engage American Culture?," *Church* (Spring 2004), 10.

26 Ibid., 6.

27 John A. Coleman, S.J., "Retrieving or Re-inventing Social Catholicism: A Transatlantic Response," in *Catholic Social Thought: Twilight or Renaissance?*, ed. J.S. Boswell, F.P. McHugh and J. Verstraeten (Leuven: Peeters, 2000), 289–92.

28 Hehir, "Can the Church Convincingly Engage American Culture?," 10.

29 Ibid.

30 Francis Schussler Fiorenza, "The Works of Mercy: Theological Perspectives," in *The Works of Mercy*, ed. F. Eigo (Philadelphia, PA: Villanova Press, 1992), 31–71 (60).

31 George De Schrijver, *The Use of Mediations in Theology* (Leuven: Centre for Liberation Theologies, 2001), 58.

32 Karl Rahner comments on the shift in theology as many tools, methods, and approaches to understanding reality were incorporated into theological expression. "Pluralism in Theology and the Unity of the Creed in the Church," in *Theological Investigations* XI (New York: The Seabury Press, 1974), 3–23.

33 Hehir, "Can the Church Convincingly Engage American Culture?," 10.

34 Joseph Cardinal Bernadin, *A Moral Vision for America*, ed. John Langan, S.J. (Washington, D.C.: Georgetown University Press, 1998), 15.

35 Steck remarks, "The order of grace does not overturn the order of creation. Rather, creation is the 'thick' presupposition that makes the next, wondrous act possible: God's convenantal relationship with what is 'other.' God's Word in Christ does not relativize the claims of the created order, but rather amplifies them and charges them with the dignity of a personal address." Christopher Steck, *The Ethical Thought of Hans Urs Von Balthasar* (New York: Crossroad, 2001), 121.

36 Similar movements also went on in other first world societies. See: Staf Hellemans, "Is There a Future for Catholic Social Teaching after the Waning of Ultramontane Mass Catholicism?," in *Catholic Social Thought*, op. cit., 20–24.

37 See Frans Jozef van Beeck, S.J., *Catholic Identity after Vatican II: Three Types of Faith in One Church* (Chicago: Loyola University Press, 1985).

38 William Henn, "Pluralism," in *The New Dictionary of Theology*, ed. Joseph Komonchak, *et al.* (Wilmington, DE: Michael Glazier, 1989), 770–72.

39 See: Judith A. Merkle, *From the Heart of the Church: The Catholic Social Tradition* (Collegeville, MN: Liturgical Press, 2004), 241–65.

40 For Aquinas, justice is "a habit whereby a man renders to each one his due by a constant and perpetual will" (II–II Q 58.1). Justice concerns the recognition of what is objectively due another; their "right." Justice concerns what we actually do to another, rather than our intentions. It is always directed toward another, and it is one of the few general virtues capable of imposing a new orientation on all actions. While other virtues have as their goal the perfection of the person, justice focuses on the good of the other.

41 Perceiving is an act of love whereby we come to the "extremely difficult realization that something other than oneself is real." Iris Murdoch, "The Sublime and the Good," in *Existentialists and Mystics*, ed. Peter Conradi (New York: Penguin, 1998), 215, as quoted in Steck, *The Ethical Thought of Hans Urs Von Balthasar*, 126.

42 Bellah, *Habits of the Heart*, 143.

43 Alasdair MacIntyre, *Dependent Rational Animals: Why Humans Need the Virtues* (Chicago: Open Court Press, 1999), as quoted in John A. Coleman, S.J., "Making the Connections: Globalization and Catholic Social Thought," in *Globalization and Catholic Social Thought: Present Crisis, Future Hope*, ed. John A. Coleman and William F. Ryan (New York: Orbis Books, 2005), 16.

44 Gerard Beigel, *Faith and Social Justice in the Teaching of Pope John Paul II* (New York: Peter Lang, 1997), 97.

45 Robin W. Lovin, *Christian Realism and the New Realities* (Cambridge: Cambridge University Press, 2008), 132.

46 John A. Coleman, "Making the Connections," 21.

47 See: Samuel Huntington, *The Clash of Civilizations and the Remaking of the World Order* (New York: Simon and Schuster, 1966). See also: Gregory Baum, "The Clash of Civilizations or Their Reconciliation?," *The Ecumenist*, 39 (Spring 2002), 12–17.

48 Richard Falk, "The Religious Foundations of Humane Governance," in *Toward a Global Civilization? The Contribution of Religions*, ed. Patricia M. Mische and Melissa Merkling (New York: Peter Lang, 2001), 52.

49 "Religion is understood here as encompassing both the teaching and beliefs of organized religion and all spiritual outlooks that interpret the meaning of life by reference to faith in and commitment to that which cannot be explained by empirical science or sensory observation, and is usually associated with an acceptance of the reality of the divine, the sacred, the transcendent, the ultimate" (ibid., 57).

50 Ibid., 57–59.

51 Susan Shapiro, "Hearing the Testimony of Radical Negation," in *The Holocaust as Interruption, Concilium*, 175 (October 1984), 3–16.

52 David R. Brumenthal, *The Banality of Good and Evil: Moral Lessons from the Shoah and Jewish Tradition* (Washington, D.C.: Georgetown University Press, 1999), 5.

53 John Perry, S.J., *Torture: Religious Ethics and National Security* (Maryknoll, NY: Orbis Books, 2005).

54 Hannah Arendt, "The Banality of Evil: Failing to Think," in *The Many Faces of Evil: Historical Perspectives*, ed. Amelie Oksenberg Rorty (London: Routledge, 2001), 265–68.

55 Rowan Williams, "A Theological Critique of Milbank," in Robert Gill, *Theology and Sociology. A Reader*, new and enlarged edition (London: Cassel, 1996), 440.

56 De Schrijvar, *The Use of Mediations in Theology*, 57.

57 The future needs to be approached through a critical reason, which accepts that the future promised by God cannot in any way be adequately conceived under the conditions of the present. Johann Baptist Metz, "Political Theology," in *Encyclopedia of Theology: The Concise Sacramentum Mundi*, ed. Karl Rahner (New York: Seabury Press, 1975), 1240.

58 John Paul II, *Veritatis Splendor* (Vatican City: Libreria Editrice Vaticana, 1993), no. 4:8.

59 Stephen Carter, *The Culture of Disbelief* (New York: Basic Books, 1993).

60 Karl Rahner, "Institution and Freedom," in *Theological Investigations*, 8, trans. David Bourke (London: Darton, Longman and Todd, 1975), 119.

PART III

TOWARD THE FUTURE OF THE CHRISTIAN LIFE

Chapter 9

THE SCAFFOLDINGS OF THE FUTURE: PRAYER, ENGAGEMENT, AND COMMUNITY

Refusing to conform to the standards of the world, they will change their whole outlook so as to know the will of God, what is good, pleasing to Him, and best in every way.

— St. Gregory of Nyssa

We have examined in brief various contexts of modern living to better understand the challenges of moral commitment in society today. We have suggested that traditional understandings of Catholic morality support the central issues of a moral life, but need also to incorporate the significance of context more formally in its understanding of the Christian journey. Now we want to ask specifically, how does incorporation of context have significance for morality? In the spirit of the method of this book, we will not offer a systematic outline of this difference; rather we will glean from the previous chapters a more heuristic insight into the question. What aspects of moral experience does an inquiry into context bring to light? These are best described in a movement from a sole reliance on traditional definitions to explain moral experience, to the integration of new factors into understanding the moral person and the moral project of the Christian life. Understanding of faithfulness is influenced by this mental shift. On the one hand, faithfulness is comprised of something as old as religious response, the acceptance of the gift of salvation, and the love to live one's life according to this knowledge. Yet, on the other, faithfulness takes its shape from the challenge of living in this world, at this time, and requires new skills of Christian living to carry out its commitments.

It is important to note that our references to four contexts of modern life have simply been a device to gain understanding of moral experience today. None of our descriptions exactly replicates the reality of these dimensions of life, rather they provide a model which brings to light elements of these experiences which may go unnoticed. We live simultaneously in all four contexts of modern living. No one lives a total Context A life, nor is solely the isolate of Context C. We move in and out of these contexts, participating in some more than others. We experience their inherent logics and expectations as forging a unique matrix of moral demands and responsibilities. At times these contexts conflict, as we have pointed out along the way. The inherent logic of one context is in tension at times with the assumptions of how life is organized in another.

The Church in some form exists in each context, although time and space does not allow a full development of this insight. At minimum we can say that church life needs to address each context by fostering the contribution it offers to human life, and assisting those in it to grow. The Church makes a unique contribution to its members. The Catholic Church has a characteristic manner of doing so marked by mediation, sacramental life and communion. These vehicles of its mystery are also styles of its presence in the life of its members. They not only feed the life of the members in their effort to be faithful, but set some criteria by which they are to act. These general remarks will be built upon as we discuss how our understanding of moral experience is enriched by insight into context.

Toward a More Inclusive Consideration of the Person

Attention to context focuses understanding of the person in a situation which requires moral deliberation. It provides a deeper assessment of the impact of the situation on the person. Attention is given to patterned and repeated factors and behaviors which order and constrain freedom both within the human personality and in social experience and interaction.

We move from the more traditional focus on an *inalienable freedom of will* which is neutral in respect of situational influences, to a will which is in relationship to a social matrix which communicates what is good, life-giving, and true.[1] Attention to context alerts us to the situated will which has the potential to internalize a distorted self-understanding and export these distortions to others through systematically distorted relationships.

Attention to context suggests we include in our *understanding of impediments* to moral willing more than those things which note restrictions on self-directedness, like fear or lack of knowledge. We also need to include those factors which disorient freedom from within by means of a social practice through which processes of subjective intentionality are socially acquired. Here the focus is not one of establishing an uncoerced self-decision which could have been otherwise, but rather one of how life-intentionalities are attracted to and captivated by a presentation of a life path or form of relationship. This presentation can be repeatedly reinforced by the codes, institutions, and processes of communication and action which reinforce how subsequent action should be taken.

This means a move solely from a *sense of the will as having more or less power of self-direction* to a will which is distracted rather than obliterated. A traditional focus has always been how much is the will involved in this action? Is the person free to act one way or another? However, attention to context also attends to the will which is pre-occupied, rather than disabled. For example, Gerard May claims that through addictions the will is nailed to a substance, process, or relationship. All addictions are replacements for God. In his words:

> . . . addiction attaches desire, bonds and enslaves the energy of desire to certain specific behaviors, things or people . . . These objects of attachment then become preoccupations and obsessions; they come to rule our lives. Or again . . . addiction is the most powerful psychic enemy of humanity's desire for God.[2]

May implies that addictions simply attach energy to a substance or process in such a manner that is it not available or under the influence of conscious willing.

Toward a More Inclusive Consideration of the Moral Project

Attention to context also shifts understanding of the project of the moral life. We move from a sole emphasis on a *universal human identity and moral project*: that is, the person as one member of the human species sharing with all human persons one ultimate goal. This classical understanding upholds the truth that all human beings are rational animals who share with all others common faculties. However, it also implies that human fulfillment is a linear project of development of human capacities that all people share.

Attention to context integrates into a sense of the moral project of one's life story as a moral journey and as a standard of moral truth in decision making. It adds "coming to an identity in Christ," a true sense of self, one in relationship to others, Christ, the Church, and the world as a moral project. Becoming oneself in Christ becomes the goal of the Christian life.

There is a shift therefore from *a sole emphasis on the individual* in an internal battle of body and soul for self-transcendence, to the interweaving of personal and situational dynamics to envision a situated moral agency. There is a move from a *vision of human becoming which focuses on a personal model of human perfection* to one where human becoming depends on one's response not only to the traditional moral restrictions of various forms of egotism, but also to the social conditions which mark one's own or another's possibility of human flourishing. For instance, it is one thing to ask how to help the poor. It is another to ask about the role of the economy in their poverty.[3] Taking responsibility for this context and one's place in it is also a standard of moral progress. This requires different role expectations of one who is responsible for a life situation and one who is dependent on it.

These shifts arise from a change in theological emphases, as in how one understands grace and nature. There is a movement from an *understanding of the supernatural* as only beyond history. This theological formulation focuses the moral life on withdrawal and avoidance of evil and fear of the world. A shift in understanding grace and nature promotes a morality of action with Christ through grace to confront evil, in spite of the forces of sin in the world. Here the focus is on how love becomes part of history.[4]

There is a movement from a *sense of salvation* as freedom from sin, yet *unrelated to life context*, to acceptance that the salvation God offers in and through Jesus Christ requires a change in one's perception of reality and value system. An interpretation of the salvation which addresses the concerns of life context will depict the gift of salvation as addressing a variety of life experiences which concretize the presence of evil in people's lives.

Toward a More Inclusive Consideration of Norms

Certainly the tradition offers a perennial and challenging vision of a fully human life. However, attention to context enriches this vision, and relates it to the challenges of modern living. Our study indicates that this involves a move from a sole emphasis on *conventional understanding of right and wrong behavior* to alertness of the way "good behavior" can be defined in culture, by a system which is inconsistent with human dignity. Such a cultural system can actually dismiss the notion of moral fault by redefining moral truth simply as what is. Some have called this a new type of colonization, where pressures to conform are not imposed by external authority, rather through internalization, the internal shaping of cognition, desire and (therefore) will.

This involves a move from a sole analysis of *a moral action as being comprised of an act, intention and circumstance* to include awareness of the ideological framework which shapes and influences the understanding of the act. The ideological framework is not chosen directly, but rather it is chosen in and with every choice that operationally assumes it. Examples are racism, an overstated sense of autonomy in health care decisions, nationalism, a recreational attitude toward human sexuality, patriarchy, etc. We socially reproduce these beliefs every time we follow them.

Attention to context requires a shift from a *sole emphasis on the personal choice of motivation for action* to awareness that the ideological framework which guides our actions does not present itself as one object in relation to which the will is neutral. It functions as the basis and foundation of all choosing and acting, as the rules by which one makes choices, which are not open to scrutiny or direct choice.[5] If one takes this seriously, one must relinquish the assumption that *withdrawal from the society locates one in a "neutral" zone* free from the influence of others, and come to an awareness that all choosing is caught up in a force field of social expectations. For example, we have indicated that a situation of low group and low grid, Context C, can lead to spiritual deepening and new forms of community or to dissipation and desolation. In the latter case there is not necessarily passivity but a great possibility for an active incorporation of the whole person, including their intentionality as well as their action, into the pathological dynamics of individualism and/or consumerism.

Toward a Shift in Understanding of the Role of Relationship in Morality

The Church has always had a vision of the whole of the moral life as an expression of one's relationship to God, and not just on providing its norms. However, in the last centuries the need for clear guidelines on moral behavior which suited the assessment of sin in the confessional impacted the style of moral theology. Growth in the Christian life was often relegated to ascetical theology. Attention to context helps to restore a balance in moral theology. There is a shift in emphasis on the Church *solely as a maker of moral rules* to the Church as a nurturer of the heart of morality, the faith and hope that leads to love. The ground of this optimism in the Christian life cannot be scientifically proven but is celebrated sacramentally, mediated in the life of the Church, and fostered by its movement of communion in the world, in part through the ethical response of its members. The Church then informs the horizons of our moral actions not only by offering a condensed code but by confirming the partial satisfactions of the end goal of the Christian life as happening along the journey. The Church confirms, as Bernard Lonergan puts it, that grace as the state of being in love is a response to Real Presence among us and the heart of morality. This shifts understanding of the role of relationship of the Church in morality. It sets a standard for the Church's own morality and that of its public institutions.

Attention to context shifts understanding of the role of other relationships and their quality in morality. There is a move from a sole emphasis *on a self which is formed through performing right actions* to a self which is formed also through dynamics of particular significant relationships. When context is integrated into moral vision, it is possible to ask whether one can lose selfhood while performing conventionally good actions. This is implied in the feminist critique of sacrifice as socially expected of women, rather than as mutually expected of men and women. In this case "good action" contributes to an interpersonal dynamic in which one's own powers of full selfhood are not nurtured, nourished, or intensified. This loss of the power of genuine selfhood generates the loss of possibility of genuine relation.

Latin American theologians share this insight in calling for an anthropology where becoming a person, becoming free, and becoming conscious of one's powers of self-direction are primary in moral development. In cases of economic oppression, they point out that systemic poverty colors interpersonal dynamic. This condition of poverty is supported by institutions set up to do violence to others simply by ignoring their real needs, and using them for selfish advantage.[6]

Toward a Shift in Understanding Sin and Evil

Attention to context creates a shift in how one discerns good and evil. There is a move from discernment of good and evil only before the reality of *original sin in its personal manifestations and tendencies* to discernment of good and evil before the reality of sin of the world, as a manifestation of original sin. The first implies a focus on sin mainly in one's personal life and in terms of the standards of traditional morality. This remains a necessary element in the moral life. However, when discernment also includes a sense of the sin of the world, there are ramifications for various areas of the moral life. For example, one's notion of conversion is broadened. Spiritual conversion is not just interior; rather it involves concrete manifestations in individual and community. John Paul II calls for a new moral imagination capable of problem solving in society as an aspect of conversion. This is not just a marker of an authentic conversion, but is necessary for the conversion of others since our social life sets the conditions which foster or hinder moral, intellectual, affective, and religious responses to what is good and true.

There is a changed notion of imitation of Christ. Jesus too faced sin of the world. Jesus' life involved activity and passivity before that which was contradictory in life. Christians are called to do the same. Attention to sin of the world raises awareness of the propensity in the world for evil as well as real progress. It shapes an understanding of the cross as walking with Christ in that equilibrium between living with human finitude and answering the call to transcendence, accepting the suffering this involves.

Attention to the sin of the world alerts one to new faces of good and evil. Faithfulness involves the drive to be whole and genuine in living before the possibility of the banality of good and evil in oneself, in others and society. It supports the realization that overcoming evil is not just a social and political project but an anthropological one as well. It holds on to the links between evil in society and the personal reinforcement of it. It broadens the notion of sin to include the image of sin as addiction. Sin is not just a crime or misdeed. It is a displacement of energy on that which cannot save; a participation in the sin of the world.[7]

Attention to the sin of the world changes the emphasis in understanding the nature of moral perfection. The warning "You cannot serve God and mammon" (Mt. 6.24), captures the challenge of the Christian before the sin of the world. If this is true, faithfulness takes on a new light. Faithfulness is not just moral perfection, but the challenge to bring all of self to moral decisions, despite the impact of the sin of the world, as it exists in situations and has its hold on the person. This is not a project of moral determination alone, but requires the grace of God. The evil carried by the likes of mammon is that mammon makes the one who thinks he or she controls it a slave.[8] Taking seriously the sin of the world leads a Christian to trust in God.

Attention to the sin of the world leads the Christian from *a sole focus on committing sin*, acts of commission, to attention to acts of omission, a willful choice to participate in or indifference to an oppressive or idolatrous system. People can passively wait on the agency of God or the conversion of others who maintain a life system which denies to them their personal intentionality or agency. Being a victim can be an active stance, even though one's subjectivity is adversely affected. One can simply "give up" and refrain from personal willing in resistance, hiding, refusing help, or abdicating responsibility.[9] Participating in one's own self-destruction reflects a modern face of evil as that which subjects its victims to a process designed to destroy the very concept of humanity within them.[10] In this case, the decision to drift is highlighted.

Attention to sin of the world moves one away from the notion that a *personal practice of Christian ethics is sufficient* to humanize the world. It fosters awareness that strategies for overcoming personal sin are insufficient for transformation at the social, cultural and political levels of life, even though these evils have their roots in human sin.[11] The use of power and coercion can be used on a social level to promote justice or the common good. The necessary use of power can appear to stand in conflict with the goal of unselfishness at the personal level.[12] Attention to the sin of the world alerts us to the necessity of a change not just in attitudes but in structures and relationships in order to "reproduce" social, cultural and political relationships in a new way. Taking seriously the sin of the world also makes more tentative the impact of Christians on this world. They often cannot make a complete change in relationships and conditions once and for all. Rather they seek to establish social and cultural ideals and processes through relationships to the world of resistance, appropriation, subversion and compromise.[13]

Attention to sin of the world forces a shift in focus solely on *culpability in sin*. This is a key concern of the confessional, and is based on a vision of the free will as more or less neutral in respect of situational influences. It focuses on an uncoerced self-decision which could have been otherwise. Assessment of culpability remains a necessary aspect of the moral life, however, it is not enough for a faithful life today. There needs to be a focus on the capability of the person, the capacity to act in a centered manner where the energies of head and heart are able to discern what is right and accomplish it.[14] The focus here is on the Christian identity of an individual vis-à-vis their environment, and their ability to express this identity in this world.[15]

For example, racism does not appear to the conscience as one choice standing alongside others. It is already within the dynamics of self-orientation and life intentionality in global society, as mentioned in our discussion of norms. Racism slips into the basis and foundation of all choosing and acting as the rules by which one makes choices. One must be converted away from forces like racism,[16] and open to the intellectual, affective, moral, and religious conversion this entails.[17] Theologian Juan Luis Segundo sees this process of conversion as the heart of a religious posture to life: "Religious faith in the fullest sense of the word is a faith which is the source of a new meaning structure."[18] Capability is the graced ability of the person to respond to God, beyond the banality of good and evil confronted in self, life, and society, and to act beyond it, in spite of it and its rewards, in ways consistent with the gospel.[19]

The process of conversion at both a personal and communal level is difficult to define. It involves various complex processes of transformation of conscious operations of the human person. The transformation influences the personal, social, and cultural dynamics of being and acting within history and includes the ability to move beyond the distorting power of bias and search for the moral truth as discussed above. The work of Lonergan frames conversion in terms of movement from an established horizon to a new horizon of knowing, valuing, and acting which involves intellectual, moral, affective, and religious conversion.[20] Capability is to be interpreted in light of a wider biblical meaning of conversion, as involving the capacity at any given time of life, through grace, to respond to God's ongoing offer to both the individual and community to become a new creation. Those who operate primarily from psychological foundations might find an analogy between aspects of this process and "soul making."[21]

Structures of Devotion in a Modern Age

From the years 1375 to 1600 there was a movement in the Church called *devotio moderna*, a movement of internal reform in which notions of the service of God, *devotio*, were translated into a practical way of Christian living for the times. Because this movement existed on the boundaries between the world and the cloister, it was instrumental in the establishment of mysticism as a social reality. The aim of this movement was to affirm love as a permanent collaboration with the desire for God to be found in the person's soul.[22] Desire was the heart of this love and was to lead to a process of conversion and transformation. The natural space for this process, however, was not the cloister, but the "common life" shared by all. Through this transformation a person became one of action and contemplation while they embraced God and neighbor in one single movement of love. One of the best-known exemplars of this movement in the Catholic community was Thomas a Kempis in his manual the *Imitation of Christ*.

Later Francis de Sales (1567–1622) furthered this movement, through his contribution to the seventeenth-century French spiritual renaissance, which had its roots in *devotio moderna*. Along with his collaborator, Jane Frances de Chantal (1572–1641), de Sales offered a vision of the world as conjoined human and divine hearts. The spiritual life of living in this union was open to all men and women of every station and walk of life. The goal was to raise up "devout souls" in every corner of the Church to be a leaven in a renewed Christian society.[23] De Sales' *Introduction to the Devout Life* encouraged a spiritual maturity adapted to the demands of work and family. It became one of the most published and translated of spiritual classics — by the end of the nineteenth century over four hundred editions had appeared. Lay people, religious orders, and clergy were affected by this spiritual renewal.

The concern to relate Christian faithfulness to life in society, we can see, is not new in the Church. These movements, however, highlight the role of affectivity or the heart in the spiritual life. Knowledge of the need to change oneself or the world is important, however, without the desire to do so it remains a nice sentiment with no energy to bring it about. Awareness that one should be faithful is not sufficient motivation for the type of conversion *devotio moderna* embraced. The head and the heart were engaged in both the desire and the search to be faithful and that is still the case today.

Traditionally devotions in the Church were expressions of a heartfelt reverence toward God, Mary, and the saints. While today some see devotions as part of the "old Church" their function of focusing on human life touching the divine is irreplaceable. Today, however, we recognize that a spirit of prayer is inseparable from the search to be faithful. Key to public prayer is an affective engagement of the community through good liturgy, music, art, and common prayer which is culturally sensitive. Yet "devotion" for the life of the world also calls Christians to engagement as well as to community, away from the individualism of our age. As we look at the Church as sacramental, mediation and communion, we see the blend of these dimensions of the Church and the new calls to prayer, engagement and community as a matrix which speaks uniquely to the call to be faithful today. They point to Catholic identity as well as indicate markers of the ethics of a Christian as he or she stands alongside others of good will and knows that in the best ethical reasoning they are also addressed by God. While the outlines of how to create a blend of these factors are beyond the scope of this text, some major directions can be noted.

Mediation

We have spoken of the Church's providing of a condensed code by which the elaborated codes of our pluralistic ways of living are grounded as an important mediating function it provides in modern living. The Church in this sense is a school of modern living and virtue. This happens not just through its codes and laws, but through its community of witness. The Church mediates the salvation offered in Jesus Christ which makes the Christian journey possible, as well as providing a way, through its life and tradition, to love of God and neighbor. The tension facing the mediating role of the Church in the search to be faithful today is between its capacity and right to speak on moral issues, and the search for what the answers are to the complex problems of the day.

While the Church mediates the law of God, it is not accurate to equate this with a complete correspondence between it and what the Church teaches at all times. In the Church's history, changes have occurred in individual and moral questions, and that change must occur.[24] Since insight and the word of the Church are also human insight and human word (also supported by the Spirit of God), the Christian needs to avoid both dismissing the Church and approaching its teachings in an unthinking way. Josef Fuchs comments on the law of God:

> It is hardly (or better still, only in rather rare cases) to be understood as a positively given and revealed commandment of God; for there are no such commandments which correspond to the unlimited variety of problems regarding the realization of human reality . . . Therefore "divine law" can mean only that moral order which God has written "as law" into the human heart and into human nature, and which is also called the moral natural law.[25]

The moral knowledge of the Church, while guided by the Holy Spirit and done in the light of the gospel, must necessarily reckon with human and time-conditioned inaccuracies in the interpretation of the law written on the heart. As a tradition, it can change, and yet hold on to guiding principles of its belief and thought, principles which in fact are not created but given.

This does not mean that the Church is just one voice of moral wisdom among others for the Christian. Rather it is recognition that only a small number of the truths of the natural law are clearly evident in comparison to the complexity of problems regarding human life today. Human knowledge, evaluation, and judgment are needed to access how the wisdom of the moral tradition, experience, Scripture, and human reasoning lead us to the moral truth as we proceed. This means too that all Christians are responsible to search for moral truth in their lives. *Gaudium et Spes* 43 acknowledges that even in the Church the answer to all questions is not known, and that alternative solutions by conscientious Christians are possible. In Fuchs words, "This, then, is the church of Christ, the church that is led by the Spirit and yet lived by human persons themselves: as such, the church is the guide to conscientious, morally right behavior in our world of human persons."[26]

The challenge for the Christian in the world facing moral pluralism and various explanations of right and wrong behavior is to avoid two extremes. The first is a "more severe" approach which relies solely on authoritative stances and tries to fit every nuance of a situation into them. This can reflect more a personal need for security than an understanding of the particular sense and determined boundaries in which these stances are to be understood. A second approach is to just assimilate the plural opinions around them, without having sufficient reasons to follow them, in place of what is normally taught; to be simply attracted to their unconventionality. Both approaches lack a proper orientation to truth, providing a one-sided need for security or an unlimited desire for arbitrariness.[27]

A more contextual understanding of Christian morality highlights the need to make strong links between evangelization and inculturation, taking seriously the multiple cultural contexts in which the gospel is preached and understood and the ethical issues which are central to that milieu. It also draws attention to engaging a variety of peoples in the work of evangelization and moral discernment in the Church.

Communion

The Eucharist is the heart of the call to communion in the Church, for the grace received in the sacrament is given also as a task to accomplish in this world. The Church calls Christians to communion in terms of the world, the *saeculum*, the world that believer and non-believer share. Faithfulness therefore involves a way of living which fosters a respect for what is human in society. This is more than a healthy humanism. Shared meaning and consensus on a value system are essential features of any society, and form part of what the heavenly city recognizes, sanctions, and fosters for its own ultimate purpose: true worship of the one God. Christian faithfulness in the *saeculum* involves the fostering of a sense of transcendence and compenetration on the part of believers and the Church. The spiritual path of solidarity or communion is reflected in a new imagination that creates systems that are more interdependent in economic, cultural, political, and religious ways. These moral changes involve growth in the spiritual path of communion — solidarity — for engagement in the activities of communion has a political-mystical dimension: it gives one access to God. As we find worth in our neighbor, respond to her or him as "other," we find God. The bonds formed in this way are deeper than the natural or human bonds we hope bind the world (SRS 40). These are the bonds of communion. This communion is that mix of the heavenly and earthly city, one that requires the structures of a healthy *saeculum* but also is dependent on that gift of faith, hope, and love which is only God's to give. The Church fosters this communion through its life and mission.

Sacramentality

The Church points the Christian to the sacramentality of life and celebrates the sacraments themselves as encounters with God. Encounter with God's gaze, a sense of standing before God who loves us, is an experience which can lead to a reaching out to value, to transcend ourselves. The sacramental experience can concretize this pull to transcendence. The call is not to leave this world, but to face the gaps between what is and what ought to be, in ourselves, in others and in the world, knowing God's presence on the journey. The God whom we encounter in Jesus Christ is one who lives present to the suffering in this world and is the one who calls all to life. "I came that they may have life, and have it abundantly" (Jn 10.10).

A sacramental vision highlights that a Christian ethic of faithfulness has love as its form, responding to the priority of God's love. The liturgy is the place where this priority of the love of God is freely bestowed and received through the gesture of Eucharistic communion. A sacramental vision confirms that Christian identity is a structure, not just a self-creation. A structure is a whole of which each component is an integral part and in which each component finds its value only by reference to the others. Finding God in all things centers life in the Mystery of the Trinity, and offers to each Christian the possibility of being an everyday mystic. The Eucharist is also the structure of Christian identity in its desire to be faithful. There is the gift, its reception and the returning gift of concrete action in society which forms the ongoing process of Christian search to be faithful, not only internally but in the world. Instead of justifying ourselves through our desire to be faithful, we welcome daily the Spirit of the Risen One into our lives and join ourselves to His presence in the world.

Virtues for a New Age

Prayer, engagement, and community are counter-intuitive in a world without God, and focused only on upward mobility, which leads one away from the influence of others. The call to community is a kenosis, a self-emptying. Yet it is the emptying oneself of a false identity. The culture says if one joins a group, a religious community, or marries or makes a commitment, he or she is not "free" to do whatever he or she wants. When freedom is considered an absolute value, giving up any facet of freedom does not make sense in a cultural understanding of life. To act in solidarity with others, to found a family, to improve a professional climate, to insist on the true identity of one's race, class or gender, to be an advocate for the poor, for the earth, for peace, one must consciously set aside some legitimate freedoms, in order to take up the greater truth which attention to the other represents. Taking responsibility to shape this world, whether it is the world of family, profession or society, requires that the needs of the other transcend the pleasure of the individual.

Perhaps the most profound commitment of faithfulness in society today is the openness to conversion. This call to conversion is even more critical today because of the complexity of our world and society. Conversion today involves facing the colonization of the mind and spirit which the complex systems of modern society impose on its members through ideals and strategies of living which are an idolatry of expediency. Through healthy religious practice, engagement, and community, one can participate in alternative practice which questions this unspoken ideal of culture. The challenge of morality today is more than doing the good that one knows. It is also discerning the false consciousness which clouds our minds and weakens our wills to pursue the constructive good which is possible in our relationships, communities, and world today. Bernard Haring reminds us that moral theology's purpose is the fostering of right vision in our world today. Faithfulness involves alertness to the thought patterns, assumptions and practices of our societies, their ideas of family life, success, and human fulfillment to test whether they are in tune with the gospel.

The quest to be faithful today requires a movement away from a vision of ethics where the "good" is only a known quality, to stress that insight into the good grows with the process of conversion of life. The problem is that the good is difficult to know, especially when it is embedded in new social contexts with complex and competing understandings of the factors which comprise it.

Attention to context in moral theology does not negate the Church's first language of morality as it is held within the tradition. However, it enhances the meaning of moral truth in the Church, as the truth of the incarnation is the incarnation of the truth in the face of human suffering in the world, at all levels of life. If the concern of ethics is the authentic life and the development of persons and societies toward the *humanum* within history and ultimately to a future with God, attention to context helps to put flesh on this project. If the call of the Church at Vatican II is to reform moral theology to help Christians bring forth fruit "for the life of the world," attention to context brings to this project a narrative of human suffering and the hope in the face of it, which the life of Jesus Christ affirms and establishes. The development of self is linked to the development of the conditions in which others can flourish. The challenge we have investigated is the promise and pitfalls of putting these two truths, of the *humanum*, and *in history* together. As Christians pray, "Thy Kingdom Come," attention to context puts flesh on the significance of this imperative in the lives of every Christian and community.

Every age calls forth from the Christian community a challenge to be faithful. Ours is no different. The call to prayer, engagement, and community today rouse us from a self-satisfaction that can cloak itself as happiness. These practices can foster in us a restlessness that will not settle for a decent life instead of a faithful one. They can stretch our imagination to believe that we can shape our world to be a better place, in spite of all the visions of the contrary. But most of all they can confirm that the path of faithfulness is not a solitary one, but one where God is most intimate to our personal and communal journey. We hear the promise of this in St. Paul: "The one who calls you is faithful, and he will also accomplish it" (1 Thess. 5.24).

Notes

1 Hence the recent focus of the Church on the role of culture in moral experience and evangelization.
2 Gerald G. May, *Addiction and Grace* (New York: Harper, 1988), 3.
3 See: Joerg Rieger, *No Rising Tide: Theology, Economics and the Future* (Minneapolis, MN: Fortress Press, 2009), 26.
4 Marc Oraison, "Psychology and the Sense of Sin," in *Sin*, trans. Bernard Murchland and Raymond Meyerpeter (New York: Macmillan, 1962), 13.
5 Alistair McFayden, *Bound to Sin: Abuse, Holocaust and the Christian Doctrine of Sin* (Cambridge: Cambridge University Press, 2000), 148. I am indebted to Prof. McFayden for his analysis of the feminist critique of patriarchy as an example of the above dynamic. This also refers to unconscious motivations springing from one's psychological history. Ideological and psychological dynamisms, however, do not have to remain unconscious; they can be changed, by different means. On a psychological level, instead of being motivated by fear and anxiety, one can see life and actions in it as a continual exchange of interpersonal relationships: ". . . the subject will tend toward a profound change in the motivation of his moral regulation: instead of agonizing, primitive and instinctual panic, a positive emotional stimulus becomes operative . . . Love, is the only finality that is capable of completing the psychological evolution of the human person in a continual transcendence of infantile and regressive attachments." Oraison, "Psychology and the Sense of Sin," 18. The pedagogy of the Church regarding morality therefore needs to appeal to mature sensibilities and not infantile and regressive needs. On a social level the unpacking of ideology requires a complex of attitudes, among them John Paul II's call for solidarity, mercy, and desire for truth and Benedict XVI's call for hope and love.
6 See for instance: Dawn M. Nothwehr, *Mutuality: A Formal Norm for Christian Social Ethics* (Bethesda, MD: International Scholars Publications, 1997).

7 See: Patrick McCormick, *Sin as Addiction* (Mahwah, NJ: Paulist Press, 1989).

8 *The New International Dictionary of New Testament Theology*, Vol. 1. ed. Colin Brown (Exeter: The Paternostic Press, 1975).

9 McFayden, *Bound to Sin*, 147.

10 See: John Perry, S.J., *Torture: Religious Ethics and National Security* (Maryknoll, NY: Orbis Books, 2005).

11 Changed social relationships simply improve the conditions where individuals still must choose egotism or love; they do not remove this personal challenge. See: Chapter Four in this book.

12 Reinhold Niebuhr claims, "There is not enough imagination in any social group to render it amenable to the influence of pure love." *Moral Man and Immoral Society* (New York: Scribner's, 1960), chapter X: "The Conflict between Individual and Social Morality."

13 Kathryn Tanner, *Theories of Culture: A New Agenda for Theology* (Minneapolis, MN: Fortress Press, 1997), 58.

14 This is also a necessary focus in moral education.

15 This is a concern of Lieven Boeve in his text, *God Interrupts History: Theology in a Time of Upheaval* (New York: Continuum, 2007), although he develops this thesis around a different range of questions.

16 Racism is a distortion which is not a rational idea, rather an irrational one which contributes to a self-validating circle. As Juan Luis Segundo writes: "Far from being a neutral photograph, cognition can present one and the same reality to me as either a triumph or a defeat — be it death, money, imprisonment, or whatever. It is not so much that I start right out evaluating them as such, but rather that I already perceive them in that way. They enter my cognitive field as data which, straight out of reality, either oblige me to revise my way of acting or confirm the latter as consistent with the data . . . The 'circle' . . . embraces something much more basic than the difficulty of reasoning clearly." This "thinking" is learned from others. Since the problem is deeper than learning to reason clearly, ratiocination seems to be able to do very little to "convert" human beings from one meaning structure to another. It also requires a movement of the heart. See the discussion of "transcendent data" in Juan Luis Segundo, *Faith and Ideologies*, trans. John Drury (Maryknoll, NY: Orbis Books, 1984), 92–93.

17 See: *Interrupting White Privilege Catholic Theologians Break the Silence*, ed. Laurie M. Cassidy and Alex Mikulich (New York: Orbis Books, 2007).

18 Segundo, *Faith and Ideologies*, 71.

19 The term "capability" here echoes the capabilities approach to development of Martha Nussbaum and Anatyra Sen. It is beyond the scope of this book to note its convergences and disjunctures.

20 Richard N. Fragomeni, "Conversion," in *The New Dictionary of Catholic Spirituality*, ed. Michael Downey (Collegeville, MN: The Liturgical Press, 1993), 234.

21 See: Robert M. Doran, *Psychic Conversion and Theological Foundations* (Chico, CA: Scholars Press, 1981).

22 Rudolph Van Dijk, "*Devotio Moderna*," trans. Philip Endean, in *The New SCM Dictionary of Christian Spirituality* (London: SCM Press, 2005), 236.

23 See: Wendy Wright, "Salesian Spirituality," in *The New SCM Dictionary of Christian Spirituality*, op. cit., 559–60.

24 The negative commands of the Old and New Testament remain stable. However, in each age, these commands must be interpreted. Thou shall not kill is a constant moral imperative. However, the determination of an issue such as capital punishment requires scrutiny in each age of the Church.

25 Josef Fuchs, *Christian Morality: The Word Becomes Flesh* (Dublin: Georgetown University Press, 1987), 34.
26 Ibid., 140.
27 Ibid., 139.

INDEX

CPSIA information can be obtained at www.ICGtesting.com
Printed in the USA
LVOW020747260613

340262LV00005B/116/P

9 780567 095046